Southern Literary Studies
Fred Hobson, Editor

The Road from Pompey's Head

The Road from Pompey's Head

The Life

and

Work of

Hamilton Basso

Inez Hollander Lake

LOUISIANA STATE UNIVERSITY PRESS

Baton Rouge

Copyright © 1999 by Louisiana State University Press
All rights reserved
Manufactured in the United States of America
First printing
08 07 06 05 04 03 02 01 00 99 5 4 3 2 1

Designer: Amanda McDonald Scallan
Typeface: Palatino
Typesetter: Coghill Composition
Printer and binder: Edwards Brothers, Inc.

Grateful acknowledgment is made to Etolia S. Basso for permission to reproduce excerpts from Hamilton Basso's published and unpublished writings. Portions of Chapters 1 and 2 were first published as "Paris in My Own Backyard: Hamilton Basso," in *Literary New Orleans in the Modern World*, edited by Richard S. Kennedy (Baton Rouge, 1998), and are reprinted by permission. Portions of Chapter 3 were first published as "Thomas Wolfe and Hamilton Basso: A Story Never Told," in the *Thomas Wolfe Review* (Spring 1993), copyright Thomas Wolfe Society, and are reprinted by permission of the editor. Parts of Chapters 2 and 4 first appeared as "Home Is Where the Heart Is: Small-Town Experiences in the Fiction of Thomas Wolfe and Hamilton Basso," in *The Small Town in America: A Multidisciplinary Revisit*, edited by Hans Bertens and Theo D'Haen (Amsterdam, 1995), and is reprinted by permission of Vrije Universiteit Press. A small portion of Chapter 4 was also published as part of "A Tale of Two Cities: An Analogy Between Thomas Wolfe's Exile in the American and European City," in the *Thomas Wolfe Review* (Spring 1996), copyright Thomas Wolfe Society, and is reprinted by permission of the editor.

Library of Congress Cataloging-in-Publication Data

Lake, Inez Hollander, 1965–
    The road from Pompey's Head : the life and work of Hamilton Basso
  / Inez Hollander Lake.
      p.   cm. — (Southern literary studies)
    Includes bibliographical references and index.
    ISBN 0-8071-2294-7 (alk. paper)
    1. Basso, Hamilton, 1904–1964.   2. Novelists, American—20th
century—Biography.   3. Southern States—In literature.   4. Southern
States—Biography.   I. Title.   II. Series.
    PS3503.A8423Z75   1999
    813'.52—dc21
    [B]   98-34406
                                                              CIP

For my husband, Jonathan,
because he cared

Ham later confided in me, in open candor, that as a youth his dream was to be one day written about at book-length in American Literature. "Then I scaled my hopes down to a paragraph. Now I'd settle for a footnote."

"Oh, for God's sake," I said then, and clairvoyantly enough. A solid oeuvre stands on the shelf, and a scholar is writing a book.

—Peter de Vries, April 2, 1992

Contents

Illustrations

Preface

At the time of his death in 1964, Hamilton Basso was a celebrated author. He received a lengthy obituary in the New York *Times,* whose
best-seller list ten years earlier had included his best-known novel, *The
View from Pompey's Head,* for forty weeks. The book was translated into
seven languages and was considered popular enough to be converted
into a Braille version. In 1998, however, the name Hamilton Basso has
left few traces in the public memory. In the thirty-four years since his
death only two works have been written on this southern novelist; one
is an unpublished Ph.D. dissertation by Clarence Frye Ikerd and the
other is a volume in the Twayne series by Joseph R. Millichap.[1] Both
works appeared in the seventies, and nothing substantial has been
written about Basso since.

My work on this book began in 1990 at the Catholic University of
Nijmegen in The Netherlands upon the recommendation of my adviser, G. A. M. Janssens. Because my foremost objective was to put this
forgotten southern author back on the map of American letters, this
book is not so much a literary biography as a critical biography in
which the oeuvre figures more prominently than the life of the author.
Also, knowing Basso's distrust of Freudians and theorists, I have attempted to stay away from psychoanalytical and literary theory. As a
literary historian I prefer facts to suppositions, and thus I hope to have
written the kind of biography that Basso himself would have had
in mind.

I am indebted to above-mentioned scholars Clarence Ikerd and Joseph Millichap for the preliminary research they undertook, which was
very helpful to me. At the same time, I had access to much more archi-

1. Clarence Frye Ikerd, "Hamilton Basso: A Critical Biography" (Ph.D. dissertation,
University of North Carolina at Chapel Hill, 1974); Joseph R. Millichap, *Hamilton Basso*
(Boston, 1979).

val material, and this has made my study more definitive. Although I never had the privilege of meeting my subject in person (he died one year before I was born), I have nonetheless tried to give a lively picture of the man behind the writing, an effort facilitated by my reading of his correspondence as well as the countless interviews and conversations I had with his widow, Etolia Simmons Basso. But loose ends remain, and no doubt more material will surface in the future to round out our picture of Basso even more.

Although Basso is mostly known as the author of eleven novels, his nonfiction attests to his works' political-historical merit and reveals his social commitment, sharp political instinct, and an abiding interest in the South. Often lashing out at societal wrongs and inequities, Basso did not write to please the establishment or the people in the South but let his conscience speak. A liberal but never a radical, an intellectual but never a closet scholar, a political thinker but never a dogmatist, and a southerner but most often a reluctant southerner, he not only became an articulate voice within the *New Republic* and the *New Yorker* but also used his art as an outlet for his political, literary, and deeply felt personal views. Thus while at the *New Republic* he would challenge particular public figures such as Huey Long, Father Coughlin, and William Randolph Hearst, in his fiction he railed against racism, intolerance, what he termed "Shintoism," and intellectual pretense. Like his nonfiction, his art is propelled by his love of people, his novels illuminating the plight of the lonely individual within a powerful and often insensitive society.

Equally relevant, though perhaps not so conspicuous as his "protesting" voice, is the modest yet meaningful role Basso played in the life of his more famous contemporaries. Sitting at the feet of Sherwood Anderson at the Quarter's literary gatherings and going for walks with William Faulkner on the New Orleans wharves, Basso found himself at the core of a generation of writers who gave American literature an identity of its own. Working with the editor Maxwell Perkins, the godfather of that same generation, Basso was destined to meet F. Scott Fitzgerald and Thomas Wolfe, both of whom happened to live near Basso shortly before their deaths. His relationship with Wolfe, which all of Wolfe's biographers have ignored, is especially fascinating and has fed my belief that Basso, after Perkins, may have been one of Wolfe's closest friends. Besides these literary friendships, he also had a close relationship with well-known and influential literary and cultural critics, such as Van Wyck Brooks, Malcolm Cowley, Matthew Josephson, and Edmund Wilson.

Basso's importance as a southern novelist outweighs his significance as an American author. Of his southern novels, the thirties novels, and especially *Cinnamon Seed*, *Courthouse Square*, and *Days Before Lent*, deserve renewed interest and consideration. Like no other writer of the Southern Renaissance, Basso surveyed the problems, emotional and otherwise, that a southerner confronts when he leaves and returns home. Though Thomas Wolfe has received most if not all of the credit for this motif, Basso analyzed the theme more often, more thoroughly, and less sentimentally.

Like most southern writers who came of age in the twenties, Basso "left home for a time, focused his eye on a changing South, an industrializing South, but looked as well at a South that was slipping away, and the result was a creative mixture of detachment and involvement—an escape from, then an attempt to return to the southern community." Like most of his southern contemporaries, too, one finds in Basso "numerous attempts . . . to define [and] describe the Southern Temper, the Southern Mind [as well as] efforts to capture the Southerner, to define him . . . before he slipped away." And since Basso and his generation were essentially the grandchildren (and great-grandchildren) of Johnny Reb, one also retraces in him "a greater attention to the past, an acceptance of man's finiteness, his penchant for failure [and] a tragic sense," which are "more characteristic of the Southerner than of other Americans." Last, Basso shares his belief in such determinants as place, community, family, and the past, with "the most notable southern *writers*, white and black, of the 1920s, 1930s, and 1940s," who "were far more conscious of place, family, community, religion and its social manifestations, and the power of the past in the present than were the nonsouthern American writers."[2] At the same time, Basso must be remembered for his southern "otherness"; scolding the Agrarians for breeding plantation anachronisms out of the dead land, and criticizing writers like Erskine Caldwell and William Faulkner for cultivating the other extreme of the southern grotesque and southern decay, he strived for realism and moderation.

---

2. Fred Hobson, *The Southern Writer in the Postmodern World* (Athens, Ga., 1991), 3–4.

Although Basso started out as a writer with a distinct and promising voice in the Southern Renascence, he ended up a little ordinarily, becoming a combination of what Herbert Gold has called a "Cataloguer" (i.e., an observer like John O'Hara) and a "Common Style Fellow," who, as a "just-plain-Bill of literature . . . produced an upper-middle class soap opera for the readers of Luce magazines and subscribers to the Book of the Month Club's service."[3] While the fifties and sixties saw the rise of postmodernism and the emergence of the ethnic novel, Basso leaned toward preserving the novel of manners and perpetuated the realistic tradition of such writers as James Gould Cozzens, John O'Hara, and J. P. Marquand.

Regrettably, Basso's neglect derives from the widespread popularity of his later and best-selling novels. While being classified as a practitioner of *belles lettres* rather than an author of canonical literature, he lost touch with his domain, the South, and his theme, the southerner who, in his attempt to come to terms with his picturesque but frequently flawed hometown, experienced delight, disenchantment, and finally, double exile. Like no other before him and no other after him, Basso captured the central dilemma of a southern generation that was rapidly outgrowing its Dixie environment.

3. Herbert Gold, "The Mystery of Personality in the Novel," in Gold, *The American Novel Since World War II* (Greenwich, Conn., 1969), 107.

Acknowledgments

This book could not have been written without the initiative and financial support of the Catholic University of Nijmegen, The Netherlands. Additional funds came from a Fulbright Fellowship and a William B. Wisdom Award (Thomas Wolfe Society). Of the libraries and librarians who allowed me to survey various Basso materials and other selected sources, I would like to mention the Beinecke Rare Book and Manuscript Library at Yale University; the Harvey S. Firestone Library at Princeton University; the Houghton Library at Harvard University; the Newberry Library in Chicago; the Howard-Tilton Memorial Library at Tulane University; the Patterson-Van Pelt Library at the University of Pennsylvania; the Wilson Library at the University of North Carolina, and the university libraries at Arizona State University and the Catholic University of Nijmegen, The Netherlands.

I am very grateful to Etolia Simmons Basso for her permission to quote so extensively from her husband's letters and unpublished writings. Toto was my closest link to Basso, and she was extremely helpful in answering my never-ending questions, making suggestions, and showing me letters of her late husband. In the process she has become a very dear friend and the adopted grandmother of our son William.

Of the others who knew Basso personally and so willingly shared their memories with me, I want to thank his son, Keith Basso; his sister, the late Mary Basso McCrady; the late Cleanth Brooks; and the late Peter de Vries.

Because "Basso scholars" are a rare species, I am especially grateful to Joseph Millichap for detailed discussions on Basso. His informative letters, his sharing of material, and his book, *Hamilton Basso* (Boston, 1979), have been very useful. Others who took an enthusiastic interest in my subject were Aldo Magi, editor of the *Thomas Wolfe Review*; David Madden, writer and critic; and John Easterly, executive editor at Louisiana State University Press.

As I was traveling through the United States in 1991 and 1992, I enjoyed a great deal of hospitality from family and friends. They made my search for Hamilton Basso truly memorable and alleviated the loneliness I occasionally endured. Of these, I would like to remember especially Bonnie Bertram, John and Ann Burrows, Angela, John, and Tony Calabro, Dani Ebskamp, Dale Edmonds, Paul Fischer, Monique and Eric Foster, Cookie and Lester Gross, Janet and Peter Harckham, Christian and Micheline Kirsebom, Bud and Dot Lake, Chris and Gretchen Lake, Ingrid and Mary Lohr, Bonnie and Jack MacDonald, Marion and Jack McQuade, Kevin and Debbie McQuade, and Robin and Jan McQuade. I am especially grateful for the warm hospitality I enjoyed in the beautiful home of Alice, Dick, Henry, Sandy, and Matthew Holland; being true to their name, they provided me with a Holland away from home.

The manuscript saw a number of readers, and this book could not have been realized without their valuable advice and feedback. I am especially grateful to Hans Bak, Jaap van der Bent, Matthew Holland, Laurine Hollander, Marian Janssen, and Ger Janssens. Of the people who were faithful friends when my spirits were low, I want to mention John Calabro, Suzen Davidsmeyer, Emily Embree, Monique van der Haagen, Frank van Meurs, Jerry Rosen, and Mathilde Roza. I feel especially fortunate to have made acquaintance with Richard S. Kennedy, professor emeritus at Temple University. He was very generous with sound advice and many letters of reference. In this list I also want to include my dear family, who backed me through thick and thin; they are Laurine, Paul, Matthijs, Laurine, Jr., Tim, Ellen, Arthur, Daan, Olivier, Minke, Marc, Julia, Marijke, and last but not least, Mom and Dad: I will always remember their financial and emotional support.

My adviser, colleague, and friend Ger Janssens was the driving force behind this project. Besides teaching me that patience is indeed a virtue, he was indispensable in providing advice, encouragement, and enthusiasm. Because he is such a dedicated and outstanding scholar in the field of American letters, I hope that the critical reader will trace the book's many imperfections to me rather than him.

Finally, I dedicate this book to my biggest fan and husband, Jonathan Lake. He has always been there for me, on the road, at home, and abroad. He has shared my little successes, and he has seen my tears. I could not have finished this work without his unconditional love and affection.

Abbreviations

SA   Scribner's Archives, Harvey S.
     Firestone Library, Princeton
     University, Princeton

WL   Wilson Library, University of
     North Carolina, Chapel Hill

The Road from Pompey's Head

1

New Orleans Beginnings

Touring the South in 1937, Jonathan Daniels described Louisiana as a "Caribbean republic" whose hard Anglo-Saxon tradition had been "softened by pleasant and relaxing Latin ways." New Orleans may be seen as the exemplar of this hybrid of cultures. With a Creole heritage that is Spanish, French, and Catholic rather than Anglo-Saxon and Protestant, New Orleans may even be called one of America's most un-American cities. Though it is located amid swamps and has seen many wet winters, floods, hurricanes, and yellow-fever epidemics, New Orleans has, owing to its architectural uniqueness, ethnic diversity, and enticing atmosphere, always remained the jewel of the Deep South. However, before its discovery by the tourist industry, the city remained undisturbed on the outer bayous of Louisiana, slumbering in the aftermath of the Civil War. Impoverished by the burdensome Reconstruction years, the elegant French Quarter had deteriorated into a slum of crime and prostitution. Although there was little to remind the visitor of the city's rich colonial past, the place still had an unequivocal charm, which Charles D. Warner captured when ambling downtown on an early Sunday morning in 1887: "In the balconies and on the mouldering window-ledges flowers bloomed, and in the decaying courts climbing-roses mingled their perfume with the orange; the shops were open;

ladies tripped along from early mass or to early market; there was a
twittering in the square and in the sweet old gardens; caged birds sang
and screamed the songs of South America and the tropics; the language heard on all sides was French. . . . Nothing could be more
shabby than the streets, ill-paved, with undulating sidewalks, and
open gutters, little canals in which the cat became the companion of the
crawfish, and the vegetable in decay sought in vain a current to oblivion." Warner seems to have been acutely aware of the split nature of the
town; juxtaposing picturesque and dirty detail, he was enchanted by
what he called this "thriftless, battered, stained and lazy old place."[1] It
was here, in the heart of the French Quarter when Choctaw Indians still
roamed the streets, that Joseph Hamilton Basso was born on September
5, 1904.

Hamilton Basso was the only son of Dominick Basso and Louise Calamari. To escape Napoleon's military draft, Hamilton's paternal great-
grandfather had left Genoa for New Orleans in the early 1800s. Thus
Hamilton's grandfather was born in New Orleans, but like the protagonist of Basso's debut novel, *Relics and Angels* (1929), he went to Genoa
on a lengthy visit as a young man.[2] Basso's maternal grandparents, Nathale and Annette Calamari, were also Italian and came to the New
World in the 1880s, when their daughter Louise was only three years
old. Devout Catholics, Nathale and Antoinette had both considered
joining religious orders, something they forgot the moment they became infatuated with each other. Hamilton was not oblivious to their
monastic aspirations: in his first novel, the protagonist's grandmother
becomes a pious nun after her failed marriage.

Although Basso characterized his family as patriarchal, "Mediterranean, Catholic [and] still essentially European," the family belonged to
the New Orleans middle class, which Joe Taylor describes as varying in
degree of wealth "but as a whole . . . literate, conservative, religious,
and economically ambitious."[3] Joseph Basso, Hamilton's grandfather,

1. Jonathan Daniels, *A Southerner Discovers the South* (New York, 1938) 231; Charles
D. Warner, "Sui Generis," in *The World from Jackson Square: A New Orleans Reader,* ed.
Etolia S. Basso (1948; rpr. New York, 1972), 307–308.

2. Hamilton Basso to C. B. Senhausen, October 21, 1959, in Hamilton Basso Papers, BL.

3. Hamilton Basso, "William Faulkner," *Saturday Review,* July 28, 1962, p. 12; Joe
Gray Taylor, *Louisiana: A Bicentennial History* (New York, 1976), 59.

had established a little shoe factory in their house on Decatur Street, located between Barracks Street and Hospital Street. Once the French Opera arrived in the 1880s, the family company specialized in shoes for the stage.

The opera did not only sustain the family financially. As true Italian Americans, the Bassos also had emotional ties with the opera. As a youth, Dominick ran away from home and tried to become an opera singer. He failed but continued, as an adult, to play and sing opera endlessly on the weekends, much to the annoyance of Hamilton and his younger sister, Mary. Apart from these matinees at home, Hamilton had to stomach more opera when his grandfather dragged him to the opera house, where the boy would sleep rather than sit through the performances. But if not swayed by the music, Hamilton, or "Ham" as he was soon to be called by family and friends, was nonetheless enthralled by the colorful opera stories that one of the cobblers at the factory told him while making shoes for the different performances. One day, the cobbler told him the story of Faust, and greatly intrigued by this epic of the devil, Ham persuaded his grandfather to take him to see the show. Contrary to the child's great expectations, the operatic devil "couldn't have frightened a sick cat," the cobbler's shoes being "the best part of the show."[4] Though obviously not smitten by opera, Hamilton did develop a taste for music. Growing up in the city of jazz, he became very fond of its music. He was an outstanding dancer, and his early stories are filled with dance rhythms and jazz music.

Hamilton's childhood in the Quarter was particularly carefree and idyllic. The house on Decatur Street may have had a few things in common with the house that Jason Kent, one of Basso's characters, grows up in and describes as "a rather wonderful old house" situated on "a rather wonderful street. From the attic window you could see the rooftops for miles . . . most of the nations of Europe had managed to crowd into that one block" (*DBL*, 38). The Bassos' house opened onto an inner courtyard, which, lush with vegetation, was an excellent site for games. One day when the yard had become a little too confining, Ham sneaked into the adjoining courtyard to peep in on the next-door

4. Mary Basso McCrady, interview with the author, February 1, 1992; Hamilton Basso, "A New Orleans Childhood: The House on Decatur Street," *New Yorker*, October 9, 1954, pp. 89–101.

neighbor, who was a poet. The boy's first encounter with this specimen from the literary world turned out to be a disappointing experience: the so-called poet was a man in suspenders who, with a notepad in his lap and a fat cigar in his mouth, loafed for about an hour. Many years after this uneventful meeting with the poet, Basso noted that it had had its value, since it taught him that "poetry can't be hurried and that a poet may well be a bald-headed man in suspenders, smoking a cigar."[5]

But there was more to Hamilton's childhood than the pleasant place he called home. While Clarence Ikerd has described Basso's father as a kindly man with an occasional temper and stubborn streak, Dominick Basso seems to have been both an indulgent and affectionate father. He liked to surprise his children with extraordinary pets, such as alligators and pigs, and when he found out that his son was spending time in the Quarter's seedy billiard rooms, he bought a pool table and had it placed in the small dining room. He also took his children on various outings. On one of these trips, he and Ham were rowed back home by a black fisherman. Ham remembered the trip as only a child would remember it: oars splashing in the lake, little fingers trailing through the water, and an arrival home well after midnight. Of this nighttime excursion, he further recalled that they could "have come back on the Canal Street ferry but my father never even thought of it. It was, in fact, unthinkable. He was in his shirtsleeves and in those days a New Orleans gentleman never appeared in public in his shirtsleeves."[6] It is interesting that Basso saw his father as an upper-middle-class gentleman. Though the family was unmistakably middle class, Basso seems to have thought they were of higher standing. Likewise, in his novels his protagonists are usually members of the upper middle class or southern "aristocracy."

On Sundays, Dominick took his children to the park, where he and Mary would make flower-petal bracelets and clover chains while Ham listened to the stories of Confederate veterans sitting on park benches.[7] The veterans' stories stirred up an appetite for southern history in the boy, which was further whetted by the stories his father told on their walks through the historic Quarter. Basso's love of southern history

5. Basso, "A New Orleans Childhood," 94.

6. Ikerd, "Hamilton Basso," 4; Hamilton Basso, "A New Orleans Childhood: The House on Decatur Street" (Typescript in Basso Papers, BL), n.p.

7. Mary Basso McCrady, interview with the author.

manifests itself in many of his works, from his biography of the Civil War general P. G. T. Beauregard to his penultimate novel, *The Light Infantry Ball* (1959).

Many of Basso's values were first taught to him and Mary by Dominick. Basso's father was a man endowed with a strong sense of justice who exhibited genuine compassion for other people. One of his lifelong friends was a Jewish man who ran a jewelry shop in the Quarter. As children, they had gone to school together, and because Dominick's friend had a hard time fending for himself, Dominick defended him with his fists. Fairness and tolerance, treating people with respect whatever their color, class, or background, were traits high on the list of proper conduct in the Basso household. Basso's novels reveal that he was sensitive to the issue of racial justice, which, in the southern context of the twenties and thirties, was not yet a reality for black southerners.

In contrast to his wife, who was an ardent Catholic, Dominick was a freemason and extremely anticlerical. Hamilton inherited his father's skepticism of religion. Even though "he swung the holy smoke" as an altar boy, Basso would not embrace the faith and eventually stopped attending church altogether, with the exception of one visit on Armistice Day in 1945.[8] In Basso's early, unpublished writing one can trace a strong anticlerical element, which also surfaces, albeit rather ambiguously, in his first novel.

Unlike his father, Dominick was a "terrible businessman." Faced with the management of the shoe company in 1917 when Joseph Basso died, Dominick sold the family business, an incident that would be recounted in *Relics and Angels*. Curiously, Dominick did not pursue a different career but remained a shoe broker and salesman all his life. Hamilton saw this as a distinctive weakness, and in his criticism of his father, he gradually dreamed up an ideal image of his grandfather, whom in terms of personal ambition he came to idolize: "It was never questioned in my grandfather's house that the scholar and the dedicated public servant were worthier and more admirable than the banker and the businessman. My father's father was one of the latter. He owned a small shoe factory and a few pieces of property that I wish we still had. But his ambition for my father was that he should be a col-

---

8. Etolia S. Basso, interview with the author, January 8, 1992.

lege professor. I think he must have been hurt and disappointed when my father went off in an entirely different direction, and into the first failures that I suppose I have been trying to make up for."[9]

Elsewhere, Basso confirms his warm feelings for his grandfather, whom he clearly saw as an example: "I liked [Grandfather] very much and he liked me and we would often go on little excursions together. So, at a time when I was highly impressionable, it was inevitable that I should be greatly influenced by him." Fictional evidence of this remarkable grandfather-grandson relationship can be found in an unpublished story in which we are introduced to a small boy sitting beside his grandfather on a long New Orleans wharf. The grandfather turns out to be an enchanting raconteur who stirs the child's fancy. He passes on his gift for talk and for conjuring a fairy-tale world by giving "the eyes of his imagination to the small boy who was sitting by his side." Although we should be wary of linking fiction to biographical fact, a writer's first stories and his first novel are inclined to be, as Leon Edel notes, "more transparently autobiographical than his later work."[10] Thus, the quoted passage, where a deliberate and almost ceremonial bequeathal takes place, may truthfully reflect Basso's grandfather fixation, something that is coincidentally reinforced by Basso's having been named after his grandfather. Worship of the grandfather figure is a recurring motif in Basso's novels. When reading them in succession, one detects a pattern of a grandson who tends to identify with his usually heroic grandfather. The father, on the other hand, is anti-heroic and often absent altogether.

According to Mary Basso McCrady, her mother was a vivacious and "tiny little thing." When taking out her baby son in a buggy, she would be approached by people who offered her a nickel and told her to "buy something for her little brother." Dedicated to her family, Louise was a conventional woman and a true "homemaker." She was popular in the Quarter, where she knew everybody, the prostitutes not excluded. Anyone who was ill or had the blues called on Louise. Like a good Italian mother, she doted on her son, carefully ironing and laying out the

9. Mary Basso McCrady, interview with the author; Hamilton Basso to Edmund Wilson, June 15, 1958, in Basso Papers, BL.

10. Hamilton Basso to Malcolm Cowley, January 9, 1939, in Malcolm Cowley Papers, NL; Hamilton Basso, "Holiday" (Typescript in Basso Papers, BL), n.p.; Leon Edel, *Writing Lives: Principia Biographica* (1959; rpr. New York, 1984), 127.

white linen suits Ham wore to school. According to Clarence Ikerd, Ham considered himself a "spoiled child": he was sometimes "disciplined . . . but never severely." Although Louise was a devout woman, her faith had a pragmatic edge to it. Keith, Hamilton Basso's only son, remembered how "she had a very informal relationship with God, referring to Him as if He ran the grocery store next door." In addition, her piety went only so far as convenience would allow: in the winter she preferred Episcopalian mass because the Episcopalians had central heating and the Catholics did not.[11]

The Italian atmosphere of the Bassos' neighborhood was not unusual; by 1900, "One white person in five living in New Orleans had been born in Italy." However, where most Italian immigrants to the Crescent City came from poor Sicilian and southern Italian peasant proletariats, the Bassos traced their roots to northern Italy and had already become hardworking members of the city's middle class by 1890, when New Orleans' Italian population jumped from 7,763 to 16,221.[12]

A popular destination because of its Catholicism and Mediterranean ambience, New Orleans—though already ethnically diverse—was not particularly welcoming of the new immigrant group. Whereas earlier immigrant groups like the Germans and the Irish had assimilated fully after a brief time of exclusion by Orleanians, the Italians experienced an extended period of harsh ostracism. According to David Mays, this was triggered by Orleanians' prejudices: not only did the Italians have darker skin, but they also struggled with the English language, were generally poor, and were believed to have imported the Mafia and street fights. In addition, their Catholicism had an anticlerical, ritualistic emphasis radically different from the Catholicism practiced by the Orleanians and the Irish. Forced to live in the poor Quarter, the Italians were soon blamed for having turned the "already crumbling century-old tenements of the Vieux Carré" into a Naples of the New World. Mays claims that as late as 1950, Robert Tallant, a promi-

---

11. Mary Basso McCrady, interview with the author; Ikerd, "Hamilton Basso," 5; Keith H. Basso, interview with the author, January 26, 1992; Etolia S. Basso, interview with the author, January 3, 1991.

12. David D. Mays, "Sivilizing Moustache Pete: Changing Attitudes Toward Italians in New Orleans, 1890–1918," in *Ethnic Minorities in Gulf Coast Society*, ed. Jerrell H. Shofner and Linda V. Ellsworth (Pensacola, Fla., 1979), 96.

nent local historian and a romantic, wrote that the Italians had changed his Vieux Carré into a "slum . . . inhabited mostly by lower-class Sicilians, a sinister people. There were scenes that duplicated Naples and Palermo—long lines of family wash hanging out on the once lovely iron lacework balconies; half-naked children running about; old, dark fat men and women sleeping on their stoops . . . scrawny chickens pecking at their feet. There was the odor of garlic, of rotting fruit and vegetables and manure."[13]

Especially interesting in view of Basso's progressive ideas about black civil rights as well as his genuine familiarity with black life in the Quarter is that the Italians lived alongside blacks and without reservation traded with them, befriended them, and respected them. Mary Basso McCrady recalled that her grandfather employed many African Americans, with whom he was on very friendly terms.

As can be expected, the Italians' relations with blacks only confirmed the opinion "of their fellow whites that the Italians were 'no better' than the blacks they served." This led to more prejudice and the conclusion that black stereotypes applied equally well to Italians: "To many Orleanians the Italians were illiterate, ignorant, physically dirty, clannish, poor, immoral, noisy, simultaneously servile and insubordinate, and idle. Like the blacks they seemed to take a noisy pleasure in life . . . worshiped strange saints in strange ways, and, again, like blacks, were primitive, superstitious, fecund as rabbits, and preternaturally prone to violence."[14]

Although the Bassos were financially better off, spoke the English language with ease, and had assimilated to such an extent that they might have escaped the above-cited stereotype, they must have been aware of, and may indeed have experienced some of, the racism of their fellow Orleanians. One can only speculate as to how much the Bassos were actually affected by the general animosity toward Italians, but the ethnic gap between those who lived within the Quarter (including the Bassos) and those who lived outside it must have contributed to Basso's lifelong sensitivity to the South's repeated exclusion of certain racial groups.

13. *Ibid.*, 100–101; Robert Tallant, *The Romantic New Orleanians* (New York, 1950), 308–309.

14. Mays, "Sivilizing Moustache Pete," 102.

After Joseph Basso's death in 1917, the family moved to the New Orleans suburbs. Mary Basso McCrady only remembered her grandfather's funeral by the hat she wore. Hamilton, on the other hand, evoked the sad occasion in an early story, "A Burial." Witnessing the burial of a young friend, the story's central character, Quimby, felt "like a child. Once before, when his grandfather had died, he had been in a house that was quiet with the knowledge of death. He was then a child, and now, in this new realization, he had become a child again."[15]

There is a family picture from about 1917 in which we see Mary dressed in white, squinting against the sunlight; next to her stands her brother, with his arm, slightly possessive and stiff, wrapped around her shoulder. He seems short for his age and appears to be an attractive boy with raven-black, brilliantined hair combed back with prepubescent flair; his eyes are dark, and his nose seems a little too big for his small face. He is dressed in a dark blazer that is too tight across the shoulders, and plus fours balloon around his short legs. His face and air are confident, determined, gentlemanly, and perhaps even a little dandyish—a peculiarity that cannot be seen as typical of Ham's later personality.

As a child Hamilton roamed the French Quarter. He knew all the shop owners, who, like his parents and grandparents, lived on the second floor above their shops. Although he belonged to the literary crowd at school, after school Ham liked to play with the tough kids, or "wharf rats" in the New Orleans port. Like Dekker Blackheath of Basso's second novel, *Cinnamon Seed* (1934), he would dive for bananas "thrown overboard from United Fruit Steamers." In an unpublished autobiographical sketch, Basso further describes the sensation he felt as a boy when, lying awake, he heard the "whistles of the boats as they nosed cautiously through the fog." In the daytime he would walk along the wharves and, while the "smell of sugar and tar and coffee crept into his nostrils," enjoy the bustle of harbor activities.[16] A similar impression of the waterfront is given in *Cinnamon Seed*, where Dekker wanders about the wharves that Basso must have ambled along when he was a child:

15. Hamilton Basso, "A Burial" (Typescript in Basso Papers, BL), n.p.
16. Malcolm Cowley, typescript notes for Hamilton Basso's eulogy, May 1964, in Cowley Papers, NL; Hamilton Basso, "A Momentary Digression" (Typescript in Basso Papers, BL), n.p.

The sun was shining on the river and there were many ships. He walked down the wharves reading the names of the ships, but all the names were strange and he saw none of the sailors he knew. He knew many sailors and even a captain, Mr. Gundersonn, and one of the sailors, Mr. O'Callahan, had a man-o'-war foaming across his chest into a brush of stiff red hair. He watched the negroes loading lumber on the *Apprentice*, seating himself on a hogshead in the midst of the clatter of hand-trucks and shouting negro voices and negro bodies shining in the sun, and he was reminded of an old ambition to some day become a sailor and go to foreign places and see foreign things and fall in love with a beautiful foreign woman. He had no desire, however, to have a man-o'-war foaming across his chest. (*CS*, 6–7)

Basso clearly shared Dekker's fascination with foreign places: later in life he would board the freighters he knew from his childhood and sail all over the world for travelogues commissioned by magazines such as *Holiday* and *Life*. Other childhood reminiscences go back to the so-called Elysian Fields, a gang of boys who terrorized the local kids by forcing them to pay "a nickel-a-week tribute for crossing the railroad tracks to school" or by having them surrender their lunches. In a *New Republic* article Basso recalled that whenever the Elysian Fields "emerged victorious from a rockfight, driving off the 'Irish Channels' or 'Basin Blues,' all the other kids, the 'exploited and oppressed' ones, gained a sort of victorious triumph. 'Our' gang had won. There would always be a celebration on the wharves . . . and it was always the non-gang kids who did most of the celebrating: even though one of them invariably got bashed for popping off his mouth too much."[17] This experience taught Basso that the docile following of certain group movements, whether they were childhood gangs or literary, intellectual, or political "gangs," was detrimental to the kind of free thinking and independence he hoped to cultivate.

Basso's early literary interests were broadened by one of the neighborhood bookshop owners, who generously lent him books. Even as a young boy, Basso wrote countless Peter Rabbit stories, one of which was published in the local newspaper. For an essay on Confederate

---

17. Hamilton Basso, Biographical sketch, *Wilson Library Bulletin*, XIV (1939), 186; Basso, "Italian Notebook: 1938," *New Republic*, June 15, 1938, p. 147.

general Alfred Mouton, he won a Daughters of the Confederacy Medal, which, many years later, his young son, Keith, lost in the autumn leaves of Connecticut.

Hamilton's access to books and the stories his father and grandfather told him undoubtedly helped shape his story-telling talent. Being a creative child, he liked to draw, had pet names for everybody, called his sister "Stump-Jumper," and told story after story to family and friends. His facility with language became even more apparent when, in eighth grade, he became champion orator of his class. Mary Basso McCrady remembered the day her father came upon a crowd in Canal Street. Pushing his way through, he saw his son and Ham's clarinet-playing friend Pinkie at the pavilion: while Pinkie played his tunes, Ham eloquently persuaded the crowd to buy more war bonds. That very same day, the sale of war bonds went up significantly. The adult Basso would often be remembered for his power of speech. One of his Tulane yearbooks, *Jambalaya*, reveals that he was an oratorical celebrity: an entry for 1924 shows that "J. Hamilton Basso and Leon Cahn completely submerged the representatives of Vanderbilt and came home bearing a unanimous victory over the Nashville school." Peter de Vries, friend and fellow writer on the *New Yorker*, recalls how Basso's gregariousness was apparent in his "ready fluent speech" and "the give-and-take in conversation, whether one-on-one or at a party, which he often dominated."[18]

Basso probably owed his happy and harmonious childhood to his parents' loving attention and the extraordinary locale of the Quarter. In addition to having a lasting effect on Basso's imagination, New Orleans would be fundamental to his literary career: serving as the backdrop in three of his novels, the city was also the venue where Basso met writers who encouraged him and helped him publish his first novel.

We have virtually no information on Basso's adolescent years. We know that he graduated from Warren Easton High School in 1922 and that same year entered Tulane University, where, in accordance with his father's wishes, he pursued a law degree. (The law program started at the undergraduate level.) Leafing through the Tulane yearbooks of

18. Tulane University *Jambalaya* (New Orleans, 1924), 331; Peter de Vries to the author, April 2, 1992.

the time, one discovers, besides boblines and Charleston dresses, that though Hamilton seems to have been a quiet student at first, occasionally appearing as a listed member of a debating or drama club, he gradually gained stature among his peers.

Grandly situated in the Uptown area, the Tulane campus was the playground for many of Basso's pranks. These ranged from nailing professors' erasers to the floor to arranging a jazz serenade to be played beneath the dean's window. Though not a favorite student with his professors, Basso became tremendously popular with his fellow students when, in midwinter, he stripped to his shorts and dove into the Audubon Park lagoon.

Charles Dufour, a college friend, later boasted that he and Basso were expelled from college. However, Basso declared that although he knew that lawyers "made a living, and writers did not," he dropped out voluntarily four months before graduation. "It is hard to say what happened," Basso later joked, but the "best explanation I can give is that New Orleans is a very social place. Something like the law is apt to get in the way." In a 1954 interview with the *Saturday Review of Literature*, Basso said that the hope for a legal career began with his grandfather, who had a good friend in a law firm: "I could see myself graduating, joining the firm, spending my life there. Everything just seemed so darn final to me, and I wasn't even twenty."[19]

Whatever the circumstances of his premature departure, he had left a marked impression on Tulane, becoming the editor-in-chief of the 1925 *Jambalaya*. This yearbook contains stories that reveal the same sophomoric humor of Basso's pranks and displays his witty drawings. Overall, it is difficult to distill Basso's contributions from this issue, as most pieces are unsigned. Nevertheless, the yearbook was considered so unique that Basso was placed in the Tulane Hall of Fame in the 1926 *Jambalaya*. Underneath Basso's picture, which shows a short young man with dark hair, a beaming smile, and a wrinkled suit too short in the sleeves, we read:

J. HAMILTON BASSO

Because, as editor-in-chief of the 1925 Jambalaya he has given Tulane the greatest annual she has had. Because his volume was

19. Hamilton Basso, "Some Important Fall Authors Speak for Themselves," *New York Herald Tribune Book Review*, October 24, 1954, p. 4; Robert Cantwell, "A Southerner Returns," *Saturday Review of Literature*, October 23, 1954, p. 15.

the first in the history of the Jambalaya to ever receive national recognition for excellence. Because he has distinguished himself as a writer by his great imaginative style. And finally because he has been elected to the Kappa Delta Phi, that honor than which there can be no greater bestowed upon a Tulanian by his fellow students.

However promising Basso seemed to his fellow Tulanians, his decision to shelve his law studies baffled his father. It was clear that, though he would develop several scholarly interests, ranging from anthropology to history, like Leon Falkes in one of the writer's early unpublished pieces, Basso could not take college seriously: "Finding himself in an unsympathetic atmosphere, where values were most frequently determined by lettering of fraternity pins, automobile designs and social position, he was rejected and an outcast." Quimby, another of Basso's alter egos in his juvenilia, resents college, too: he "does not see the good of cramming and wonders why he has gone to college in the first place."[20]

Already during his law school semesters, Basso had traded in his lectures for the smoke-filled rooms of the city's newspaper offices. Working for three newspapers, the *Tribune*, the *Item*, and the *Times-Picayune*, Basso thought that a career in journalism would be the proper path for an aspiring writer like himself to take. Or as he pondered in one of his autobiographical pieces: "Often because he believes that merely dealing with words will be pleasurable, the young man who wishes to become a poet finds employment on a newspaper. He looks upon his occupation as an 'apprenticeship.' In his mind it takes on a romantic glow and he always tells himself 'I am on the way to becoming a poet.' "[21]

Basso started out as a feature writer covering the waterfront run and city crime, and his talents were soon recognized by the city desk. Sent out to report on the meteoric rise of Huey Long, Basso was once thrown out of the governor's hotel room, an incident he would later recall with pride as his antipathy toward Long grew over the years. Although he enjoyed his newspaper work, he was ready to pursue the

20. Hamilton Basso, "Attitude" (Typescript in Basso Papers, BL), n.p.; Basso, "Exam" (Typescript in Basso Papers, BL), n.p.

21. Hamilton Basso, "An Epilogue" (Typescript in Hamilton Basso Papers, BL), n.p.

true passion of his life—literature. His timing was fortunate, for in the twenties New Orleans was becoming one of the literary centers of the South.

In the French Quarter, then still known as a prostitution quarter, the Louisiana writer Lyle Saxon had started a literary salon as early as 1919. Saxon predicted that "in the trail of artists" who had already settled there in the war years "would come the writers and soon we would boast of our own Place D'Armes as New York does her Washington Square." By 1922, Saxon's prediction had come true. The Quarter saw the opening of photographers' studios and bohemian tearooms, and one year earlier, John McClure, Julius Friend, and Albert Goldstein had founded New Orleans' first literary magazine, the *Double Dealer*. Attracting many artists for whom Paris was too far and Greenwich Village too expensive, New Orleans offered a reasonable alternative. Depicting the city as a "Creole version of the Left Bank," Basso wrote many years after he had left the Big Easy: "If I never much hankered after Paris in the 1920s it was because . . . I had Paris in my own backyard."[22]

James Feibleman, who was one year younger than Basso and who also frequented the *Double Dealer* hangouts, described the city as an art colony where, despite Prohibition, "liquor was cheap and plentiful." The plenitude of liquor was best explained by William Spratling, a young architecture professor at Tulane: besides distilling Pernod, the popular drink, Spratling notes that "we also made gin in the bath tub using five-gallon cans of Cuban alcohol and adding the proper little bottle of Juniper essence, which you could get at the corner store." The boyish and boisterous atmosphere, which Basso happily participated in, is also conveyed by Oliver LaFarge: "Our parties were generally held in my apartment, since as a bachelor in the French Quarter I had a place in which we could laugh and sing without causing parents to protest or scandalizing the neighbors."[23]

As in college, Basso was known for his humor and liveliness; Clarence Ikerd writes that "he was known particularly as a dancer and had

22. Cathy Chance Harvey, "Lyle Saxon: A Portrait in Letters, 1917–1945" (Ph.D. dissertation, Tulane University, 1980), 71; Basso, "William Faulkner," 11.

23. James Feibleman, *The Way of Man: An Autobiography* (1952; rpr. New York, 1969), 271–72; William Spratling, *File on Spratling: An Autobiography* (Boston, 1967), 28; Oliver LaFarge, "Completely New," in *The World from Jackson Square*, ed. Basso, 362.

the reputation . . . of being able to dance all night." Still fond of pranks, he and his friends "had a brick baked in the oven of a New Orleans restaurant with sauce covering it, and then set it before Sherwood Anderson to carve." Basso may also have been guilty of shooting a BB gun at passersby from Spratling's apartment: "We had a system of premiums, or points, which was pasted to the walls. . . . If you managed to pink a Negro nun, that rated ten points (for rarity value) and that was the highest you could go."[24]

Regardless of and perhaps due to the Quarter's derelict state, the neighborhood had a captivating charm that Sherwood Anderson, one of the older and more established writers on the *Double Dealer*, laid down in his story "A Meeting South": "We walked slowly . . . through many streets of the Old Town, Negro women laughing all around us in the dusk, shadows playing over old buildings, children with their shrill cries dodging in and out of hallways. . . . Families were sitting down to dinner within full sight of the street—all doors and windows open. A man and his wife quarreled in Italian. In a patio back of an old building a Negress sang a French song." Oliver LaFarge underlines the socially tolerant atmosphere of the Quarter as the "art colony centering around Jackson Square," surrounded by "negroes, Creoles, Cajuns . . . Italians, Greeks, Jews . . . and a great many Latin Americans. There were sailors of all kinds, antique dealers, second hand dealers, speakeasies galore, simple workmen, a fair variety of criminals, both white and colored nuns, the survivors of a few aristocratic families . . . merchants, and whole blocks of prostitutes."[25]

The Quarter's easygoing atmosphere was also one of the hallmarks of the *Double Dealer* group and its magazine. Despite the editors' resolute literary ambitions, the magazine was not averse to an element of fun. As the editors wrote in their first issue: "A skit, a jest, a jingle, making no pretense to the name of literature, is . . . a more honorable display of ink than a literary failure." Basso emphasized the *Double Dealer* stance: "We were not a literary clique, we were not a movement, and God knows we were not a school. . . . What held us together was a mutual friendliness and good-will." It is in this spirit also that the

24. Ikerd, "Hamilton Basso," 13; Hamilton Basso to Frances Bowen Durrett, August 5, 1952, in Basso Papers, BL; Spratling, *File on Spratling*, 28.

25. Sherwood Anderson, "A Meeting South," in *The World from Jackson Square*, ed. Basso, 345; LaFarge, "Completely New," *ibid.*, 365.

group gathered at the Pelican Bookshop on Royal Street after closing hours. The shades would be drawn, wine was produced, and, sitting down with a salami and some bread, the group would have their "tea." It was a happy hour and not, as we would perhaps be ready to believe, an intellectual hour. The Royal Street locale was later described by Basso as "a good part of town. It was old and broken-down and not even the imitation artists and Bohemians could spoil it. They had done their best to spoil it but somehow or other . . . the Quarter managed to absorb all its invaders and come off relatively unscarred" (*DBL*, 59). Also, telling Frances Bowen Durrett, one of the first *Double Dealer* chroniclers, that she should not make the *Double Dealer* members "sound too earnest," Basso criticized the novel *Green Margins* (1936), by fellow member E. P. O'Donnell, for portraying the New Orleans literary community of the twenties as the center of "Big Thoughts": "By the time we reach page 300, we are beginning to wonder whether we are in the Louisiana delta or Greenwich Village."[26]

In spite of Basso's attempt to demystify the *Double Dealer* experience and contrary to the apparent frivolity of Spratling's and LaFarge's stories, we should not underestimate the importance of the magazine. Fred Hobson claims that southern magazines like the New Orleans *Double Dealer* and the Richmond *Reviewer* emerged as important rebuttals to H. L. Mencken's invective that the South had turned into a "Sahara of the Bozart." In reply to Mencken's Dixie bashing, the editors of the New Orleans publication avowed that southern culture did exist and endowed their efforts with a considerable degree of self-importance by subtitling the *Double Dealer* a "National Magazine of the South." In their repudiation of certain southern stigmas, they further stated that it was a "high time . . . for some doughty, clear-visioned pen man to emerge from the sodden marshes of Southern literature." "Sick to death of the treacly sentimentalities with which our well-intentioned lady fictioneers regale us," the editors claimed that the old traditions and the Confederacy should no longer be on southerners' minds: "A storied realm of dreams, lassitude, pleasure, chivalry and the Nigger no longer exists."[27]

26. *Double Dealer*, I (March 1921), 83; Basso, "William Faulkner," 11; Etolia S. Basso, interview with the author, January 3, 1991; Hamilton Basso, "No Decision," *New Republic*, November 11, 1936, p. 55.

27. Fred Hobson, *Serpent in Eden: H. L. Mencken and the South* (Chapel Hill, 1974), 33–56; *Double Dealer*, II (June 1921), 2.

The *Double Dealer* influenced the young Basso at a time when he had only begun to form his opinions of southern literature. Accordingly, Basso still thought in terms of the *Double Dealer* when he wrote that he wanted to depart from Dixie's "romantic . . . emotionalism" and tell about a South that was to be different from Julia Peterkin's and Lyle Saxon's "pretty wallpaper" versions. Similarly, his continued insistence on wanting to capture the "essential reality of the South" and his desire "to get rid of all the old sentimental truck and explain, by using facts instead of poetry, what has happened here in the South and why this romantic conception is so untrue" go back to the rhetoric and founding principles of the magazine.[28]

Besides leaving a mark on Basso's early poetics, the *Double Dealer* had a catalytic influence on the Southern Renascence. Although the magazine was constantly short of funds and struggled to survive, Hobson notes that the magazine "urged a critical examination of Southern tradition, and in doing so infused young writers centered in New Orleans (including Faulkner) with a sense of excitement and new purpose concerning the possibilities of Southern literature." Despite the magazine's initial regional orientation, by 1922 it had turned to the national scene and, in tune with the modernist zeitgeist, started to publish experimental fiction by writers such as William Faulkner, Ernest Hemingway, Jean Toomer, and Thornton Wilder. Basso thought the opportunity to experiment one of the merits of this little magazine.[29] His own inclination toward experimentation, especially noticeable in his early work and first novel, may have stemmed from the *Double Dealer*, too.

Frances Bowen Durrett ranks the magazine "as one of the most important organs for the development of struggling artists during the period [of the] Southern literary renascence." She has calculated that of the 293 contributors, 55 were sufficiently prominent to make *Who's Who in America* thirty years after the *Double Dealer* had first been published. From established authors like Anderson and Hemingway to writers like Basso and Faulkner, who owed their very first publications to the *Double Dealer*, the magazine attracted a wide variety of authors and artists. It was "fun," Basso wrote, and "something to be in on. . . .

28. Hamilton Basso to Maxwell Perkins, February 1, 1930, November 30, 1931, August 13, 1932, in SA.

29. Hobson, *Serpent in Eden*, 48; Hamilton Basso to Frances Bowen Durrett, July 20, 1952, in Basso Papers, BL.

It was a kind of cross between student days in Paris in the 1890's, and the Jazz age of the U.S. in the 1920's."[30]

Durrett places Anderson at the hub of the magazine and draws a rather flattering portrait of him: "His hospitality was without bounds, as was also his lack of social discrimination. No one was too dull or too conceited or too undesirable to be interesting. He was never hurried but listened endlessly to anyone who sought him out, and demonstrated a genius for smoothing out human snarls." Anderson's contemporaries give a somewhat different picture. Spratling writes how Anderson was not at all interested in a young Mississippi "squirt" named William Faulkner. Although Faulkner and Anderson would halfway mend their initial and mutually felt animosity, the two would remain at odds with each other, especially when either one wanted to be the center of attention; Spratling writes that Anderson could not stand it when Faulkner "spoke out of turn or distracted Sherwood's listeners."[31]

Another example of Anderson's smugness is provided by Spratling, who, together with Faulkner, offered Anderson a little book of caricatures entitled *Sherwood Anderson and Other Famous Creoles* (1926):

> [Spratling] made the drawings of all the "artful and crafty ones" in our group, Faulkner did the editing. We paid to have this thin little book of caricature—a spoof at Sherwood—printed . . . Though certainly not literature, it may now be considered a sort of mirror of our scene in New Orleans.
>
> When it arrived from the press, we very proudly visited Sherwood that evening and handed him his copy. He turned it over, looking inside, scowled and said, "I don't think it's very funny." Sherwood was taking himself very seriously at that time. He had recently been referred to by a critic as the "Dean of American Literature."

Among the rather benign caricatures there is a dazzling portrait of Basso "dancing the Charleston with the Muse." The caption reads: "A

30. Frances Jean Bowen Durrett, "The New Orleans Double Dealer," in *Reality and Myth: Essays in American Literature*, ed. William E. Walker and Robert L. Welker (Nashville, 1964), 212; Basso to Durrett, July 20, 1952, in Basso Papers, BL.

31. Durrett, "The New Orleans Double Dealer," in *Reality and Myth*, ed. Walker and Welker, 222–23; Spratling, *File on Spratling*, 22.

happy conception of the artist, the significance of which has slipped his mind in the interval. Picture has to do with superiority of agile heels over the keenest brain in captivating that elusive female, success."[32] Clearly, this alludes to Basso's dancing talent as well as his serious literary ambitions.

Basso's relationship with Sherwood Anderson seems to have been a trifle ambivalent. As one of the youngest members of the *Double Dealer* group, Basso naturally looked up to the peremptory personality of Anderson, at whose feet he literally liked to sit. Consequently, he acclaimed Anderson in his early career. Also, in correspondence with the *Winesburg* author, he envisioned Anderson to be the model leader of an "Intellectual Party," which Basso had thought up in a mood of young idealism. In another and rather humbling letter Basso reveals endearingly: "I couldn't be more deeply devoted to you. . . . I owe you a debt that I can never even hope to repay." In later years he was to omit the superlatives. Upon visiting the "glamor-starved" countryside of Kansas, he recorded that he was reminded of Anderson, who, in his own "clumsy, groping, fumbling way," was after "a kind of glamor." Mockingly, he added in his diary: "If I lived in Haddam (Kansas), I don't think I'd ever dream about characters in Winesburg . . . I'd dream about Rita Hayworth." Basso's gradual reconsideration of Anderson's art and personality coincided with the downward curve of the latter's reputation. In a letter to Thomas Wolfe, Basso actually regretted Anderson's fading fame. Influenced by Anderson himself, he observed that younger writers showed ingratitude where they ought to have shown indebtedness. To Basso, Anderson was one of the older American writers who "invented the tools," handed them down, and then found that the younger generation had become "more expert in using them."[33]

At the same time, Basso was, like Hemingway and Faulkner, unrelenting in his criticism of his older friend: musing how some writers become their own characters, he described Anderson as "one of those

32. Spratling, *File on Spratling,* 28–29; William Faulkner and William Spratling, eds., *Sherwood Anderson and Other Famous Creoles* (New Orleans, 1926), n.p.

33. Hamilton Basso to Sherwood Anderson, August 6, 1931, and undated letter in Sherwood Anderson Papers, NL; Basso, "An American Notebook: USA 1950–1951," July 7, 1950 (Typescript in Hamilton Basso Papers, HT), n.p.; Basso to Thomas Wolfe, July 3, 1937, in William B. Wisdom Papers, HL.

half-articulate, muggy-minded people that turn up in Winesburg." He depreciated his former mentor further in a letter to Elizabeth Nowell, in which he attributed a quarrel Wolfe and Anderson had had in the past to Anderson's "streak of malice" that occasionally turned him into a "trouble-maker." Yet in the same letter, he admitted squarely that Anderson "too is dead now, and was kind of generous to me back in the old days in New Orleans, and I wouldn't want to injure him in any way. The blunt truth of the matter is that all literary men are apt to be extremely disagreeable at times, and that's all there is to it."[34]

Basso was also relatively close to Faulkner, who lived "within shouting distance" of him in the French Quarter. He was first introduced to the Mississippian in 1924, when he and Faulkner were dinner guests of the Andersons. What he remembered best of that evening was not only Faulkner's gentlemanliness, which surfaced in his "beautiful manners, his soft speech," and "his controlled intensity," but also his not-so-gentlemanly "astonishing capacity for hard drink." Although neither Basso nor Faulkner had published any major work at this point, Basso especially felt his youth in Faulkner's company, as though he had been "admitted to the ball park by mistake." He felt particularly wet behind the ears when he discussed literature with Faulkner: while Faulkner had most of the modernists (Verlaine, Eliot, Pound, and Joyce) under his belt, Basso was still struggling with Conrad and Melville. He also noticed their different southern background: while Basso identified with a Mediterranean, Catholic, and European tradition, Faulkner's hinterland was "much less diluted, *sui generis*, Anglo-Saxon, Protestant, and, as it were, more land-locked, turned inward upon itself." This difference triggered many a conversation between the two writers, who would sometimes go for long walks on the wharves. Their friendship intensified when they went flying together with the Gates Flying Circus. This circus of reckless aviators, flying rickety planes, was a novelty in town. Since Basso served as a feature writer on the New Orleans *Times-Picayune* and was therefore considered to be "the least expensive" and most "expendable" of the paper's journalists, he was sent out by his city editor to report on the spectacle. Faulkner, who had a lifelong fascination with aviation, accompanied

34. Hamilton Basso, typescript notes for a *New Yorker* profile on Eugene O'Neill in Basso Papers, BL, n.p.; Basso to Elizabeth Nowell, April 27, 1949, in Basso Papers, BL.

Basso on these flights. "Nobody *else* in our crowd had gone looping-the-loop in a bucket seat and open cockpit over the Mississippi River," Basso later observed.[35]

After Basso left New Orleans and Faulkner returned to Oxford, Mississippi, the two lost touch but ran into each other again years later on a New York–bound train. The two men greeted each other as people who shared some fond memories but also as "two provincials" who found comfort in each other's company en route to that "large, unfamiliar city." Basso nicknamed Faulkner the "little Confederate" because he happened to be even shorter than himself. The two would send "occasional" messages to and fro via John McCrady, painter of the Deep South and husband of Basso's sister, Mary. After their meeting on the train, they ran into each other once more in the downstairs lobby of Random House, whose offices were on Madison Avenue: "I said, 'Well, now' and Faulkner said 'Good morning to you sir'; and then in full sight of a small audience, we rather formally embraced." Many years after this second chance encounter, Basso approached Faulkner and asked him if he could interview him for a *New Yorker* profile. Faulkner, who valued his privacy, answered, "Oh hell no!" and told Basso he would be welcome to visit but that interviews would be out of the question.[36]

When Faulkner died in 1962, Basso wrote a sympathetic obituary in the *Saturday Review*. Recalling their New Orleans days, he confessed that Faulkner's oeuvre was too complex for him; he attributed this to Faulkner's modernist techniques and mythologization of the South, which was not, in Basso's eyes, the South but "Faulkner's vision of the South. . . . Those who read him as a 'realistic' novelist might just as well read Dante as a Baedeker to the nether regions, and Milton as a Michelin going in the opposite direction."[37] Notwithstanding this droll criticism, which reveals Basso's penchant for a more straightforward and realistic mode, he respected Faulkner's work highly, and whereas his praise for Anderson would peter out over the years, his admiration for Faulkner continued to grow.

A last but not unimportant contact was the writer Lyle Saxon.

35. Basso to Perkins, April 2, 1934, in SA; Basso, "William Faulkner", 11–12.

36. Basso, "William Faulkner," 11–12. William Faulkner to Hamilton Basso, postmarked September 23, 1948, in Basso Papers, BL.

37. Basso, "William Faulkner," 13.

Basso's senior by thirteen years, Saxon was, like Anderson, a father figure for young and struggling artists; proof of this can be found in a letter in which Basso thanked Saxon for helping John McCrady: "Your belief in his stuff has helped him immensely—just as your belief, and your great encouragement, have always helped me." Basso was obviously part of both Saxon's and Anderson's social set; in a letter to Noel Straus, Saxon mentions how at a tea hosted by the Andersons, he ran into "Bill Spratling and young J. Hamilton Basso . . . then there was a strange couple . . . socialists, one a Russian Jew [Michael Gold] very dirty looking, but rather handsome in a Cossack way." Cathy Chance Harvey claims that Basso was a "sad kind of person" and that Saxon would "keep him bucked up." Although we should probably question Harvey's assumption that the older writer kept Basso "bucked up long after he left Louisiana," it is true that Saxon's support was generous and never wavered. In a *Herald Tribune* book review of Basso's *Courthouse Square* (1936), Saxon was even so magnanimous as to argue that the novel placed Basso "among the significant writers of the South" and incorporated "the fine fulfillment of the promise given in his earlier books."[38]

Saxon's benevolence was not always reciprocated by Basso: When it was his turn to write a critique of Saxon's only novel, *Children of Strangers* (1937), he produced a very flat-sounding review in which he made fun of Saxon's expert knowledge of Louisiana: "Mr. Lyle Saxon . . . knows more about Louisiana than many people know about their apartments." Although Basso apologized for the review with an ingratiating letter in which he told Saxon that the *New Republic* had cut one third of the piece without notifying him, one may question Basso's sincerity. Not only did Basso dislike Saxon's flighty plantation idylls, he was not very forthcoming either when he described Saxon to Thomas Wolfe as "a sort of the Ward McAllister of the New Orleans intellectual circles and not such a bad guy if you don't expect too much: maybe a little old ladyish."[39]

38. Hamilton Basso to Lyle Saxon, November 29, 1937, in Basso Papers, HT; Lyle Saxon to Noel Straus, December 21, 1925, in Lyle Saxon Papers, HT; Harvey, "Lyle Saxon," 138 (Etolia Basso disagrees with this and believes that Saxon was less influential than Harvey claims); Lyle Saxon, "Uneasy Blood in Their Veins," *New York Herald Tribune Book Review,* November 1, 1936, p. 8.

39. Hamilton Basso, "Bayou People," *New Republic,* September 1, 1937, p. 108; Basso

Basso's ambivalence may be ascribed to the fact that Saxon was a relative outsider to the *Double Dealer* circle. Although the group feigned a spirit of camaraderie and mutual encouragement, which Faulkner described as a fellowship of art and Oliver LaFarge endorsed with his claim that "when one of us achieved anything at all, however slight, the others were delighted and I think everyone took new courage," Harvey insists that there was no such bonding and that the formation of cliques of those who came from New Orleans and those who came from out of town was inevitable: "The inner circle of the *Double Dealer*, composed of members of established New Orleans families, was not always open to outsiders. For example, although Saxon served on the magazine's staff for seven months, he was not close to founder Julius Friend." As a New Orleans and Quarter native, Basso *was* part of the literary community.

Though Basso was still full of doubts about his own artistic talent, he was trusted by his peers for his literary judgment: besides advising LaFarge on his Pulitzer Prize–winning *Laughing Boy* (1929), he was very supportive of his friends and of other struggling writers. When he became an acclaimed author with the breakthrough of *The View from Pompey's Head* (1954), he did not lose his ability to stimulate young people and help them find their niche in life. Thus Robert Cowley, Malcolm Cowley's son, who remembered Basso as "one of the gods" of his childhood, recalled that "once, just before my senior year at college, Ham and I got into a long discussion about the Civil War—he was then writing the *Light Infantry Ball*. He talked about the problems of writing historical fiction. How, he asked by way of example, did people light fires or cigars in 1861? He said he had spent days finding the answer. Then one morning before I drove home he called me into his study and wrote out a check for $100—a princely sum in 1955. 'Here,' he said, 'use this to go to some battlefields.' I did, spending a week with my father in places like Gettysburg, Antietam, and Spottsylvania. I think that is where I came by my fascination for military history . . . [and] I started a magazine on the subject."[40] He was equally instrumental to his own son's anthropology career: when Keith's adviser wanted him

---

to Wolfe, October 20, 1936, in Wisdom Papers, HL. Remarkably, after visiting Saxon, Wolfe used Basso's very words in his notebook: "An old lady—not a phony" (Harvey, "Lyle Saxon," 358).

40. Robert Cowley, letter to the author, March 18, 1998.

to stay at an Apache reservation to do research, Basso bought his son a car and sent him away with his blessing, despite the doubts expressed by Keith's mother.

Basso's involvement with New Orleans' literary crowd explains also why his first publications—two mediocre poems—appeared in the *Double Dealer*.[41] At the outset of his career, Basso may have thought that he had more talent as a poet than as a prose writer. The early pieces that he wrote in New York are mostly poems, too, and when Basso tried to interest a publisher, he showed his poetry first and his prose second.

A titillating piece from Basso's *Double Dealer* days, giving a good impression of his strolls around the Quarter when he was a reporter, is the short story "I Can't Dance." The narrative, which marvelously conveys the French Quarter atmosphere on a hot summer night, is the kind of story that would have appealed to the *Double Dealer*: rather than presenting a glorious and romantic Old South, the story is set in the contemporary South, which figures as a seedy locale of sensuality and decay. Macolm, the central character, is a young newspaperman who wanders past a speakeasy in the Quarter's red-light district. "Speakeasies," the narrator tells us, are "wild and wicked places . . . bagnios where naked women sang and danced their own peculiar dance."[42]

Walking down the street, Macolm is caught in a dilemma: though immensely curious about the goings-on in the speakeasy, he is held back by the thought of his forthcoming marriage to the saintly Katherine. When he finally summons up the courage to enter a speakeasy, he is accosted by the husky voice of a prostitute who invites him to her place instead. He declines her offer with an embarrassed and apologetic "I just want to talk to you" and is bawled out. A second prostitute approaches him, yet finding out that her potential customer is a cheapskate who merely wants to talk, she also ridicules him and tells him to hurry home to his "Mamma." Ashamed, Macolm walks down the street, past the prostitutes who "began to vile [*sic*], scattering him with filth. Once or twice he winced, their obscenity so extreme, but he con-

41. Hamilton Basso, "Brain," *Double Dealer*, VII (April 1925), 139; Basso, "Questioning," *Double Dealer*, VIII (May 1926), 339.

42. Hamilton Basso, "I Can't Dance," *transition*, XVI (June 1929), 127–32.

tinued on his way, never looking up, thinking of penance and the price one paid for sin."[43]

Humiliated by the streetwalkers, Macolm passes the last house, where a black prostitute sits on the dilapidated steps of her porch. In contrast to the offensive white women, who prefer a quick buck to a small gesture of fellowship, this black girl invites Macolm to sit down next to her and tell her what is on his mind:

> Brown as an autumn leaf, brown as a cane-stalk in the dust of a country road. She raised her arms and her arms were like dark shadows upon the yellow brightness of the room. Kindness dripped from her voice. Her words were thick and sweet as the syrup ground from cane. Hungry for kindness, he stopped. It was the last house on the street. The cries and the laughter had died away. The street was quiet and dark again.
>
> "What yo' want ter talk about. Cum sit on de steps. Us'll talk ertil the moon goes down."

Macolm welcomes this token of sympathy, but as his desire to see the naked dances lingers on in his mind, he spoils the serenity of the moment. He gives the girl a dollar and asks her to dance for him. Throwing off her clothes, the girl sways her body from side to side while humming a jazz song. This does not satisfy Macolm, who asks her why she does not dance. The story ends with her self-conscious, "I can't dance, Mister. . . . I ain't never danced before. I jist can't dance."[44]

Unlike most of Basso's early and sophomoric compositions, "I Can't Dance" is a well written and carefully composed story. Powerful and straightforward, the narrative does not rely on sentimentality or melodrama, which is an occasional weakness of Basso's early work. Moreover, its realistically drawn local color characters carry the action convincingly to the story's unanticipated ending and leave the reader with something to think about.

The story is very similar to a fragment in Thomas Wolfe's *Look Homeward, Angel*. Although the two pieces can be read as intertexts of each other, since both publications go back to 1929, it is improbable

43. *Ibid.*
44. *Ibid.*

that either influenced the other. In Wolfe's novel, the young protagonist Eugene is sent out to collect money from newspaper subscribers. His route takes him to "Niggertown," a segregated part of Altamont. Here Eugene calls on a black prostitute named Ella. Unable to pay the bill, Ella hints that she might settle it otherwise. Eugene, who appears embarrassed and awkward, then demands that she dance for him.

As in Basso's story, the scene is imbued with overtones of white male supremacy. Although both Macolm and Eugene are conspicuously immature, exhibiting a puerile and compulsive hunger for sensuality, they assume airs of white superiority and "experience": whereas Macolm has the woman dance for him and tells her bluntly that she cannot dance, Eugene orders the woman around, tells her to take off her clothes, and yells hysterically that she should dance. The men are equally unsympathetic in their rude treatment of the two women, but Macolm's bad manners are a little more disguised than Eugene's: he yells, "Get-'way-nigger. Get-'way."[45] Also, Basso's portrayal of the black prostitute seems more sympathetic than Wolfe's: whereas the New Orleans callgirl is a slender, beautiful, and compassionate girl, Ella is fat and intimidating; once she starts dancing for Eugene, she turns into a "devouring" creature who smothers the boy in her embrace, whirls him around "like a chip," and grips "his slender arms round like bracelets." Escaping from her flabby arms and shabby apartment, Eugene dashes out and does not stop running until he has reached the town square, from where he looks back on Niggertown, which with its "rich, jungle-wild" laughter stands out in all its demonic otherworldliness.

As opposed to Basso's story, the scene in Wolfe's novel illustrates that Eugene, who represents white man in general, is an alien in the exotic world of Niggertown; it is a world he does not know or understand, and the incident seems to show that the abyss between blacks and whites was still wide at the time Wolfe was writing. This divide is further accentuated by the narrator's use of black stereotypes; Ella's naïveté, her black-mamma qualities, along with what Eugene perceives as her diabolic quality, turn her into a type rather than a human being. In Basso's story, on the other hand, the prostitute has very few stereotypical traits. Although she is extremely sensual, she is never dimin-

45. Thomas Wolfe, *Look Homeward, Angel* (1929; rpr. London, 1930), 323–26.

ished into a black archetype. On the contrary, her characterization bears more resemblance to the characters the African American writer Jean Toomer created in *Cane* (1923). One should further note that whereas in Wolfe's story the black and white parts of town are worlds apart, in Basso's story, black and white people live in the same neighborhood and seem to be on speaking terms with each other. Not only do black prostitutes go about their business on the same street as white whores, but the conversation between Macolm and the black girl also seems indicative of the more relaxed atmosphere of race relations in downtown New Orleans.

In addition to writing short fictional pieces and poems, which he attempted to sell to magazines and newspapers, Basso busied himself with journalism. Although he never spoke highly of his early newspaper work, remembering it as "space rate journalism" and a "short unhappy time on the late night shift," this work did increase his appetite for writing and gave rise to the dream to run his own newspaper business. In a letter to Matthew Josephson, he expressed doubts about the literary profession: "I would rather, a thousand times, to have my own newspaper." He tried to realize this in 1932, when his writing career advanced too slowly. He intended to be the editor of a weekly in Abingdon, Virginia, but after having consulted Sherwood Anderson, who had already started a newspaper in Virginia, Basso came to the conclusion that he did not have sufficient funds to launch such an enterprise. Etolia Basso denies this and believes that her husband's newspaper ambitions were "just talk." Nonetheless, Basso's reporting taught him that journalism came relatively easy to him; it would always be something to fall back on.[46]

Despite the good times Basso had in New Orleans, he understood that the Crescent City was by no means the literary mecca of the United States. He knew that if he wanted to become a serious writer, he should either join the expatriates in Paris and try to get published in one of the little magazines issued from the Left Bank, or rent a garret in the heart of Greenwich Village and try to interest a New York publisher. Basso finally departed for New York on June 7, 1926. Appar-

46. Basso to Wolfe, October 20, 1936, in Wisdom Papers, HL; Basso to Matthew Josephson, July 4, 1932, in Matthew Josephson Papers, BL; Basso to Perkins, June 2, 1932, in SA; Etolia S. Basso, interview with the author, January 3, 1991.

ently, Lyle Saxon had lined up a newspaper job for him at the *Sun*. His correspondence with Anderson, however, reveals that employment eluded him for months.

Basso dramatized his trip from New Orleans to New York City as a spiritual journey from childhood to adulthood: leaving home meant cutting ties and saying farewell to the carefree days of childhood and adolescence. In Basso's life and oeuvre, journeys usually take on a sentimental air. Just as the narrator of *Courthouse Square* (1936) records upon his hero's journey home that he "was not old but so much of youth had already gone" (*CTS*, 10), so did Basso observe upon his outward-bound journey that, with his twenty-second birthday coming up, his "boyhood" was essentially over:

> New York City, Oct. 30th, 1926: I write with the approach of my twenty-second birthday staring into my face. My boyhood is over. By the turn of the wheel I am a man. A great man has written "There comes a time in every young man's life when he first takes a backward view of life."
>
> I have known that moment. It came, I think, when I stood on the deck of the steamer that bore me from New Orleans. My previous years seemed to float past me like the plume of the funnels smoke. Beyond the conflicting emotions of parting I saw my whole past life.[47]

Never an optimist at heart, Basso experienced his journey as a rather somber one. With an Italian sense for drama, he wrote Anderson on the eve of his departure: "Tomorrow the young man departs for the guillotine." Half in earnest and half jokingly, he also asked Anderson if he would light some candles for the "innocent" who was about to set foot "abroad." The next morning, nervous but also excited, Basso boarded his steamer to New York City.

47. Hamilton Basso, Diary (Typescript in Basso Papers, BL).

2

Portrait of the
Artist as a
Young Man

When Basso arrived in Greenwich Village in 1926, its lively artistic climate was already past its apogee. No longer was the Village the site of the militant *Masses* or of Mabel Dodge's and Margaret Anderson's literary salons. The Golden Boy of the Village and poet-radical, John Reed, had died in Moscow; the *Little Review* had suspended publication; and many of the earlier artists who created that exceptional Village atmosphere had moved elsewhere. In a last attempt to resuscitate their glory days, the New York aesthetes tried to resurrect magazines of the arts such as they had known in Paris. However, the old maverick spirit was ebbing and making room for the discovery of the Village by the public: crowds of people poured in, and rather than practicing or discussing art, they came for cocktails, good dinners, and the special ambience. When Basso disembarked his steamer from New Orleans, the place was rapidly changing from a center of bohemia into a center of entertainment for lost artists, fad followers, and dilettantes. With the Jazz Age in full swing, Greenwich Village became a pre-Depression paradise of hedonism:

> While the rest of the nation tried to escape reality in a mad whirl
> of spending and Charleston dancing, the Village did precisely

the same—only more so. . . . In all sections of the Village natives
and Bohemians had grasped the opportunity to make money by
flaunting the Prohibition. . . . Probably the world will never
again see the sort of frenzy that swirled and eddied among the
diverse Village joints. No less than the uptowners in search of
excitement or the Bohemians out for a good time, the intelligen-
tsia fell under the spell of mad hysteria. Still nursing the belief
that older generations had let them down, and that the future
was empty of hope, they drank, made promiscuous love, and
danced with the abandon of every one else.

In contrast to this drunken revelry, Basso's experiences in Gotham
were soberly spartan. In letters to Anderson, he complains of loneliness, listlessness, illness, and a general sense of uprootedness. Alone
and lost, the young provincial from Louisiana bemoaned how it "gets
lonely as hell up here. Sometimes I just walk and walk and walk—
trying to make myself become part of things."[1]

Lyle Saxon, who happened to be in New York City at the same time,
had similar impressions of the metropolis. Writing about swarming
masses, noisy traffic, and subway entrances that "belch up thousands
of people from underground at every corner," he commented that life
in Greenwich Village was not as "romantic" as it sounded. Basso's and
Saxon's discomfort with the big city may be attributed to their both
having come from the protected world of *Double Dealer* coziness; in
New Orleans they had known the artistic community inside out, but in
New York they were without friends, family, and in Basso's case, soon
without money. Catherine Harvey notes that Saxon's perturbation may
also have been triggered by his aversion to the commercialization of the
Village, a development that he feared for his beloved Quarter. Basso's
worries, on the other hand, were more personal and immediate.[2]

Unable to find appropriate employment and too proud to run back
home, Basso took on jobs such as trucking freight and working in a department store. At the same time, he tried to approach a publisher with
references from Edmund Wilson, whom he knew from New Orleans,

1. Allen Churchill, *The Improper Bohemians: A Re-creation of Greenwich Village in Its
Heyday* (New York, 1959), 293–94; Hamilton Basso to Sherwood Anderson, June 22, 1926,
in Anderson Papers, NL.
2. Harvey, "Lyle Saxon," 207–208.

and Sherwood Anderson. A few letters to Anderson and a handful of diary notes are the only sparse documentation available regarding Basso's life in the Village; from it one learns that Basso was working on a novel that he intended to send off to a publisher. However, always diffident about his work, he delayed mailing it. Having asked Anderson for a letter of introduction on July 8, 1926, two weeks later, on July 22, Basso was reluctant to mail his manuscript, because he had found some "really bad parts." Swings of mood, oscillating between confidence, doubt, and dejection, typify his starting out as a novelist. Questioning the legitimacy of his vocation, Basso depicted himself as the prototypical struggling young writer trying to keep his head above water: "Three years of life pass smoothly. Old haunts change, old faces fade, old names are forgotten. The young man grows older. In a few years he will no longer be young. The wind whistles through his sleeves and there is bread and butter to be earned. Clothes and bread and butter do not come easily to a poet. He must seek a more substantial means of livelihood."[3]

Basso liked to play up a sense of urban loneliness, a sentiment that reverberates in the writings of the lost generation: "Throughout the day, mingling with crowds of people, he has felt lonely and desolate. Though he has rubbed shoulders with hundreds of men and women, he seems to be living in a remote world that is not the sphere they inhabit." One does not have to go far to find the same young man and the same cityscape in the work of Basso's contemporaries. While F. Scott Fitzgerald reminisces in "My Lost City" how drab his life in New York City was before he made his roaring debut in the literary world, one of John Dos Passos' characters roams a similar landscape of despair: "The young man walks fast by himself through the crowd that thins into the night streets; feet are tired from hours of walking; eyes greedy for warm curve of faces. . . . At night, head swimming with wants, he walks by himself alone."[4] The image of a young man lost in a dehumanized urban reality is especially poignant in one of Basso's poems:

3. Hamilton Basso, "An Epilogue" (Typescript in Basso Papers, BL), n.p.
4. Hamilton Basso, untitled typescript in Basso Papers, BL, n.p. F. Scott Fitzgerald, "My Lost City," in *The Crack-Up* (1945; rpr. New York, 1959), 23-33; John Dos Passos, *The Big Money* (1936; rpr. New York, 1979), xviii-xix.

I know that somewhere
Past sky-scrapers
Past subways
Past the thunder of wheels
There is silence

I know that somewhere
Quiet women
With quiet eyes
Are folding
And putting things in chests

Men are coming home
Blessedly weary
After a day in the fields
Happy in the bounty that they have
. . .

I know that somewhere
These things exist
And yet I sit here
My head in my hands
Dark and unhappy.[5]

The poem seems to have been engendered by Basso's homesickness, longing for a familiar face, and desire for a sense of community. The tension between home, here portrayed as a kind of pastoral myth, and the big city of skyscrapers, subways, and "thunder of wheels," returns more explicitly in *Courthouse Square* and *The View from Pompey's Head.* But homesickness was not the sole source of Basso's melancholy. His loneliness was undoubtedly exacerbated by his stubborn refusal to immerse himself in New York's literary scene. In a revealing diary fragment, he condemns the modernist "disease" and wishes no part of it: "All the young men suffer from the same disease. Everything we write is symptomatic of the current world and disorder. It's so easy to get lost. My friends in Paris, Jolas and the rest of them, call them Surrealists, issue proclamations saying that the revolution of the Word is an accomplished fact and promptly lose themselves, following their savior in the impossibilities of an unsound theory . . . on the other side, I

---

5. Hamilton Basso, "Litany" (Typescript in Basso Papers, BL), n.p.

find my other friends, Saxon, Lafarge, Bradford etc. selling art on the streets. A few young men, Matthew Josephson, Bill Faulkner, Edmund Wilson are really plowing a field."[6]

Basso did not relate to his fellow artists: "I suppose I've never liked groups or cliques and find it a sort of fierce necessity to walk alone." His claim to independence, often causing unwanted loneliness, prevails in his life and work. While Basso complained in later life that "I write, I suppose, out of this loneliness I always feel in New York . . . and the awareness that, among people who write books and paint pictures I have so few friends," in his third novel David Barondess tells the reader that it is "better to get off in your own room and be your own self and do your own work" (*CTS*, 28–29). It may be for this reason also that David, like Basso in 1926, "tried to become part of the literary life but it did not work out very well."[7]

Basso shared his dislike of the Village with Thomas Wolfe, who, like his alter ego, George Webber, also denounced New York bohemia. In *You Can't Go Home Again* (1940), George does not want to have anything to do with either the "phoney passions, and six-months-long religions of fools, joiners and fashion-apes" or the "franky-panky, seldesey-weldesey, cowley-wowley, tatsey-watesy, hicksy-picksy, wilsony-pilsony, jolasy-wolasy, steiny-weiny, goldy-woldly, sneer-puss fellows." Though forced to play along at first, Basso and Wolfe soon tired of the pretenses of the artistic crowd. Their southern provincialism, which may have been accentuated by the metropolitan context of New York City, can be seen as characteristic of southerners of their generation. C. Hugh Holman suggests that the southerner, once he arrives in the city, is a provincial par excellence: "When the Southerner has gone to the metropolis, when he has felt the strong pull of the cultural and intellectual forces concentrated in the big city, it has been to what was in many respects to him a foreign land." Basso, Wolfe, and their characters David and George find out gradually that the city is a land of broken promises, and although they moved to the city in the hope of gaining professional and personal recognition, they return to their hometowns disillusioned. Holman further believes that because

6. Basso to Anderson, [*ca.* 1926], Anderson Papers, NL.

7. Hamilton Basso to Matthew Josephson, [*ca.* 1947], in Josephson Papers, BL; Hamilton Basso, *Courthouse Square* (New York, 1936), 29.

the southerner views the city as a foreign and sometimes hostile reality, he remains an outsider, a provincial and mere "sojourner."[8]

Basso's sense of exclusion is conveyed especially well in one of his autobiographical pieces. Overlooking the bustling Thanksgiving crowd from a shabby room with stained curtains, the young author feels disconnected and expresses disdain: "I often wonder whether these good people think of nothing save their bellies. . . . N. told me my own feeling of superiority was naught but an indication of madness, but mad or not mad the fact remains that they are a terribly depressing lot." Basso's feelings of homelessness and isolation were probably intensified by his rejection of starry-eyed artists and New York intellectuals. Although an intellectual himself, he resented the breed that acted intellectually for intellectuality's sake: "The inhabitants of the Village are not so bad or not so original as one has been led to believe. I see them every night when I go into 'Hubert's Cafeteria' about twelve o'clock for a cup of coffee. They sit around the somewhat greasy tables reading and talking. Some of them have the expected long hair but a great number of them are as closely-tonsured as I. It is impossible for me to believe although I would like to, that they are worth very much. They seem generally to be of the most shallow and sterile types, talking about cleverness and what-not-else, reading all the things they are expected to read."[9]

These observations and frustrations of 1926 would ultimately be vented by Basso's character David Barondess, who remarks that "there was nearly always a party where you met writers and painters and radicals and whole crowds of people who wanted to be painters and radicals and publishers" (*CTS*, 28). Like his fictional brother, Basso was skeptical of would-be artists and presumptuous intellectuals. For established artists, on the other hand, he had deep respect. Chasing away the loneliness of his New York City evenings, he had watched Eugene O'Neill's play *The Great God Brown* (1926) and had subsequently bumped into the playwright at a subway entrance when he was loudly repeating an appealing line from the play to himself. O'Neill had

8. Thomas Wolfe, *You Can't Go Home Again* (1940; rpr. New York, 1989), 376; C. Hugh Holman, "The Southern Provincial in Metropolis," in Holman, *Windows on the World: Essays on American Social Fiction* (Knoxville, 1979), 160, 166.

9. Hamilton Basso, "Greenwich Village" (Typescript, Basso Papers, BL), n.p.

smiled, as Basso recounted twenty-one years later, in 1947, while inter-
viewing the playwright for a *New Yorker* profile.[10]

Basso's disillusionment with the Village and anxiety over jobless-
ness became so chafing in the end that he began to pen apocalyptic visions of despair: in the story entitled "Holiday," the world is portrayed
as an "evil" and "greedy woman," while in the poem "A Spatial Arrangement," the world has become a "Patronymic spider" that likes to
swallow screaming man with its "distended abdomen." Aware of his
son's discontent and financial difficulties, Basso's father finally persuaded him to come home. By the winter of 1926, Basso had returned
to New Orleans, revisiting the quarters of the moribund *Double Dealer*.
His sojourn in New York City amounted to less than half a year and
not, as Clarence Ikerd claims, two years. About thirteen years after his
stay in New York, Basso described the metropolis as "an oyster" that to
his "hurt astonishment wouldn't open."[11]

Of his return to New Orleans we have no actual records, but Etolia
Basso remembers that Basso felt depressed and disappointed in his
hometown. Edmund Wilson must have sensed his friend's discomfort
as he responded to one of Basso's letters with "I can see how New Orleans would get on your nerves, but would give anything to be able to
go there myself." The best impression of Basso's feelings at this time is
provided by an insightful letter he sent to the former *Double Dealer*
member Eugene Jolas, who published it in his little magazine, *transition*. The letter gives a marvelous glimpse of Basso's personality, for
underneath that gracious, sociable, and polite southern gentleman was
hidden a feisty and combative critic who, like Leon Falkes in Basso's juvenilia, aspired to emulate H. L. Mencken: "[Mencken] was the most
important critic in America. There should be a few more like him. A

10. Besides using this story for his O'Neill biography, Arthur Gelb borrowed extensively from Basso's interview notes, as he had been one of the last reporters to interview
O'Neill. See Arthur Gelb, *O'Neill* (New York, 1962).

11. Ikerd, "Hamilton Basso," 10. For verification one should consult Basso's correspondence with Sherwood Anderson: we know that he sailed for New York City on June
7, 1926; he must have arrived in Manhattan about a week later. His first letter to Anderson is dated June 22, 1926; his last letter, October 24, 1926. As we now know, Basso was
plagued by unemployment, illness, and depression. He left soon after his last letter,
which means that he had been in New York about five months. See "Hamilton Basso,"
Wilson Library Bulletin, XIV (1939), 186.

few more Menckens to jolt this self-satisfied set of boobs who thought the whole world revolved about them. . . . Some day, he would write about them. He'd bounce a regular Mencken bladder upon their heads. He'd show them in all their pimply nakedness for the asses they truly were."[12]

In his "New Orleans Letter" Basso not only conveys his feelings of alienation, which seem typical of someone who has been weaned from his former habitat, but also lashes out against the gentrification of the Quarter and, like Mencken, derides the clique of artists who, drawn by the reputation of the fading *Double Dealer*, sat around in bookshops, swapping ideas: "They make me feel as though I ought to hurry home and take a bath," Basso told Jolas. Self-effacing about his own literary ambitions, he further challenged John McClure, who had defended the poet John Fineran because of his young age. Basso believed that youth should never be "an excuse for poor poetry." He added that though he himself felt the process of youth "very keenly," he would "vomit" if anybody told him that he was "a promising young writer." Conceivably, Basso's vehement attacks against the Quarter crowd arose from the rancor he had developed in New York. However, one should also see his disappointment in the light of how the Quarter was changing. Like Basso, Roark Bradford observed in a letter to Lyle Saxon that "too many country boys and girls are coming in to be Bohemians and immorality lacks that calm, professional dignity it held in the corrupt era prior to 1927."[13]

Shortly after Basso returned from New York City, he was hired again by the New Orleans *Times-Picayune*. Taking mostly night shifts, he tried to do some serious writing of his own in the daytime. However, since his night shifts and busy social life were not conducive to

12. Etolia S. Basso, interview with author, May 4, 1992; Edmund Wilson to Hamilton Basso, January 25, 1927, in Edmund Wilson, *Letters on Literature and Politics, 1912–1972,* ed. Elena Wilson (London, 1977), 132–33; Basso, "New Orleans Letter," *transition,* XV (February 1929), 149–50; Basso, "A Debutante" (Typescript in Basso Papers, BL).

13. Basso, "New Orleans Letter," 149–50. Harvey, "Lyle Saxon," 208. Despite the embittered and pessimistic tone of Basso's letter, his gloom is reversed when in the closing paragraph he speaks of his hope for a new generation of writers. Basso's wish for new writers who would not be crippled by affectation but who would come from more ordinary backgrounds—making their living in factories or, like himself, by writing "obits for newspapers and ads for ladies' underwear"—anticipates the emergence of the proletarian literature of the thirties.

creative writing, Basso decided he needed another place to get pen to paper: in a letter to a friend, he inquired after a cabin in the Louisiana countryside. Looking forward to having time off and finishing a novel he had been composing for months, Basso joked that his sociable temperament might be incompatible with the isolation a writer has to endure: "I am essentially a creature of civilization, with a penchant for debutantes or part debutantes who smell nice, jazz, booze and all the other awful, awful vices."[14] He expected that by the summertime he would have saved enough money "to bide off a year or so." This plan failed: *Relics and Angels* was not completed in the Louisiana countryside but in Grand Isle on the Gulf of Mexico in 1928.

Tony Clezac, the main character of Basso's first novel, returns to New Orleans after having lived with his grandfather in Italy for eight years. The city is never mentioned by name, yet one recognizes New Orleans by the proximity of the river, the bayous, the balconied streets, the gray cathedral, and the overall setting, which the narrator summarizes as looking like some "very sentimental and romantic play" (*RA*, 36).

Upon his arrival, Tony first visits his grandmother, who entered a convent after her husband ran off with his mistress. In an awkward reunion Tony tells his grandmother of his grandfather's death and of his resolve to fill the executive position at the shoe factory that the Clezacs once owned. The attentive reader may notice autobiographical parallels. Both the Clezacs and the Bassos have roots in the Old World, and both make their living in shoe manufacturing. Aged twenty-five (Basso's age when he was writing the novel), Tony, like Basso, has one younger sister, is raised a Catholic, and comes from New Orleans. Moreover, Tony's grandmother, named Antoinette, resembles Basso's, whose name was Annette. Like Basso, Tony is named after his grandfather, Antoine. Finally, whereas the Bassos sold their company to Steinberg, the man in charge of the Clezac company is named Epstein.

Tony's homecoming, its tone having been set by the uncomfortable reunion with his stern but noble grandmother, is a typical Basso homecoming: the protagonist is overwhelmed by contradictory feelings. While Tony acknowledges a sense of connectedness as he enjoys revisiting the scenes of his childhood, he also feels alienated in a world that

14. Hamilton Basso to Eugene Matrange, April 22, 1927, in Basso Papers, HT.

is no longer his own. For example, when he sees his sister Laurine again, he finds it difficult to believe that she "was his sister. They were barricaded by hemispheres" (*RA*, 33–34). Tony's estrangement is further displayed in his reserve toward Laurine's fun-seeking country club friends. His feelings probably reflect Basso's own discomfort upon his return home from New York. Like Basso, who was no longer comfortable with the artists who made the French Quarter their home, Tony experiences a similar kind of awkwardness in his former home environment.

Julius Epstein, the new owner of the Clezac company, gives Tony the somewhat redundant position of second vice-president. At this point his dilemma starts to take root, because although he feels the call of familial duty, he cannot warm to business, having been trained as a scientist. Tony's conflict between propriety and true ambition may have resembled Basso's predicament in 1929: like Tony, Basso felt divided between the obligations of a job he held but did not care for and the aspirations of a career he wanted but did not (yet) have. A similar vocational dilemma would recur in Basso's 1939 novel, *Days Before Lent*. Though the protagonist of this novel is considerably more mature than Tony, his choice between research and the practice of medicine is equally thorny and reveals Basso's continued preoccupation with the discrepancies between theory and practice, the intellectual way of life and a more pragmatic way of life.

Tony's homecoming also involves romance, a fixed ingredient of Basso's novels. His first love is the married Helen Montross, who is initially flattered by Tony's loving attention, an affair being a welcome diversion from her dull middle-class life. The romance, however, turns sour when Tony proposes they elope. Suffering from what Basso later termed "Shintoism" in his best-seller *The View from Pompey's Head*, Helen refuses to give up her marriage as well as her position in society and simply rejects Tony. Enter Camilla Thorne, whose name emblematizes guarded innocence. Although she is attracted to Tony, she keeps him at a distance. Camilla is a favorite Basso heroine: beautiful, genuine, virtuous, and invariably gray-eyed. Curiously, though, despite his infatuation, Tony cannot muster the energy or courage to court her. A third young woman drifts in and out of his life at a moment of weakness, Marianne Slade. As her last name perhaps hints (it alliterates with "slut" and "sleazy"), she is preoccupied with sex. Basso's portrayal of Marianne and Camilla, who clearly serve as antitypes of each other, sets a pattern of shallow and antonymous female characters in Basso's novels: having very little substance altogether, they are either madonnas or whores.

Tony's miserable love life is exacerbated by his unhappiness at the Clezac factory, Forward Shoes. His misery reaches a nadir when he delivers a speech to the laborers. Confused by his own argument, Tony pleads against consumerism and other evils of industrialized society. His listeners, who do not understand half of what he is saying, nonetheless single him out as someone loyal to their cause and go on strike. Reprimanded by the board of directors, Tony uses the occasion to quit his job but then wonders whether he has done the right thing; he is reminded of his grandfather's warning that one should never become a wanderer in life or a "gypsy in a yellow wagon." Conversely, enlightened by Camilla's advice, Tony also realizes that he must remain true to his ambition. So he writes his European mentor, Hugo Mullendorf, and asks if he can become his research assistant. As Tony attempts to solve the complications of his homecoming, which essentially revolve around his uncertainty about his own identity, the family (identity) slowly disintegrates; while Tony intends to abandon the family and return to Italy, his spinster aunt, Hermine, dies of a neglected pneumonia, and Laurine marries and moves out of the house.

The novel could have ended there, but the narrator confronts the protagonist with a rather forced reversal of fortune—at Laurine's wedding, Marianne informs Tony of her unwanted pregnancy. Although the child is not Tony's, Marianne claims it is and requests fifty dollars for a clandestine abortion. In shock, Tony only hears the news of the pregnancy and sees his future ruined by an untimely marriage. After having been reimbursed fifty dollars for the planned trip to Italy, he meets Marianne and, in an all-too-contrived incident, the dollar bills fall out of his pocket. This satisfies Marianne but leaves him standing bewildered in the street. In a trancelike state, he wanders through the busy streets of New Orleans, sits in on a Negro tent revival, and finally falls asleep. His dream reveals "the shadowy figure of the priest, a later portrait of himself" (*RA*, 286).

The bizarre ending jars with Tony's (and Basso's) anticlerical views. As one of the novel's many inconsistencies, it can best be explained by Basso's inexperience as a novelist. Rather than taking the conclusion

literally, we may agree with Joseph Millichap that Tony's final vision
should be read as a metaphor for his shouldering of a "mature responsibility."[15] For it is highly improbable that someone like Tony, who
sneers at "the voluptuousness of high mass, the color and the music,
and the barren rigor of monastery walls" (*RA*, 252), would embrace the
faith so emotionally in the end.

Clearly, the protagonist's epiphany should be considered within
the framework of the *Bildungsroman*: although Tony's "education"
does not lead to the realization of his vocation in life, the novel does
progress toward his ultimate maturity. Accordingly, Tony's vision
should not be interpreted as a reconversion to the Church but as his
way of finding his feet again. This reading would be in harmony with
Basso's views on religion: in 1939 he told Malcolm Cowley that man's
"instinct for religion" was no more than "a longing for order."[16]

Tony's initial skepticism toward the Church and his problems fit-
ting in with society are typical of the twenties zeitgeist. In Anderson's
Winesburg, Ohio (1919), Sinclair Lewis' *Main Street* (1920) and *Babbitt*
(1922), and Wolfe's *Look Homeward, Angel*, as well as Van Wyck Brooks'
America's Coming of Age (1915) and Harold Stearns' *Civilization in the
United States* (1922), much of the twenties spirit amounts to a rebellion
against the trappings of dull, middle-class, small-town America. The
revolt from the village and the rise in secularization among the young
are recurring twenties motifs and evince what Malcolm Bradbury
called "the idea of a distinctive modernity of the times" as well as "the
desperate novelty of a generation feeling the distinctiveness of its own
conditions and searching out the emotional and moral terms of a new
life, free of provincialism" and "regressiveness." Although Tony's
struggle is mostly a private affair, his difficult acclimatization to home
and American society lie at the base of what Bradbury describes as the
need experienced by many at the time to break away from the established order.[17]

Tony's defiance surfaces most prominently in the speech he delivers
at the factory and in the grudge he bears against the entrepreneurial
class in general and Julius Epstein in particular. Upon a first reading of

15. Joseph R. Millichap, *Hamilton Basso* (Boston, 1979), 37.
16. Basso to Cowley, July 17, 1939, in Cowley Papers, NL.
17. Malcolm Bradbury and David Palmer, eds. *The American Novel and the Nineteen
Twenties* (London, 1971), 16–17.

the speech, which is enfeebled by Tony's emotional rhetoric, one may be puzzled by its apparent contradictions: whereas Tony praises the machine and laborers' skill in working with the machine, he ultimately denounces industrialized society. Echoing Henry Adams' belief that industry has become the new religion, the machine having replaced the "statue of St. Paul and the Virgin Mary" (*RA*, 142), Tony seems to unnerve his own industrial optimism when he speaks out his fear of unbridled consumerism and materialism. Preaching that the "art of character . . . [and] ethics and morality" are more "important than the art of being comfortable" (*RA*, 143), he warns the laborers against Henry Ford's hollow promises of the middle-class American Dream: "If there is a need for revolt it should be against the urge of well-being. You are paid well for your services here and so you are content to remain. You want an automobile, a home, new clothes for your wives and by working in the factory those things are brought within your reach. You have neither time nor patience for anything else" (*RA*, 140).

One may understand Tony's mixed feelings better in the context of what Richard Pells calls the twenties' inability to "decide whether [the machine] represented the most sophisticated achievement of the modern mind or a supreme expression of evil." In the same vein, Malcolm Bradbury has argued that the machine turned into an "ambiguous image" as it came to represent both "a novel vortex of energy and a destructive element." Tony's contradictory tirade may further be illuminated by a letter that Basso wrote to Sherwood Anderson in 1931. Citing Anderson's belief that a machine will only "produce whatever man wants to produce," Basso does not blame the machine so much as man's inadequacy to deal with industrialization: "It's man's fault. The people who have gotten hold of the machines are such fools. Properly directed the machine will show us the way out—to communism perhaps, socialism surely. I see a planned society, some kind of social order—borrowing from the Russians—with the machine to give man the thing he has had before:—leisure, the time to think and feel and live." Once the Depression became a reality, Basso was to view the machine in a much darker light; in 1932, he warned that it "may destroy us all; leaving only empty shells to perform, in grim mockery, the functions of men."[18]

18. Richard Pells, *Radical Visions and American Dreams: Culture and Social Thought in the Depression Years* (New York, 1973), 27; Malcolm Bradbury, "The Name and Nature of

Although Basso and Tony seem to have identified with the intellectual point of view of the day, they are not enamored with the milieu per se. In a fragment that is obviously based on Basso's experiences with the avant garde communities of New York City and New Orleans, Tony observes that the reality of the factory floor has very little in common with the parlor socialism of his friends: "Once, in the international company of several young men who were painters and poets, [Tony] had used certain expressions: 'man becoming subject to inorganic forces'—'the destruction of manual individuality'—but now, with the sound of the monster crowding his ears, he never once thought of such expressions. They seemed pale and unhealthily green, nurtured in a baleful atmosphere where high-voiced youths and posing newspaper women talked and became hysterical over the things they were going to do" (*RA*, 140).

Tony's hatred of the establishment is also aroused by the man who is in charge of the machine, Julius Epstein. His animosity is typical of the antagonism that twenties writers and intellectuals displayed toward the entrepreneurial class. Maxwell Geismar even attributes literature's "failure of nerve" to the tensions of the time, between the "guiding spirit of society" (i.e., the intellectual) and "its productive forces" (i.e., the entrepreneur).[19]

What is disturbing about Epstein's portrait is not so much Tony's renunciation of the capitalist class as his blatant anti-Semitism. While the depiction of Epstein as the ugly Jew and stereotypical cigar-smoking capitalist is more pronounced in earlier typescripts of the novel, all typescript versions share sentiments like, "he was a Jew and to Antoine Jews were lower in the scale of things than the niggers who carried boxes in his factory." Although anti-Semitic statements and innuendo abound in twenties novels generally, comments such as "Who was this Jew to patronize him" are extremely disconcerting given Basso's frequent and vehement repudiation of racism.[20]

Modernism," in *Modernism, 1890–1930*, ed. Malcolm Bradbury and James McFarlane (1976; rpr. Harmondsworth, Eng., 1987), 49; Basso to Anderson, August 6, 1931, in Anderson Papers, NL; Hamilton Basso, "Cotton Blossom: The South from a Mississippi Showboat," *Sewanee Review*, XL (1932), 393.

    19. Maxwell Geismar, *Writers in Crisis: The American Novel Between Two Wars* (Boston, 1942), 277.

    20. Hamilton Basso, "Relics and Angels," (Typescript in Basso Papers, HT), 51, 174.

At the same time, one should ask whether it is fair to associate Tony's anti-Semitism with Basso's actual views. Although Tony resembles his creator, it would be incorrect to claim that he is Basso's alter ego. Indeed, Basso's beliefs are more clearly indicated in his short story "The Fabulous Man." In that story, an expatriate American is shocked by the inflammatory anti-Semitic propaganda of his German girlfriend. The American protests and elicits his girlfriend's snide comment that he must be a Jew-lover when he defends Albert Einstein and attacks Adolf Hitler. The story, which was written as early as 1935, shows that Basso seems to have been keenly aware of the dangers of anti-Semitism and fascism, and unlike a majority of Americans, citizens and statesmen alike, he foresaw the impending disaster of Hitler's regime.[21]

As for Epstein, he is depicted as an amiable and generous man who welcomes Tony as a prodigal son. In contrast, Tony's conceit and resentment of Epstein reveal his intolerant and spoiled demeanor. Significantly, in two earlier typescript versions of the novel, but not in the published version, Tony's job resignation goes hand in hand with a painful row with Epstein. At Laurine's wedding, a tender reconciliation occurs, in which Tony finally acknowledges that Epstein deserves more credit for having remained such a loyal friend of the Clezacs. A similar role reversal takes place in *The Light Infantry Ball*, in which a mulatto, who is also despised by the main character, turns out to be the savior of the family. With this kind of turnabout antipathy, one should ascribe Tony's anti-Semitic feelings to his immaturity and his inability to judge other people. These failings are of course also painfully brought to light by Tony's failure to fathom either Helen's false intentions or Marianne's lie.

Though he is surely opposed to capitalism, Tony's social conscience lacks depth. As with most twenties characters (and unlike most thirties characters), Tony's contempt for society does not lead to a willingness to tackle its problems but to a disinclination to conform to society altogether. Instead of facing the world's difficulties, Tony looks inward: not only is *Relics and Angels* filled with mirrors and reflecting surfaces, but in the opening line of the novel we also find Tony "looking into

---

21. Hamilton Basso, "The Fabulous Man," *Scribner's Magazine,* XCVII (April 1935), 217–18.

himself" (*RA*, 9). This narcissistic quality, so different from that of the socially and politically engaged characters in proletarian fiction of the thirties, has been described by Malcolm Bradbury as the twenties character's "ethic of solitude." Suffering from self, solitude, and a society from which they remove themselves, these characters (and writers) lose themselves in a kind of social vacuum, a state that Henry Idema and Harold Stearns have described as "anomie."[22] It is obvious that Tony has fallen victim to anomie: like Hemingway's Jake Barnes in *The Sun Also Rises* (1926), he wanders aimlessly and is tormented with self-doubt and inertia. Restless and rootless, Tony experiences feelings of alienation upon his arrival home, aggravating his predicament. But his homecoming also gives him the chance to rid himself of his anomic condition. Or rather, Tony's homecoming is the precondition for his spiritual regeneration.

The latter is reinforced metaphorically by images of darkness, light, and rebirth. When Tony arrives home, he is literally plunged into darkness: visiting his grandmother, he is led, via descending, narrowing staircases, to the dark heart of the convent. Exiting the convent, Tony is again enveloped by darkness, as "the sun was gone and the sky . . . filling with night" (*RA*, 23). On his way home, he meets a blind beggar, who, groping his way through the darkness, asks for a penny and makes an obscure reference to Hamlet. Like that of Tiresias in T. S. Eliot's *Waste Land* (1922), the beggar's blindness is a "seeing blindness": he knows more about Tony than Tony does himself. Unaware of his fate, Tony is mentally blind. Contrary to Joseph Millichap, who argues that the protagonist's visit to his grandmother is the beginning of his rebirth in which the grandmother figures as a kind of spiritual guide, I would argue that Tony's homecoming is a necessary descent into darkness, blindness, and confusion prior to his personal renascence.[23]

The darkness starts to lift after Tony has his first breakdown. Having spent a pleasant day on an island off the Louisiana coast, he is called to the bed of a ferryman's wife, who is in labor. Having assisted in the delivery of her child, Tony wanders off to the beach. Contemplat-

22. Malcolm Bradbury, *The Modern American Novel* (Oxford, 1983), 77; Henry Idema, *Freud, Religion, and the Roaring Twenties: A Psychoanalytical Theory of Secularization in Three Novels: Anderson, Hemingway, and Fitzgerald* (Savage, Md., 1990), 145; Harold Stearns, *America and the Young Intellectual* (1918; rpr. New York, 1921), 69.

23. Millichap, *Hamilton Basso*, 30.

ing the trauma that an infant must suffer during childbirth, he thinks of his own mother, becomes very emotional, and finally collapses on the beach. Cursing the light of the rising sun, just as a baby would curse the light upon its entrance into the world, he reproaches the daylight with its reminders of the truth. Like the infant who has to descend from prenatal bliss and darkness into the reality of pain and light, Tony moves from the opiate darkness to a painful but authentic reality: "A great loneliness filled him. It was just as though he was walking a barren place. The barren place was filled with fog. He could not see. . . . He wanted someone to love and someone who would understand. . . . 'Get away, you bastardly light,' he shouted. 'Get the hell away from here.' . . . He could only think of birth's agony and the terror of bringing a child into this world. He began to pound the sand with his fists. He still looked at the stars. The stars had never seemed so far away" (*RA*, 100–101).

After this cathartic experience, Tony has truly become a new person. Realizing that his "personal salvation" is more important than anything else, he quits his job and by the end of the novel he looks back on his homecoming as an event that greatly contributed to his "education": "It was not to be supposed . . . that he would be able to return to that peculiar identity which he possessed upon returning to his own country. Many months had passed, there had been adventures and encounters, some discordant, some pleasant, and he had been changed" (*RA*, 180).

Tony is a typical solipsistic twenties hero, and Basso's female characters also have features of that era. Unlike the Prufrockian Tony, who is passive and indecisive, his sister Laurine has a mind of her own. As such, she fits in perfectly with the flappers of Fitzgerald's fiction and some of the more forceful of Hemingway's women; much more liberated than their Victorian mothers and grandmothers, these women exemplify the decade's feminism: they are tough and truly deserve to be called "New Women." Having broken with their Victorian forebears, they smoke and dance; they are assertive, sexually liberated, and rebel against their all-too-feminine roles. Thus, while in Fitzgerald's *This Side of Paradise* (1920), Rosalind declares that there "used to be two kinds of kisses: first when girls were kissed and deserted; second when they were engaged. Now there's a third kind, where the man is kissed and deserted," in the same novel Eleanor resents that women, notwithstanding their intelligence or ambitions, are "tied to the sinking ship of future matrimony."[24] Basso's Camilla condemns marriage in a similar fashion. Describing the institution as a "rotten thing" that does "awful things" to people and "especially to women," Camilla does not want to get married at all (*RA*, 237). But she is not the only one with feminist impulses. Laurine shows that emancipation has not left her unaffected either: in contrast to her uptight brother, she is uninhibited, smokes, and says that she is "sorry as hell." The secretary in Tony's office gossips that she is "free and easy. . . . It ain't worth being good and moral these days. Men don't want good women anymore" (*RA*, 170). Even the feminine Helen shows that the twenties woman can be calculating: like a Fitzgerald heroine, she confesses unashamedly that she broke up with her lover in college because he was "too poor" (*RA*, 87).

Whereas Laurine, Camilla, Rosalind, and Brett are portrayed as independent and strong figures, the male characters Tony, Amory, and Jake seem to have lost some of their masculinity. The subversion of these traditional role patterns goes hand in hand with the decade's demystification of romantic love; thus, in *The Waste Land*, a carbuncular clerk copulates with his bored typist, love having come down to the level of trivial routine. Likewise, in novels of the twenties, love and sexuality are no longer dark and mysterious forces but dreary and sham commodities: Lady Brett in *The Sun Also Rises*, Rosalind in *This Side of Paradise*, Carol Kennicott in *Main Street*, Daisy Buchanan in *The Great Gatsby*, Margot Dowling and Mary French in *The Big Money*, and Helen in *Relics and Angels* do not seek romance but diversion, convenience, money, or improvement of social status. Tony's deplorable love life can be blamed on the atrophy of romance. While Helen makes love to Tony because she wants attention, Tony makes love to Marianne because he is bored, and Camilla, the woman who has an authentic and romantic love potential for Tony, does not want to get involved for the reasons mentioned above.

Both Clarence Ikerd and Joseph Millichap have argued against a classification of Basso's first book as a southern novel, yet it contains some important southern elements that reverberate in Basso's later work and the works of his contemporaries. One of the most significant such features is the protagonist's sense of a family identity. Southern

24. F. Scott Fitzgerald, *This Side of Paradise* (1920; rpr. New York, 1986), 181, 237.

historians and critics have elaborated on this notion. C. Vann Woodward argues that whereas a Hemingway protagonist is usually deprived of any familial or cultural context and thus finds himself, like a
character out of Edgar Allan Poe, "alone with his problems, in the wilderness or with God," the southern character is usually burdened with
a familial and historical past; that is, he is not "alone in the wilderness,
at sea or in the bull ring [but] an inextricable part of a living history and
community, attached and determined in a thousand ways by other
wills and destinies of people he has only heard about."[25]

And just as C. Hugh Holman has claimed that the idea of family solidarity goes back to the agrarian origins of southern society, so has
M. E. Bradford written that the southern hero has such an engrained
sense of duty toward his family and society that he is essentially part of
a "corporate identity." A southern character with a corporate identity
represents rather than *is*, or, as the narrator of *Relics and Angels* clarifies:
"No man can lead his life independently of all other men. Life is not
simple like that. History is a fabric woven from the lives of all the men
who ever lived" (*RA*, 42). Unlike the "urban cosmopolites" of twenties
fiction, who, according to Malcolm Bradbury, are "freed from their
economic and moral roots, and so permitted to explore the pleasures of
time," Tony Clezac is checked by familial, cultural, and historical re-
straints. Moreover, Tony needs both society and family as touchstones
and consolidating forces of his identity, and to recover his true identity, he must return home. As in *Look Homeward, Angel*, the protagonist's confrontation with (and subsequent rejection of) the home is intertwined with the substantiation of his personal identity.[26]

What is more, Tony has a remarkable relationship with his grandfather, not dissimilar to Basso's relationship with his own grandfather.
Not only does Tony try to be a gentleman like his grandfather, but his
emulation of the pater familias goes so far that he perceives running off
with Helen as a perfectly justified act against the background of his
grandfather's adulterous affair. In Basso's later novels, the grandfather

25. C. Vann Woodward, "The Historical Dimension," *Virginia Quarterly Review*,
XXXII (1956), 260.

26. C. Hugh Holman, *The Immoderate Past: The Southern Writer and History* (Athens,
Ga., 1977), 9; M. E. Bradford, *Generations of the Faithful Heart: On the Literature of the South*
(La Salle, Ill., 1983), 40; Bradbury and Palmer, eds., *The American Novel and the Nineteen
Twenties*, 27.

takes on legendary proportions and becomes an almost inimitable example for the protagonist. Bertram Wyatt-Brown explains that this is a southern phenomenon, too—the veneration of forefathers coming out of a "genetic foundation that provided sons with inspiration but also the formidable challenge of living up to almost mythological heroes from the family."[27]

In addition to his exaggerated identification with his grandfather, Tony's corporate identity also manifests itself in his sensitivity toward family obligations, responsibility, and respectability. Concerned about the family's reputation, Tony initially attempts to save the family name by returning to the shoe company. It is there as well as in the old Clezac house that the family portraits "gazed dolefully" (*RA*, 30) down at him as if trying to remind him of his duty. However, in the end Tony realizes that being true to his family involves a life of "sham" (*RA*, 259) and "subterfuge" (*RA*, 228), for saving the family identity means sacrificing his own.

Besides Tony's realization that he may not be able to live up to his family's expectations, there are obvious signs that he has, in fact, come too late: the Clezac house is already moribund, containing the "final signal of a fading house" (*RA*, 167) and the "sense of man's defeat [hanging] like a pall in every room" (*RA*, 187). While the house is generally described as a scene of death, the garden likewise is withering, the banana leaves "torn like old clothes," no birds singing, and the fountain broken. Epstein notes that "a germ of decay had gotten in the Clezac family. . . . They were not on the verge of ruin but the infected spot was widening" (*RA*, 52). And yet even after Tony has reconciled himself with the fact that the Clezac era has gone, he cannot help feeling nostalgic: "He loved the house. It contained Clezac lives whose ghosts, living in the plaster of the walls, would soon be disturbed. Another name would make it theirs, there would be alterations and repairs, and all the things they had built, the things they cherished and admired, the colors they had selected and the wood they had bought, would be gone" (*RA*, 250–51). Until the end of the novel, Tony remains conscious of the family identity; at Laurine's wedding, he withdraws to the library to take a guilt-ridden look at the family portraits: "He felt as

27. Bertram Wyatt-Brown, *Southern Honor: Ethics and Behavior in the Old South* (Oxford, 1982), 118.

though he should tell them how sorry he was that everything had happened" (*RA*, 252).

The decline of the family, or fading out of an old order, is a prevalent theme in various Southern Renascence writings. As Richard Gray has written in his *Literature of Memory*: "During the 1920s, the years when people like William Faulkner, Thomas Wolfe and Robert Penn Warren were beginning to write and examine their regional environment, the South was at last acknowledging the death of its traditional way of life, based on the small farm and the great plantation, and recognizing its absorption into the strange new world of industrialism and advanced capitalism."[28]

Basso saw this motif of change as symptomatic of the New South. Like the two sisters in his unpublished novelette "The Ladies of the Land," the Blackheaths in *Cinnamon Seed*, and the Barondesses in *Courthouse Square*, the Clezacs have been replaced by a new entrepreneurial class. For this reason, Basso's first novel may also be classified as a novel of manners, which, according to James Tuttleton, tends to focus on "classes which have existed briefly or during transitional periods when one group is in the process of decay while another is rising to supplant it."[29] Since southern society has always been especially conscious of class and manners, the southern novel may be a novel of manners par excellence. In *Relics and Angels*, the reader is certainly made aware of class differences among the genteel world of the Clezacs, the money-grubbing world of the Epsteins, and the lower working-class milieu of the Slades. In Basso's later novels such class distinctions would persist, the protagonist's family usually occupying an island of enlightened thought amid a sea of up-and-coming white trash. Basso may be called a J. P. Marquand of the South, for not only did he, like Marquand, use the flashback as a recurring novelistic device, he also mocked and criticized the ways of the South, just as Marquand made fun of New England society.

As for the African American experience, unlike the black characters in Basso's thirties novels, the black characters in *Relics and Angels* play a minor part. Living in the shadow of their white employers, they are

---

28. Richard Gray, *The Literature of Memory: Modern Writers of the American South* (London, 1977), 2.

29. James W. Tuttleton, *The Novel of Manners in America* (Chapel Hill, 1972), 13–14.

discreetly present yet more attuned to the family's affairs than the family itself is aware of: "Colored folk are like that. They come into a white family, knowing all their secrets, all their joys and sorrows and ills. Then at night they go home again, to the cluttered house lit by candles and lamps, and lead their own lives, the whites know nothing of what goes on" (*RA*, 217). Despite their marginal and anonymous presence in the novel, they have strong identities of their own, and whenever the narrator brings them to the foreground, the prose attains a lyrical and incantational mode reminiscent of Jean Toomer's *Cane* (1923):

> —*Dream, brown mother, dream. Let your worshipping thoughts drift over the cane fields, into the dusky sky. Let them become of the redness of the rising moon and of the rustles of leaves of cane. What your dreams are, I know not. That knowledge is denied me. But dream them, whatever they may be. Be drunk with them.*
>
> —*Your nipples will soon be rid of his gnawing. The dust of the road lose the marks of his feet. He will be gone and forgetting . . .*
>
> —*Dream, brown mother, dream. Always and always. Until you die. Never open your eyes. Your dreams would be spilled. Were I cruel I would spill them. They would be spilled like the milk that drips from the corners of his greedy mouth.*
>
> —*I would say: That babe of yours, do you know what he will be? A low down buck nigger, stinking of sweat, his hands broken to the shape of a scythe. He will be consumed with brute passions. He will sing songs. White men will beat him. With whips sometimes, with words and looks more often. Even, I, unwittingly, will beat him.*
>
> —*He will get into a brawl with a white man. The white man's throat will choke with blood and your babe will throw the knife in the road. He will take to the swamps. Men and dogs will hunt him. Mosquitoes will torture his flesh. The miasma of the swamps will rise about him. He will be beset with primitive fears. Devils and demons will yell at him. He will try to escape.*
>
> —*White men will see him dashing across a road. Dogs will howl after him, bring him to earth. After that the end will be swift and frightful.*
>
> —*Only once in his life will he know tenderness. A brown girl will love him. They will go to the clearing where the canefield ends. Crickets will sing. The wind will whisper to them.* (*RA*, 121–23)

The Toomeresque flavor, which has been enhanced by simple sentences, repetitions, dreamlike atmosphere, poetic local color, but

also the awareness of the ill fate of the black southerner, is not coincidental. Basso was familiar with Toomer's writings: not only must he
have read some of *Cane*'s stories and poems that appeared in the *Double
Dealer* of 1923, but he also praised Toomer as one of the few writers
who truly grasped the black situation in the South. By 1926, Basso was
writing in the same vein and showed an interest in a similar subject
matter. Like Toomer, he affirmed the African American identity, and
rather than typecasting the black character as a jolly old simpleton, a
potential rapist of white women, or a benevolent black mamma, he
portrayed his fellow southerners as people whose emotions were genuine and whose rural lives bordered on the pastoral. Toomer achieved
the same in *Cane* by setting off black rural life against the dystopia of
the urban and white Northeast. While both writers acknowledged the
abuse of blacks and their exposure to constant surges of violence, they
also implied that the rural way of life and blacks' closeness to the soil
was to be preferred to the uprootedness of city life. To strengthen the
claim that Basso may have been influenced by Toomer's unique style,
one should compare the following passages, the first by Toomer and
the second, an early and unpublished piece by Basso:

> A pianist slips into the pit and improvises jazz. The walls awake.
> Arms of the girls, and their limbs, which . . . jazz, jazz . . . by lift-
> ing up their tight street skirts they set free, jab the air and clog
> the floor in the rhythm to the music . . . they press John towards
> a center of physical ecstasy . . . The glitter and color of stacked
> scenes, the gilt and brass and crimson of the house, converge
> towards a center of physical ecstasy. John's feet and torso and
> his blood press in . . . The walls press in singing. Flesh of a throb-
> bing body, they press close to John and Dorris. They close them
> in. John's heart beats intensely against her dancing body. Walls
> press his mind within his heart . . . Mind pulls him upward into
> dream. Dorris dances . . . John dreams.

> Jazz surging, jazz pounding, jazz breaking on the walls. Walls
> becoming soaked with jazz.
> Feet scraping, heels pounding, drums rolling, cornets mouth-
> ing . . .

Hey! Hey! Shake that thing! Rattle those cans! Hands clap.
Feet stamp. Voices shout.

. . .

Aimee, black eyes shining, becomes part of Quimby. Slender,
nigger-girl hips, swing next to his. Firm nigger-girl breasts,
crush upon him. Jazz jumbles words in his brain. She hums the
music but Quimby does not hear her. He is lost in a field of
cane.[30]

Progressing from entrancing jazz rhythms to the rhythms of seduction,
these passages are remarkably similar. Basso's "Nocturne" seems to
have been inspired by Toomer's "Theater" and "Carma," in which the
uninhibited Carma is seen dancing in pagan ritual. In "Nocturne," we
encounter the same ritual. Whereas "Carma" opens with "Wind is
in the cane. Come along / Cane leaves swaying, rusty with talk, /
Scratching choruses above the guinea's hawk, / Wind is in the cane.
Come along," Basso's piece closes with "Cane rustles in the moonlight.
Wind sings to it. Cane rustles and grows and is broken."[31]

Relics and Angels is remarkable for its unadorned and detached
style. The novel's simple, declarative sentences and its straightforward
dialogue are reminiscent of Hemingway's prose. It is not improbable
that Basso was influenced by Hemingway: Dan Piper claims that while
the first reviews of Hemingway's work go back to 1923, "By 1929 he
was already exercising considerable stylistic influences on such writers
as Dashiell Hammett, Raymond Chandler and John O'Hara." At the
same time, one could ascribe Basso's austere and paratactic style to
Sherwood Anderson's influence. Not only was Anderson an exemplary
author for many writers in the twenties, he had taken a personal interest in Basso while in New Orleans. Another influential writer is James
Joyce, whose *Portrait of the Artist as a Young Man* (1916) influenced *Look
Homeward, Angel, Cane,* and *Relics and Angels.*[32] However much Basso
may have shared with his modernist contemporaries, his experimental

30. Jean Toomer, "Theater," in *Cane* (1923; rpr. New York, 1969), 92–98; Hamilton
Basso, "Nocturne" (Typescript in Basso Papers, BL), n.p.

31. Toomer, "Theater," 16; Basso, "Nocturne," n.p.

32. Bradbury and Palmer, eds., *The American Novel and the Nineteen Twenties,* 65,
Louis D. Rubin, Jr., "Twentieth-Century Southern Literature," in *Southern Literary Study:
Problems and Possibilities,* ed. Louis D. Rubin, Jr., and C. Hugh Holman (Chapel Hill,
1975), 135.

style is not always successful like Hemingway's. Whereas Hemingway is adept at employing what some critics have called an "anti-style," which is especially powerful in its understatement, Basso's simplicity interferes with the narrative's implied tragedy. That is, Tony's self-dramatization and the melodrama of the forced and unanticipated epiphanies are incongruous with the novel's sober style.

A similar conflict of style and content is created by the narrator's stream of consciousness technique: Tony's "thought flows" do not necessarily impel the reader's closer involvement with him. On the contrary, Tony's motives are too obscure, his behavior is too erratic, and his acts are too unpredictable to win the reader over. This is also what makes *Relics and Angels* a mediocre novel, because regardless of its many twenties' insights, its Southern Renascence motifs, and its modernist style, the book never rises above the level of apprentice work. But as a formative work, it deserves some attention, for it clearly foreshadows some of the themes and characters of Basso's thirties novels. In the later novels, one finds the same troubled and homeward-bound protagonist, the same sense of family identity, the same society in transition, the same local color, and the same unfulfilled romance. However, despite Basso's tenacious use of similar characters, themes, and settings, his style would change from a modernist base to a more straightforward realism.

Upon its publication, *Relics and Angels* garnered little praise. In contrast to a complimentary *New Republic* review by Edmund Wilson, who lauded the book rather generously as having "grace, charm and a distinction which seem to mark the author as an artist rather than just another young man who has written a novel," the *New York Herald Tribune Review of Books* lambasted the novel's poor conception and characterization and decried Tony's naïveté as plain "horse sense."[33] Although the novel has value as an early work, the *Tribune*'s criticism was valid and would be endorsed by Basso's growing dislike of the book: in later life, he excluded the work from his list of publications altogether.

While Basso was putting his first novel together, he was falling in love with a woman named Etolia Simmons. Ham and Etolia, or Toto, had

33. Edmund Wilson, "Reveries and Surprises," *New Republic*, October 23, 1929, pp. 274–75; "Relics and Angels," *New York Herald Tribune Review of Books*, September 8, 1929, pp. 19–20.

both attended Tulane, yet they knew each other only vaguely from parties. This changed when Toto started working for the Pelican Bookshop on Royal Street, one of the locations where the *Double Dealer* crowd occasionally gathered. According to Toto, she and Ham became friends very gradually. Although she was attracted to his good looks, his white linen suits and maroon ties, romance was slow to unfold. However, when Ham returned from New York, they met again and "became very good friends."[34]

Toto was the only daughter of a well-to-do St. Louis family. Her father, Roger Simmons, became a national hero after he witnessed the October Revolution and survived a narrow escape from a Moscow prison. Upon his return to the United States in 1918, he and his family moved to New Orleans, where he became prosperous in the lumber business. Etolia attended Newcomb, the women's college at Tulane, and graduated in 1926. From the Tulane yearbooks we know that she was an active young woman, taking part in many clubs and sports events. While Etolia Basso denies having been a sought-after beauty, Malcolm Cowley has written that Basso stole her away "from twenty or thirty young lawyers and newspapermen who had the same glint in their eyes." He finally proposed to her during a romantic dinner at Galatoire's. Toto's parents were not pleased with the prospect of giving away their daughter to a struggling young writer. As Toto herself remembered in her customary deadpan manner, "They did not think much of it."[35]

The two were wed in the summer of 1930. Because Ham was Catholic and Toto Protestant, they chose the quiet countryside of North Carolina for the ceremony. The wedding was held outdoors in the beautiful garden of Toto's friends, Mr. and Mrs. Henry Carriere. The announcement in the *Times-Picayune,* stating that Ham and Toto's wedding was going to be "one of the very interesting out-of-town nuptials of the early summer," indicates that they were a popular New Orleans couple. The wedding itself occurred when the bishop arrived on horseback to witness the couple exchange their vows in the open air. Toto may have wondered what she was getting herself into, for although her hus-

34. Etolia S. Basso, interview with author, January 3, 1991.

35. Malcolm Cowley, draft for Basso's eulogy, in Cowley Papers, NL; Etolia S. Basso, interview with author, January 16, 1992.

band had taken on a job as a copy writer with a New Orleans advertising agency, he really wanted to become a full-time novelist. At this point, *Relics and Angels* had already come out.

The couple moved into an apartment on Milan Street, where Ham tried to write a new novel as well as find another publisher. Although Macaulay, the publisher of his first novel, was ready to take on another manuscript, Basso was shopping around, sending outlines, ideas, and full stories to various publishers. As early as 1927 he had approached Maxwell Perkins, the renowned editor of Fitzgerald, Hemingway, and—supremely—Thomas Wolfe. In a letter of February 1, 1930, Basso informed Perkins that he was writing a novel that in typical *Double Dealer* fashion, would be a radical departure from antebellum myths and southern "emotionalism." In a subsequent letter he hinted to the Scribner's editor that he had broken with Macaulay, as he was tired of "laying in the same bed with Peggy Joyce, etc." He casually mentioned that he had "chunked the manuscript of a perfectly lousy novel into the river," and although Perkins responded to this with confusion, Basso exclaimed, "What the hell! There are too many incompetents slinging ink."[36]

Basso nonetheless strained to get both his longer and shorter fiction accepted by Perkins. Failing to do so and worrying about the wife he now had to support, he was afflicted by a bad case of stomach ulcers in August 1930. Reporting to Perkins that he could have no more than a pint of milk every twenty-four hours, he lamented: "I think with great despair about the many good things there are in life to eat and what a gorgeous pleasure eating is [but] All this gastronomical preamble is but a way of approaching the question of 'Did you ever get a manuscript titled 'Cotton Blossom'? . . . I fear for its safety as I kept no carbon of it.'"[37] Perkins rejected "Cotton Blossom" together with Basso's other (lost) sketches of the South.

Following Edmund Wilson's advice "to keep at it, in spite of hell," Basso then sent Perkins the manuscript of another novel, "A Room in the Sky." At this point, Basso worried that he would fail to publish anything after the meager success of *Relics and Angels.* Perkins' response was painfully short but honest: "In spite of its unusual talent

36. Hamilton Basso to Maxwell Perkins, February 1, May 17, 1930, in SA.
37. Basso to Perkins, August 1930, in SA.

cannot think publication practicable. Deeply sorry." Although this sounds like the typical editorial response, Perkins' replies were usually heartfelt. He was an extraordinary editor, who, more "actively than any of his colleagues . . . scouted the work of new authors from all corners of the country [and] sought out authors who were not just 'safe,' but who spoke in a new voice about the new values of the post-war world." His genius lay not merely in his ability to spot new talent but in his punctilious diplomacy and his genuine concern for the well-being of the novelist and his work. Some of that diplomacy and concern are already present in the letters that he wrote to Basso at a time when there was not yet a contract.[38]

Basso must have felt Perkins' good will, and although much of his early work was rejected, he continued to send Perkins his efforts. The editor's many responses ranged from "I think it is full of very very beautiful writing but really it is more a poem of some sorts than a story" to "the book was extremely well-written and the characters were well realized [but] we are in a depression, and we have to consider that aspect more than in better times."[39] With the Depression worsening every day, Perkins had to be careful, selective, and parsimonious. Adding to Basso's difficulty in getting a foot in the door at Scribner's or at any of the other New York publishing houses was the fact that his full-time job as a copywriter at the Fitzgerald Advertising Agency distracted him from doing anything substantially literary.

Basso truly disliked writing copy for Fitzgerald's. Despising hucksterism in general, he told Anderson in a letter of August 6, 1931, that he was trying to fight off the "bourgeois norm" but that working for Fitzgerald's was necessary: "It becomes increasingly important, as time goes on, to first establish an identity as a man. It comes before the erection of an identity as an artist." In December 1931, Basso approached Perkins to ask if he could work in the advertising department of Scribner's: "After all, I should be of considerable value. I believe I have a rather deep appreciation of things done into covers, etc., and have some very definite and rather sound (I think) ideas as to how they should be advertised. I have had some four years or so of intensive

---

38. Wilson to Basso, May 9, 1929, in Wilson, *Letters on Literature and Politics*, 173. Perkins to Basso, June 3, 1931, in Basso Papers, BL; Scott Berg, *Maxwell Perkins: Editor of Genius* (New York, 1978), 40–41.

39. Perkins to Basso, February 24, 1927, June 23, 1931, in Basso Papers, BL.

advertising work, working on a number of national accounts, to say nothing of my time served on the newspapers."[40] He was never hired by Scribner's.

Basso would later use his advertising experience in his novels, but not so much to elevate the profession as to ridicule it. In *Cinnamon Seed*, the antagonist and opportunist Harry Brand believes that legal services and politics are "just like a can of beans. . . . You've got to sell them both. . . . You've got to advertise!" (*CS*, 119). Likewise, in *In Their Own Image* (1935), "Mayonnaise Queen" Emma Troy has gained her nouveau riche status through smart advertising. John Pine, artist and mouthpiece for Basso, is a kind of anti-Babbitt who blames mass industry and the advertising business for turning "America into a three-ring circus" (*IT*, 137); he further rejects the old highbrow and genteel culture as represented by the faint-hearted and foppish Europeans in the book and heralds art as the new high culture and authority. This corresponds with Richard King's argument that in the twenties and thirties, advertising and open consumerism "became a much commented on phenomenon [but] the thrust was not only against industrially manufactured mass culture but also against the high culture of the genteel tradition . . . the authority of the author [becoming] a new kind of high culture . . . that would transcend mass culture."[41]

Although Basso disliked the advertising world of soups, soaps, and sodas, when the agency fired him in 1932 because of the Depression, he regretted the loss of financial security. He told Matthew Josephson that its effect was one of "emancipation, although I would have preferred to have achieved it, instead of having it thrust upon me. I had planned to leave next spring, had formally announced it, so this just hastens it by a year." With the little savings they had, the Bassos decided to leave New Orleans and settle in the North Carolina mountains. As they would not leave New Orleans until the fall because of the lease on their apartment, Basso told Perkins that they would "swelter all summer and freeze all winter." Yet the Bassos were set on leaving, as Louisiana offered no opportunities; already one of the poorest states before the Depression, the economic downswing had aggravated general conditions.

40. Basso to Perkins, December 27, 1931, in SA.
41. Richard King, "Modernism and Mass Culture: The Origins of the Debate," in *The Thirties: Politics and Culture in a Time of Broken Dreams* ed. Heinz Ickstadt, Rob Kroes, and Brian Lee (Amsterdam, 1987), 144.

Driving upriver, Basso noticed the "terror" of poverty, which, like a "giant maggot," gnawed at the dismal villages and the people. The couple left the city in a melancholy mood, but at the same time, it was evident that Basso felt urged to leave: by 1931, he denigratingly called New Orleans a "provincial backwater."[42]

Basso would ultimately develop a love-hate relationship with his hometown. Although he had outgrown New Orleans and would return infrequently, the city remained for him "the last place in the South where people know how to have fun. The rest of the South is too joylessly Anglo-Saxon." It is perhaps not so surprising that Basso projected his mixed feelings on the characters in his books. A return home, whether it was his own homecoming or Beauregard's or David Barondess', always triggered mixed feelings of alienation and nostalgia. And although Basso left New Orleans permanently in 1932, he did not sever all ties. Not until the end of his life, after he had written his last novel on the South, did Basso cut the final ties with the city of his birth. Sitting on the deck of a ship that was to take him from New Orleans to Tahiti in 1958, he wrote in his diary: "I suspect I have used up my sentiment for and about New Orleans: I *could* go home again, but I doubt that I could stand it for long: it's the provincialism, it's the provincial aspirations—like so many of its sister cities in the United States, New Orleans won't be minor league—which was its charm and its appeal. I didn't even much enjoy walking in the French Quarter this time, though that may have been because of the weather. I don't think so, however. It could be that I have used up the last of my memories, and so am free of them—in one way or another, one eventually shakes loose."[43]

42. Basso to Josephson, June 9, 1932, in Josephson Papers, BL; Basso to Perkins, July 12, 1932, in SA; Basso, "Cotton Blossom," 385; Basso to Anderson, June 19, 1931, in Anderson Papers, NL.

43. Basso to Cowley, April 29, 1940, in Cowley Papers, NL; Hamilton Basso, "Tahiti Diary" (Typescript in Basso Papers, BL) n.p.

3

Mountain Muse

Leaving New Orleans in September 1932, the Bassos moved into a cabin in Pisgah Forest, four miles from Brevard, North Carolina, and three quarters of a mile up the mountain. According to Gail Lathrop, the cabin was located on the Partridge Hill estate, "sitting well back from Everett Farm Road and above the lush farm valley of the French Broad River which eventually winds its way through Asheville and beyond."[1]

Since the couple's monthly expenses had to be cut to less than seventy dollars, the Rich Mountain Lodge, which they rented for only ten dollars a month from a friend of Toto's (who, according to Basso, was a "bum etcher but a very nice person"), offered a satisfactory way to economize. Yet despite this cutdown on their expenditures, they could not afford financial setbacks, such as the dentist bill that came in after Basso broke his front tooth on a piece of mountain candy. Nor could Basso buy the books he wanted to read so much. Once he was contracted by Scribner's, he asked Perkins in a postscript to a letter if he could not get the new Hemingway and Thomas Wolfe novels at a re-

---

1. R. Gail Lathrop, "Thomas Wolfe and Partridge Hill," *Thomas Wolfe Review*, IX (1985), 27.

duced price: "I just haven't got the money to pay regular price for them. Please don't think I'm a chiseller. I'm not. I'm just damned poor."[2]

Basso described their cabin as "not very elegant but . . . comfortable" and further noted that "there is even hot water and a bath tub." Shortly after having moved in, he recorded his excitement with mountain life: "We look down into the valley, there is also a river, and then on the other side of the valley the mountains go off purply into the distance, range after range of them. Cities seem cramped and noisy now, manifestations of meaningless frenzy, and the depression comes not only [sic] as some vague thing that is happening (or so we hear) in the outside world. There is perhaps a danger in that but for a time I propose to abandon myself to this blessed ignorance, or unconcern, in the hope that it will give me a fresh, clearer, view."[3]

When Basso was not at his desk typing, he would chop wood, do some carpentry, or climb the mountains with his dog: "And then we sit on the great rocks that hang like enormous shelves from the face of the mountains and watch the little, far world beneath us . . . enjoying a momentary, ridiculous feeling that we have been triumphant over Nature; while Nature tolerates us and is beautiful beyond all believing." Because of his sociable temperament, Basso made sure to mix with the locals; in a letter of November 4, 1932, he told Perkins that he had gone to a "mountain 'singing' where a little preaching was thrown in for good measure and it was very fine."[4]

But perhaps this rustic bliss was a trifle premature. After the rainstorms of the fall of 1932, which threatened "to take the roof off," the winter turned the Bassos into "temporary prisoners"; the pipes froze and then burst. Besides having to walk to the spring, which was "about two city blocks away," Basso had to crawl underneath the cabin to do the necessary plumbing. In times of snow and ice, the couple had to push their little Ford up the unpaved road, and when that became impossible, they had to leave the car behind and carry their provisions on foot: "Our road goes straight up and once I slipped and would have kept going until I hit the valley had I not hit a laurel thicket instead."

2. Hamilton Basso to Maxwell Perkins, November 4, September 20, 1932, in SA.
3. Basso to Perkins, July 20, September 20, 1932, in SA.
4. Basso to Perkins, September 20, 1932, in SA.

To add to their financial distress, Toto suffered a neck injury while sledding. This cost them three months of living expenses in doctor's bills and made Basso "worried and useless and resentful at the way bad luck" nagged him.[5]

In spite of these problems, the young couple appreciated country life, and the quiet was highly conducive to Basso's writing. Though he had been a noted party-goer, once Basso had settled down in marriage and the mountains, he became more serious and more committed to his craft. In fact, as he grew older, he developed a "special distaste for large parties with a lot of people drinking and talking at once." Preferring quieter, more serious conversation, he was drawn to those with whom he shared interests and experiences. Turning into what Ikerd called a "model of domesticity and moderation," Basso realized that to be a writer one has to renounce the "real world," which "is sometimes so much more exciting (and satisfying) than the literary world. . . . You'd rather go climbing somewhere than sit down and push a typewriter." A social rather than a solitary being, he was nonetheless delighted to devote all his time to his writing: "I feel a greater sense of permanency here than when I was writing advertising crap in an office and getting a check every two weeks."[6]

Before leaving New Orleans, Basso had already begun new writing projects. Disillusioned with the reception of *Relics and Angels* and Perkins' rejection of the novel "A Room in the Sky," a manuscript that appears to have been lost, he turned to nonfiction after chancing upon a number of shoeboxes containing Civil War documents in an old plantation home. An avid student of history, Basso decided to write the biography of the Confederate general P. G. T. Beauregard. With great excitement, as was customary when he envisioned a new project, he told Matthew Josephson: "But if I could afford it, I would do a biography of our own General P. G. T. Beauregard. You think that strange? It's really not because old P. G. T. was really an important person—especially because of what happened to him after the war. He's very obscure now, and completely overshadowed by Lee, Jackson and others, but he has three major victories to his credit and the perfectly masterful retreat

5. Hamilton Basso to Matthew Josephson, March 7, 1933, in Josephson Papers, BL; Basso to Perkins, February 12, 1933, in SA.
6. Basso to Perkins, December 29, 1932, in SA; Ikerd, "Hamilton Basso," 64; Basso to Lyle Saxon, November 21, 1932, in Saxon papers, HT.

from Corinth. His fame during the war was very great. You know I suppose, the story of the Creole gentleman who, hearing somebody mention Lee said: 'Lee, Lee . . . Yes, now I remember. I have heard Beauregard speak highly of him.' "[7]

Basso's decision to pick the only Creole general in the Rebel army may have had to do with his fondness for the Creole contribution to Louisiana history, or as he was to remark in a book review written at the time he was composing *Beauregard, The Great Creole*: "[Edward Larocque Tinker's *Bibliography of the French of Louisiana* (1932)] makes us realize anew how truly significant a civilization was erected in Louisiana by these Creoles and Frenchmen and how much the poorer we are because of its passing."[8]

As the Beauregard biography began to take shape, Basso approached Maxwell Perkins and asked him if Scribner's was in a "gambling mood," for he was "sure trying to get his head above the water." The biography would not be fictitious but "fully documented and definitive," as well as the first full assessment of Beauregard's life, for no other biographies of the general were in existence. With his characteristic editorial reserve, Perkins replied that the project seemed original but that "the odds" were "always against a life of a figure who is not among the most compelling in the popular mind."[9] At the same time, he clearly sensed that the young writer had to be encouraged and sent him the one hundred dollars that Basso needed to make a research trip to Charleston. In enclosing the check, Perkins insisted that the money was not meant as a pledge or advance on a possible book. Somewhat mystified by this spontaneous generosity, Basso kept in touch, informing Perkins as to how the book was progressing.

In the end the biography *was* accepted for publication, albeit on stiff terms: because of the Depression, Perkins could only consent to a limited number of copies. The news of the book's publication reached Toto

7. John K. Hutchens, "The Architect of Pompey's Head," *New York Herald Tribune Book Review*, October 31, 1954, p. 3; Basso to Josephson, August 27, 1931, in Josephson Papers, BL.

8. Hamilton Basso, Review of Edward Larocque Tinker's *Bibliography of the French Newspapers and Periodicals of Louisiana*, in *Books Abroad* October (1933), 427.

9. Basso to Perkins, November 4, 1931, in SA; Perkins to Basso, November 27, 1931, in SA.

first, and with excitement and pride, she scribbled her delight on the back of Perkins' letter: "My chest expansion has increased threefold. I'm just that proud! Bless you baby—it was coming to you. When I found this letter I sat a full 2 minutes on the steps before I could open it because I thought it must be a refusal, or it would have come by wire. So when I finally did, I let out an enormous whoop. A passing negro said, 'One white lady sho is happy!' Now you can't say any more that you want to do things for me—cause you have."[10]

Relieved that Perkins had accepted the manuscript, Basso confided to Josephson: "I had gotten to the point, what with everybody shying away from my last novel like a wild horse, that I was beginning to wonder if I'd ever get published again." When he sent off the final manuscript, he told Perkins that he did not care so much for success as for his integrity as an author: "I didn't write this book to make a pile of dough. Unlike Uncle Arnold Bennett, I don't think my manhood depends on making money by my literary efforts. . . . I hope you enjoy meeting my people. I've had a good time getting to know them."[11]

As is clear from the Beauregard outline and the comments that Basso jotted down in letters to Josephson, he wanted to write a different Civil War biography. A novelist at heart, Basso was not interested in laying out battle scenes, but was fascinated most by Beauregard as an individual. Viewing the biography's narrative in terms of a novelistic plot, which was to be determined by "characters' " actions, he told Perkins he had been primarily absorbed by "personalities and their effect upon incidents—and the effect of incidents upon personalities."[12]

Basso's objective was to show that Beauregard's life could be seen as representative of "certain attitudes which, common to a whole slice of society, explain a certain definite change in the Southern character." Depicting Beauregard as a kind of Rebel Everyman, he emphasized that the general's life after the war—his withdrawal into a world of memories and his quarrels with Jefferson Davis—was more indicative of the southern character and history than Beauregard's actual battle

10. Etolia S. Basso, penciled note on Maxwell Perkins' letter, June 28, 1932, in Basso Papers, BL.
11. Basso to Josephson, July 4, 1932, in Josephson Papers, BL; Basso to Perkins, May 27, 1932, in SA.
12. Basso to Perkins, February 1, 1932, in SA.

heroics. In the same way, Basso saw Beauregard's retreat into the past as typical of the "self-defense mechanism" of some postwar southerners who, by retiring to their disintegrating antebellum homes, allowed "the liberated poor whites" to take the helm and give "the South its direction." Condemning the Agrarians for nourishing the southern inclination to pore over the past, Basso firmly believed that one of the societal impasses of the South in 1931 was its "queer worship of the South 'before the war'": "The more truck and nonsense I read about the South," he wrote to Josephson, "the more I feel . . . I've got to get these things of [sic] my chest."[13]

Not afraid to demystify the Lost Cause mythology, Basso took up arms repeatedly against southern traditionalists and mythmakers. Whether he actually succeeded in his revisionism and call for realism remains to be questioned, for he, too, indulges in portraying Beauregard's plantation childhood as stereotypically idyllic. For the moment, however, it should be clear that in line with *Double Dealer* rhetoric, Basso at least intended to "throw as clear a light as possible upon this holy Confederacy . . . and . . . do away with the tinted illumination that has always been thrown upon it and the people who gave it its character and direction."[14] In its objective to critically examine certain southern ways and wrongs, *Beauregard* can be seen as the beginning of Basso's deracination from southern soil.

Beauregard's fame, established during the war, dwindled rapidly after his death in 1893. Overshadowed by Lee, Jackson, and Grant, the Louisiana general was soon forgotten. It is difficult to determine Beauregard's true merits, valor, and historical stature. If one is to believe Basso's premise, Beauregard was a misunderstood talent who failed to reach his full potential because Jefferson Davis disregarded all his strategies and advice. But Basso was obviously on Beauregard's side, his opinions being very much swayed by what he claimed to be his "sympathies with Beauregard" (*B*, xii).

Civil War historians are of two minds about the southern general. They all record his vanity, his rhetorical eloquence, his emulation of Napoleon, and his bravery in battle. James McPherson argues that

13. Basso to Perkins, "The Great Creole: A Biography of General P. G. T. Beauregard" [letter and outline], November 4, 1931, in SA; Basso to Josephson, August 27, September 24, 1931, in Josephson Papers, BL.

14. Basso to Josephson, September 24, 1931, in Josephson Papers, BL.

though Beauregard's victories at Sumter and Manassas have been over-rated, his sensible retreat from Shiloh is underrated. According to Mc-Pherson, Davis was extremely disgruntled when he heard of Beauregard's retreat and replaced the Creole with Braxton Bragg. For the remainder of the war, Beauregard played a secondary role. Clement Eaton has a higher opinion of the general: blaming Davis for the final defeat, Eaton believes that despite Beauregard's degradation after Shiloh, "Toward the end of the war, he emerged once more as a brilliant officer in the defense of Charleston and the skillful repulse of Butler's and Grant's efforts to seize Petersburg."[15] Robert Kean, a Beauregard contemporary and chief of the Confederate Bureau of War, pays the general the greatest compliment by saying that he preferred the letters of the Creole to those of Robert E. Lee.

For a complete picture of Beauregard, one should consult T. H. Williams' *P. G. T. Beauregard, Napoleon in Gray* (1955). This book appeared twenty-two years after Basso's life of Beauregard, so Williams' slant is bound to be more nuanced: not only did Williams have the advantage of better access to a wider range of information, but he could also conveniently draw from Basso's book. Williams thought Basso's study "interesting and full of human interest," yet also far too negligent of "many important phases of Beauregard's career."[16] The latter could be attributed to Basso's handling of the biographical method; whereas Williams aimed to write a well-documented, historically accurate, and academically sound work, Basso wanted to capture "the feeling of a time and the spirit of a man" (*B*, xiii). As Basso explained to Perkins: "I've tried to do more than write a biography. I've attempted to make something come alive, to dig below the surface, I think, seeing it *as fictively as I can*" [my emphasis].[17] Of course, from a historical point of view, Williams' book is much more objective. While Williams is very careful in his delineation of the general, Basso gets carried away by his subject's personality.

15. James McPherson, *Battle Cry of Freedom: The Civil War Era* (Oxford, Eng., 1988), 410; Clement Eaton, *A History of the Southern Confederacy* (London, 1954), 56; 115.

16. T. H. Williams, *P. G. T. Beauregard: Napoleon in Gray* (Baton Rouge, 1955), 334. Interestingly, Williams also wrote a biography of Huey Long, the Louisiana governor and senator whom Basso castigated in many articles and used as a source of inspiration for his novel *Sun in Capricorn* (1942).

17. Basso to Perkins, May 27, 1932, in SA.

Basso's sympathies with Beauregard would ultimately lead to such a coloring of the facts that his biography comes close to hagiography. Exaggerating both Davis' administrative weaknesses and Beauregard's underdog position, Basso presents Davis as an utterly unsympathetic and testy commander-in-chief. Beauregard, on the other hand, is portrayed as a sad victim of circumstance who was not allowed to carry out his brilliant strategies. Beauregard is made larger than life, with Basso highlighting his patience, his Confederate patriotism, his handsome and aristocratic demeanor, his popularity with the public, his Creole exoticism, and his powerful rhetoric. Williams adopts a much more circumspect point of view. For instance, whereas Basso sees Beauregard's role in the Mexican War as foreshadowing his fame and success in the Civil War, Williams points out that in the Mexican War Beauregard had already revealed some of the weaknesses that would prove detrimental in the course of the Civil War: a stickler for the rules and attaching more value to theory than practice, Beauregard would "slap together a plan without complete information of the enemy and without regard to the realities of his own resources and then in a glow of enthusiasm [would] claim that it would accomplish brilliant results."[18]

Basso and Williams also disagree on the so-called Petersburg myth. When Beauregard was stationed at Petersburg with as few as 2,200 men, he was attacked by General Smith's Federal army of 40,000 men. Greatly alarmed by the Union might, Beauregard sent several reports to both Bragg and Lee, asking for assistance and warning them that Grant planned to take Richmond via Petersburg. In Basso's opinion, Lee was too slow to move, ostensibly trivializing Beauregard's alert. Not until a third messenger arrived at Lee's tent did he move to Petersburg and save the town. In Williams' view, the myth arose when Beauregard, his friends, and his followers stated in their postwar writings that all along Beauregard had had the right instincts about Grant's moves. In their account (and Basso's), "Lee ignored repeated and clear warnings from Beauregard and left the latter to battle at Petersburg against great odds. At the last desperate minute, Beauregard convinced Lee and saved the Confederacy." Williams debunks the Pe-

---

18. Williams, *P. G. T. Beauregard*, 71.

tersburg myth, arguing that Beauregard was not at all clear in his reports. Since Lee was unable to find out where Grant had positioned himself, he decided to hold back. In addition, Williams explains, Lee "could not abandon the James River line until he was certain the Federals had left it." Basso, on the other hand, criticizes Lee for his apparent lethargy and praises Beauregard for accomplishing "the apparently impossible," that is, saving Richmond with so few men; yet "Mr. Davis," Basso continues, "was displeased" (*B*, 255).[19]

Besides the biographers' different interpretations of historical facts, they also contradict each other in their rendering of these men's portraits. Depicting Davis as a proud politician who approved of slavery and defended the legitimacy of the doctrine of manifest destiny, Basso believed that the Confederate commander wanted to be a "militarist rather than a president." Siding with his Creole, Basso portrays Davis as an obdurate autocrat, a "dog barking," and eventually a cowardly weakling who, at the end of the war, takes flight in his wife's clothes. Throughout the book, Davis' stature is minimized and ridiculed. Beauregard, on the other hand, emerges as the tragic hero (*B*, 73, 255).

Interestingly, where Basso disparages Davis, Allen Tate, who as an Agrarian was in many ways diametrically opposed to Basso, enhanced the standing of the Confederate leader in his biography *Jefferson Davis, His Rise and Fall: A Biographical Narrative* (1929). Like Basso's Beauregard, Tate depicts Davis as a tragic victim of circumstance and martyr of the Lost Cause. But there is something to be said for Davis and Beauregard both. Williams, who is neither a poet like Tate nor a novelist like Basso, does just that. Although Williams acknowledges that Davis was difficult and responsible for critical errors, he also argues that the Confederate president was a truly intelligent man who found himself in a precarious position. Unlike Basso, Williams does not harp on Davis' mistakes but criticizes Beauregard's misbehavior instead: "Captain Beauregard displayed a testy impatience with people, especially politicians who criticized his work or tried to interfere with him." Because Davis did not like to be corrected by his inferiors either, the two men "were born to clash." Basso ultimately agrees with Williams, describing Beauregard's and Davis' conflict as a "clash of egos" in which both

---

19. *Ibid.*, 232, 234.

parties were to blame for their vanity, pride, and desire to be the center of attention.[20]

Finally, the two biographies are distinctly dissimilar in style, for where Williams documents facts and leaves no room for fiction or myth, Basso treats his subject as a character out of a novel, dramatizes his narrative, and builds in suspense. Also, Basso frequently shifts from the past to the present tense and, to enliven things even more, interjects short, choppy sentences into his narrative. To endow the account with some degree of historical authenticity, he pastes in newspaper reports of the time. As defeat draws near, his inclination toward dramatization swells: viewing Sherman's army as a bunch of "vandals," he describes their march to the sea as the march of the bigoted mob in his unpublished novelette "The Ladies of the Land." Empathizing with poor southern whites, Basso laments their many losses in a war that was not necessarily fought in their interest. Beauregard's journey home is not without bathos, either: the trip to New Orleans triggers feelings of great emptiness, sadness, and regret. Upon his arrival home, a crowd gathers around his horse, and a tailor taking the general's measurements for a civilian suit weeps. The rendering of Beauregard's demise is equally maudlin. Retiring to his old plantation home, he lapses into narcissistic withdrawal, the memory of battle being the sorry remainder and reality of his old age: "Perhaps, as he went upstairs, the echo of Stuart's song went softly into his darkened room, perhaps the dark was poignant with the ghosts of men in weathered gray. And perhaps, as he fell asleep, there was the past again, and the days of golden glory, when his name was a banner in the Southern sun. Or perhaps there was nothing . . . only quiet and the ceasing of his heart and the peaceful coming of the end" (*B*, 311).

Not a biography in the strictest sense of the word, *Beauregard* is really a "docudrama" in which historical accuracy is secondary to a livelier and pervasively fictional narrative. Although Basso may have thought that he wrote a historical biography, *Beauregard* is closer to fiction than fact. Ikerd goes so far as to suggest that the book could be

20. *Ibid.*, 41, 67. Basso finally reduced the Beauregard-Davis strife to a conflict of civilization and race: because of Davis' Protestant and Anglo-Saxon background he could not, Basso claims, "understand" the Creole, whose background was Latin and Catholic (*ibid.*, 126, 160–61).

read as another novel in which the Beauregard figure can be seen as a typical Basso protagonist: "[Basso] presented Beauregard as the kind of man around which his novels are constructed, a man who feels a profound dissatisfaction with his situation or with society and is determined to establish his own worth rather than surrender to a system of values he despises."[21]

The biography was an acclaimed success in 1933. It was praised in some twenty reviews and made the second page of the *New York Times Book Review*. As such, the book meant a breakthrough for Basso's career. Maxwell Perkins acknowledged this in a letter written upon the biography's release: "If Beauregard has done nothing else for you it has certainly given you a degree of prestige. It is too bad, because in decent times it would have surely made you considerable money." It was too bad indeed, because on March 4, 1933, the day that the book came out, all the bookshops were open and the banks were closed: to avert a banking crisis, President Roosevelt had called for a bank holiday. Although the book did not bring in the "pile of dough" that Basso was not counting on anyway, *Beauregard*'s success was encouraging. After briefly considering the composition of a Tolstoy biography in an attempt to "confound all the garret revolutionary boys," Basso returned to his second novel with renewed confidence.[22]

While beginning his second novel, Basso worried about the Depression. He struggled to make ends meet. Because he earned a meager $35 a month tutoring, or what he referred to as "trying to ram learning down the throat of a not very bright child," Toto cobbled some money together by working as a counselor and secretary in a nearby girls' camp. The couple's financial straits worsened when they lost half of their savings in a New Orleans banking crisis. Somewhat desperately, Basso told Matthew Josephson that it felt like they were living in a new age: "We are waiting for the Fall—Here is to the New Deal—the New Era too. It can't come too soon to suit me." Despite the financial duress, however, Basso loved his life in the mountains: "Spring is beginning and we almost wear out the arbutus plants hunting for buds and last

21. Ikerd, "Hamilton Basso," 42–43.
22. Perkins to Basso, March 24, 1933, in SA; Basso to Perkins, July 7, 1934, in SA.

night from our porch, we could see acres of broom-sedge burning. We thought it was a forest fire at first and went to it, and hurried back because it looked so much more exciting from the porch."[23]

Though Basso seemed resigned when he told Perkins that "there is nothing either of us can do about the depression," and "if [the world] wants to blow up, let it," he was actually not at all indifferent to the Depression and Washington politics: starting out as a freelance reporter for the *New Republic* in the early thirties, he eventually became a member of the magazine's editorial staff. How Basso managed to get his foot in the door with the *New Republic* is open to speculation, but Josephson, who also paved the way for the publication of *Relics and Angels*, may well have drawn the editors' attention to the talented Louisianian, who, in need of quick cash, was very willing to write for the magazine. Josephson's support was pivotal to Basso, who despite his vivacious demeanor was prone to spells of dejection and doubt. Like Sherwood Anderson and to a lesser extent, Lyle Saxon, Josephson stimulated and encouraged the young southerner, a favor Basso warmly acknowledged: "If I managed to do anything at all, you have helped enormously. It was you, after all, who got me published for the first time and you continued to believe in me."[24] In tandem with his visits to New York City, where, according to Malcolm Cowley, Basso used to light up the *New Republic* office with his amiable personality and customary bear hugs, Basso delighted in visiting the Josephsons at their home in Connecticut. Sitting on the rocks by the brook in Josephson's garden or sipping applejack by the fire, the two men had animated political discussions that they resumed in an extensive correspondence during the thirties.

As the political climate intensified and more and more intellectuals were drawn to fellow-traveling and Communism, Basso dissociated himself from both the extreme left and extreme right. While sharing Josephson's (and fellow intellectuals') liberalism, Basso declared time and again that both Communism and Fascism were founded on hate, violence, rigid dogma, and the radical belief in "means justifying the

23. Basso to Josephson, April 24, 1933, in Josephson Papers, BL; Matthew Josephson, *Infidel in the Temple: A Memoir of the Nineteen Thirties* (New York, 1967), 171.

24. Basso to Perkins, February 22, 1933, in SA; Basso to Josephson, September 3, 1936, in Josephson Papers, BL.

end."[25] Rebelling against Josephson's parlor socialism, Basso argued that intellectuals' love affair with Marxist theory could not eliminate the misery of the southern mill villages he had reported on for the *New Republic*.

To Basso's mind, the conscience of the nation was represented neither by the intellectuals of the twenties, who fueled their cultural pessimism by exchanging America's Main Street for Paris's Left Bank, nor by the intellectuals of the thirties, whose social myopia led to empty discussions about the Soviet experiment and uncertifiable utopianism. Viewing the twenties and thirties as an "era of derision and denial" in which intellectuals denounced their country and challenged American democracy with "the Marxian myth of catastrophic revolution," Basso ultimately identified with the patriotism of the average American—whom he called John Applegate in *Mainstream* (1943)—and subscribed to the democratic ideals of Franklin Delano Roosevelt. Castigating Josephson's and intellectuals' support of what he nicknamed the "*un*-Popular Front," Basso himself was not conservative but "liberal for America in the late twenties and very liberal for the South at the time, but among the group associated with the *New Republic* . . . only moderately so." Or as he would describe himself in a 1939 interview: "I am, I suppose, a free-thinking liberal opposed to any kind of dictatorship whether it be of the right or the left. I believe that America has something that no other country can match—a promise, a hope, call it a dream—and that its potentialities have never been realized. My political opinions, however, are my own, and I don't want to preach them or cram them down anybody's throat."[26]

While Basso may have respected opinions other than his own, in his correspondence with Josephson he was quite adamant in getting his point across. Josephson probably tired of this because when the thirties drew to a close, Basso complained about the "silent treatment" his friend was giving him. He tried to patch up the relationship in a letter of August 13, 1940, and made another attempt a month later: "I shall argue violently with you—it has always been thus: we enjoy the strik-

25. Hamilton Basso to Malcolm Cowley, August 12, 1937, in Cowley Papers, NL.

26. Basso to Perkins, December 22, 1931, July 28, 1937, in SA; Hamilton Basso, "Franklin Delano Roosevelt: The American and the Revolution," in Basso, *Mainstream* (New York, 1943), 195; Ikerd, "Hamilton Basso," 52; "Hamilton Basso," *Wilson Library Bulletin*, XIV (October 1939), 186.

ing of mind on mind: the sparks that fly, the smoky smell of flint—but, after all the argument, I would always want to feel, and have you feel that on the inside, in the sentimental places of the heart, nothing is ever changed." Finally, in a moving letter of October 15, 1940, Basso made a last reconciliatory endeavor, which is half apologia and half mea culpa:

> You're Matty, the man who first believed in me. So how can I get off and have an "objective" look at you? How can I? . . . I'm beginning to suspect that ever since you and I disagreed about the Moscow thing, I've been over-sensitive. There was a time when, frankly, I found a note of dogmatism in many things you said that I did not like. It seemed to me you were setting up certain rigid measurements to which you felt all people must conform or else be written off. Had I not always looked upon you as one of my closest friends, one of my "backers," it would not have made so much difference. At the time it did make a difference.

Basso's apologies and suggestion that "beneath the river of words runs the deeper river of friendship" were not enough to heal the bond that had meant so much to him. The two men had grown apart, and no rapprochement could alter this. Etolia Basso, who found the Josephsons "terribly effusive" anyway, remembered how "Ham sort of steered away from Josephson" when the latter persevered in his radical beliefs.[27]

In 1961, when Josephson contacted Basso for his memoir, *Infidel in the Temple* (1967), Basso appeared embarrassed, as if he did not want to be reminded of the tumultuous thirties: "Time passes, old friend. Rain on the roof, winter on the wind, and all those who have dropped by the wayside. I think of that young New Orleans provincial coming up to the city, and the rocks in your brook—I don't know Matty. Perhaps it means something merely to have persisted and endured. You mention your foresight in relation to Burke's comment on the state of France in 1790. I think of the old gentleman who ran the bookstore across the street from my grandfather's small shoe factory when I was a boy. When the telephone 'came in,' he would have nothing to do with it be-

---

27. Basso to Josephson, August 13, September 25, October 15, 1940, in Josephson Papers, BL; Etolia S. Basso, interview with the author, January 8, 1992.

cause he thought it was only a fad. Now *that's* the kind of foresight I admire."[28]

The difference between Basso's and Josephson's temperaments surfaces rather strikingly in this final resuscitation of their correspondence: while Josephson resorts to books and uses the cerebral example of Edmund Burke to illustrate "foresight," Basso counters with a less bookish example borrowed from life. Inspired by the noble examples of rebel-writers such as Rousseau, Zola, and Hugo, Josephson became an easy pawn of the party and its ideology. Basso, on the other hand, used his pragmatism and remote existence in the mountains to put the radicalism of New York City in perspective. This also caused isolation: reluctant to be either a son of the conservative South or a convert of the radical North, Basso felt doubly isolated, a predicament his fictional heroes also suffer from as they vacillate between southern roots and northern compromise. Confessing to his northern friends that his talking to mountaineers "of crops and the Bible" rather than of "art and literature" forced him "to hack out" his own view of the world, he would nonetheless deprecate the general boredom of his country life and would speak of his longing to visit New York again. Yet to Perkins, who occupied neutral ground, he would rant about New York intellectuals: "The other day I went several miles back in the mountains to see a mountain family I know and like. It was startling, after seeing so few people with those qualities in New York, to come across human beings with simplicity and friendship and dignity and pride. Yahoos are bad but the intellectual Yahoo—Mother of God deliver us."[29]

Malcolm Cowley was another prominent *New Republic* intellectual that Basso clashed with. According to Etolia Basso, her husband's *New Republic* piece on the Scottsboro trial was instrumental in triggering Cowley's initial admiration for Basso. Cowley, in contrast, writes in his eulogy for Basso's memorial service that the two did not really get to know each other until he visited Basso in the summer of 1934: "We came, we walked in the woods under the house—high rhododendrons in bloom, we drove to Caesar's Head—not Pompey's Head—for a

---

28. Basso to Josephson, January 8, 1962, in Josephson Papers, BL.

29. Basso to Josephson, June 13, 1934, August 7, 1935, in Josephson Papers, BL; Basso to Perkins, July 4, 1935, in SA.

view over fifty miles of cotton fields, we climbed Mount Pisgah and Ham told me something about his early life."[30] Gradually, Basso was given more and more *New Republic* assignments and finally became a kind of "southern correspondent" and reviewer of southern novels.

Although Basso and Cowley remained close friends, in the thirties they had heated arguments. Besides attacking Cowley's political naïveté and flirtation with Communism, Basso believed that the *New Republic* editor relied too much on theory while being oblivious to the facts. Thus in a philosophical debate over the value of book learning versus the lessons of life, Cowley argued that books would always have the most significant influence on people's lives and minds; Basso, however, refuted the idea and declared that people rather than books had left their impact on *his* life:

> If I were asked to name the books that had changed my mind, I could not truthfully name a single one. My impulse would be to name people instead: a highschool professor who taught me the difference between good books and trash . . . then that Catholic priest I wrote a piece for The New Republic about, who opened new fields of thought and speculation; then a couple of girls: then a long break, the years of college totally wasted. Then in recent times, people I've known in New York. I got to books as it were, through people: and I should guess that the making or unmaking of a mind is far more than a mere matter of books.[31]

Although Basso could not and would not deny his own intellectuality and love of books, he was immensely drawn to ordinary people, getting along "famously well with plumbers, farmers and carpenters." Cowley became somewhat leery of Basso's mixing with commoners and wrote in a letter of January 6, 1939: "Well, baby, I wish I had your genius for getting acquainted with all sorts of people." Cowley seems to have believed that once one belonged to the self-contained class of intellectuals that magazines like the *New Republic* fostered, one simply could not step out of that milieu in what he saw as Basso's attempts to

---

30. Etolia S. Basso, interview with the author, January 3, 1991; Malcolm Cowley, typescript notes for Hamilton Basso's eulogy, in Cowley Papers, NL. Cowley is incorrect about meeting the Bassos in Pisgah Forest in 1934: the Bassos did not move to Pisgah Forest until the summer of 1935.

31. Basso to Cowley, January 2, 1939, in Cowley Papers, NL.

"relate" to people. However, for Basso, who lived among mountaineers throughout the thirties, this was not so much a choice as a way of
life. His genuine sympathy for the humble lives of ordinary people was
no posturing or putting on of false identities. It was an honest, pragmatic, and natural impulse. Hating to be pigeonholed as a "writer" or
"artist," he even confessed: "The truth is, I suppose, that I ain't an artist. I've never thought of myself as one, or because I write that I was
somehow separated from other people . . . and it's hard, because my
deepest love is for writing, and books and ideas, to be thrust into a special and (to me) false category."[32]

Unfortunately, in the world of books and art, Basso was surrounded
by people who were the very opposite of his personality, and it is especially in the correspondence with Cowley that Basso's lasting repugnance of intellectuals shows. Panning Cowley's infatuation with W. H.
Auden's modernist erudition, which was, to Basso's mind, too abstruse
for the average reader, Basso wrote "*Fuque*, Malcolm!" [asterisked
with: "spelling, throughout, by courtesy of Malcolm Cowley"]:
"Poetry is dying on its feet when poets limit their audiences to other
poets: and all this clap-trap of [Auden's] notes in the back of his book.
A line or an image isn't worth a *fuqueing* damn if it needs ten lines to
explain it."[33]

The correspondence between Cowley and Basso was a constant tug
of war, but even though they disagreed fiercely, they never lost their
sense of humor, called one another "baby," and pinpricked each other
with remarks such as, "Honey, I don't mind what you say about the
critics. I'm sick of the bastards." In later years, the quarrelsome tone of
the thirties letters lightened considerably and changed into something
more friendly and superficial. Remarkably, in these later letters, neither Cowley nor Basso ever mentioned their thirties' embroilment. The
only trace of what had occurred is to be found in a letter that Basso
wrote to his wife in 1942, when Cowley was under harsh public scru-
tiny: "I read Muriel [Cowley's wife]'s letter: it's pretty bad for them, especially for Muriel. But I still can't entirely absolve Malcolm: I too
clearly remember. No, the only way you can judge a man is by his act

---

32. Keith H. Basso, interview with the author, January 26, 1992; Basso to Cowley,
May 26, 1942, in Cowley Papers, NL.
33. Basso to Cowley, May 7, 1945, in Cowley Papers, NL.

and from his acts . . . you do wonder just what ground Malcolm does stand on. I don't blame him for anything except being such a gargantuan naif—just as so many of those people were. Word of God, I wouldn't care if I never saw another intellectual again. A bunch of observers, for the most part, lookers-on. It's that part of me, the observing part, that I don't like. Not even in me. Skip it."[34]

For those who had been so wrapped up in the events of those years, the thirties became a decade of denial, regret, melancholy, and shame. Even a writer like Basso, who had shown no interest in zealous radicalism, recalled the decade abashedly: when Josephson approached him for his correspondence in preparation of *Infidel*, he replied mournfully: "Going through these reminders of twenty-five years ago has left me a bit subdued. It has been a rocky road for us all, and, everything else aside, I think it is to our credit, if I may include myself, that we managed at least to persist."[35]

Just as Basso became disenchanted with his friends' politics and intellectualizing, so did he become disillusioned with the *New Republic*, which he ultimately called "The Cave of Winds." Initially in favor of the publication, he came to denounce the editors' reliance on "predicting" and chose to fall back on his own "political paganism . . . preferring personal values and 'exalted sentiments' over the intellectual, political values and 'cool thinking' of the *New Republic*." Otis Ferguson, a well-known critic of the magazine, shared Basso's sentiments. Sending Basso books to review, Ferguson enclosed the latest *New Republic* gossip and scoffed at the "Red Fever" of New York intellectuals. Ridiculing the Trotskyites as a "bunch of girls with an itchy girdle," he joined Basso's criticism of the *New Republic*'s predictions: "Gazing into the fate of Europe, their [i.e., the editors'] keen prognostics are never compromised by the fact that meanwhile they have somehow befouled their drawers." Ferguson's letters evince that Basso's editorial recommendations did not go unnoticed: "You started something more far reaching in The New Republic than you or its editors know, by the let's-look-at-the-troubles-in-America plan. You remember when you brought their Soviet trials duck down with that. It has been their guid-

---

34. Basso to Cowley, October 19, 1956, in Basso Papers, BL, Basso to Etolia S. Basso, March 11, 1942, in Basso Papers, BL.

35. Basso to Josephson, July 11, 1962, in Josephson Papers, BL.

ing-light ever since, though of course they don't know it and wouldn't acknowledge authorship."[36]

The "let's-look-at-America" approach Ferguson refers to was the new and first-hand way of informing readers of the national state of affairs: writers and photographers left their studies and studios and traveled all over the country to report on strikes and other incidents related to the Depression. Ferguson's claim that Basso was responsible for this prime trend of thirties journalism is probably a generous overstatement, yet it reveals that Basso, though skeptical of the *New Republic's* mainstream philosophy, offered perceptive suggestions and was heard. The total output of his writing for the magazine, from 1927 to 1942, amounts to more than thirty book reviews, twenty articles on political and cultural affairs, ten profiles of political figures, three letters to the editor, some literary essays, and one short story. Though he wrote on a great many topics, from southern schools to sit-down strikes to Huey Long's dictatorial powers to William Randolph Hearst's Liberty League, his literary criticism for the magazine is most interesting as a background to his thirties novels.

In the early thirties, Basso was most articulate about the South, his ideas having been animated by both the *Double Dealer* and his writing of *Beauregard*. After finishing *Beauregard*, he contemplated writing a book about the South to which he wanted to give the ominous title "Death over Dixie." Countering the philosophy of the backward-looking Agrarians, Basso's book was to propound the idea that the essential reality of the South did not lie in some Edenic or mythopoeic past but in a commonplace and declining present. Seeking to demystify antebellum society and expose its antidemocratic, feudalistic, and xenophobic idiosyncrasies, he was primarily interested in what happened to the South after the Civil War. Convinced that the shattering of Dixie's social stratification, from planter to poor white and slave, had a traumatic effect on the South's collective psyche, Basso argued that the region's problem was not so much its (economic) decline as its refusal to accept the new social order. It is "high time," he wrote, "to say

36. Basso to Perkins, August 7, 1939, in SA; Basso to Josephson, December 5, 1937, April 7, 1938, in Josephson Papers, BL; Otis Ferguson to Hamilton Basso, n.d., in Basso Papers, BL.

goodbye to Dixie. The South may remain, latitude and longitude fixed, but the South is no longer Dixie. . . . The South along with the rest of the country, moves toward a changed order. It is part of the United States now. It will talk about the past for a long time to come—the more the complexion of the present order changes, the more remembering there will be. Dixie, however, is gone." At the same time, he maintained that the South was denying both its past and its present: clinging to its "dreams of gone glory," the South did not want to be confronted with its "negro . . . agricultural and industrial problem," but found "release from actuality and lived again its dream of power in contemplation of things past." Impressed though he was with Basso's theory, Maxwell Perkins thought "Death over Dixie" would be "too depressing. . . . No one in the South would be willing to read it [for] Southerners would not want to contemplate their deteriation [sic]."[37]

Together with such writers as Ellen Glasgow and T. S. Stribling, Basso was one of the few southern novelists who really "concerned himself with the impact of social change at various levels." Incidentally, the sociocritical mode was virtually nonexistent in southern literature: while Louis Rubin has argued that the societal slump of the Depression did not greatly inspire or affect the work of southern writers, John Crowe Ransom considered social realism an "imported genre" in southern literature and condemned it as "militant liberal fiction." Similarly, Robert Penn Warren denounced the southern realism of a writer like Stribling as a snobbish outlet for hick-baiting, pseudo-humanitarianism, and "disordered liberalism." Basso's southern realism, which the Agrarians and others may have dismissed as unnecessary southern pessimism, places him at the center of the Southern Renascence. In contrast to the Agrarians, whose cultural ideal he castigated as "evasive idealism," "elitism," and "isolationism," Basso reiterated the Double Dealer claim that southern writers should not use the hazy lens "of the plantation and aristocratic tradition" but realize that the new South was "anything but picturesque" and had to be (re)presented accordingly.[38]

37. Hamilton Basso, "Death over Dixie" (Typescript of outline), n.p., and letter to Sherwood Anderson, December 25, 1933, in SA; Perkins to Basso, January 11, 1934, in SA.

38. Willard Thorp, *American Writing in the Twentieth Century* (Cambridge, Mass., 1960), 255; Louis D. Rubin, Jr., "Trouble on the Land: Southern Literature and the Great Depression," in Rubin, *A Gallery of Southerners* (Baton Rouge, 1982); John Crowe Ransom,

The key essay that features Basso's love of southern realism and sets the standard for his literary criticism in the *New Republic* is entitled "Letters in the South." In this essay, he examines the roots of the southern tradition—the plantation legend—and defines southern literature as either a product of or a departure from this tradition. This leads to a division into two groups—those writers who aim to preserve the tradition and those who try to demythologize it. Thus whereas the "traditionalists" or "regionalists" (the Agrarians being obviously at the core of this group) adopt the antebellum past as their fictional and poetic reality, the "realists" reject the southern past in favor of a less exalted and more authentic postbellum present. Speaking with great respect of George Washington Cable and Ellen Glasgow, whom he names the "spiritual godfather" and "godmother" of southern realism, Basso supported the realists, a group that includes such writers as Erskine Caldwell, William Faulkner, and Thomas Wolfe. Conversely, Basso did not see any merit in the Agrarian aesthetics and found Cleanth Brooks' argument that "only the traditionalists have any real and vital connection to the past" preposterous.[39]

Brooks replied to Basso's article many years later, writing that "Mr. Hamilton Basso attempted to separate the sheep from the goats, that is the progressive writers from the traditionalists." Teasing that "a good deal of squeezing and stretching was necessary to make the division work," Brooks nonetheless avowed that Basso's observation formed a central dilemma for southern writers, that is, "the Southern writer must either be white-washing the magnolia blossom or urging us to particular reform." At the same time, he mistook Basso's insistence on realism for a rhetoric of reform and bad publicity for the South. Or maybe he was merely trying to get back at Basso for stating that the Agrarian concept was "historically incorrect," a note on which Basso had concluded his article: "The Southern past bears the same relation to Southern culture as does the United States Constitution to national affairs. It can be a dead weight or a living instrument. And it is a living

---

"Modern with the Southern Accent," *Virginia Quarterly Review*, XI (1935), 186–94; Robert Penn Warren, "Some Don'ts for Literary Regionalism," *American Review*, VIII (1936), 142–50; Hamilton Basso, "Letters in the South," *New Republic*, June 19, 1935, pp. 161–63; Basso, "Deep Dark River," *New Republic*, August 21, 1935, p. 54; Basso, "Cotton Blossom," 385–95.

39. Basso, "Letters in the South," 161–63.

instrument when, instead of retreating into it as if into some half-lit acropolis away from all sight and sound to the outside world, we use it to understand the South today—which is, I believe, the most important part of our inheritance."[40]

Irked by writers' falsification of the antebellum past, Basso did not intend to ignore the past. On the contrary, he argued that the realists also utilized the historical imagination yet viewed the present as an evolutionary and at times degenerated product of the past. The Agrarians, however, seemed intent on exchanging the imperfect present with a sacrosanct past: worshiping the agrarian plantation culture of the Old South for its genteel values and paternalistic mores, they envisioned a kind of aesthetic utopia with which they would keep the ills of industrialized society at bay. Basso considered the ideals of the Vanderbilt group regressive and repulsive and mocked them as "poetic economists" who tried "to lock the barn door after the horse had been stolen." In a letter to Perkins, Basso commented, "Me and the agrarians stand at opposite poles and perhaps it's me that's nuts."[41]

More anti-Agrarian sentiment can be found in Basso's *New Republic* review of W. T. Couch's *Culture in the South* (1934), a book he praised as an appropriate response to the Agrarian manifesto *I'll Take My Stand* (1930). Unlike the cultural escapism of the Agrarians, Couch did not capitalize on the antebellum past but focused on the contemporary situation and questioned why the South had lagged behind so much. Whereas the conventional southern rebuttal blamed the war and Reconstruction, Basso and Couch attributed the South's backwardness to southerners' conservatism and reluctance to restructure their agrarian economy.[42]

Interestingly, in a 1936 letter to Josephson, Basso speaks of his contact with Couch and his intention of assisting him with another book which was to "(1) show that the Agrarians, historically, have no thesis for their position; (2) present the so called 'Southern Tradition' in the fulness of its complexity; (3) to go further and show what kinds of life can be and ought to be lived in the South." He would contribute an ar-

40. Cleanth Brooks, "What Deep South Literature Needs," *Saturday Review of Literature*, September 19, 1942, p. 8; Basso, "Letters in the South," 163.

41. Basso to Perkins, August 6, 1931, December 25, 1933, May 7, 1936, in SA.

42. Hamilton Basso, "A Spotlight on the South," *New Republic*, April 18, 1934, pp. 286–87.

ticle that was to tie "Southern letters with Southern politics." In the piece he hoped to show that "the same social economic forces that produced writers like Faulkner, Caldwell, Wolfe etc., produced politicians like Gene Talmadge and Huey Long." It is "high time," he believed, "to put an end to all this silly Agrarian pretentiousness. Those guys ought to stick to poetry and novels about the Civil War." Unfortunately, this article was never written. In a letter to Josephson of October 3, 1936, Basso explained: "My plan of counterstating the Agrarians hit a snag. . . . W. T. Couch of the Chapel Hill Press had ideas for a long professorial scholastic job on the history of the South since 1700—a book that is badly needed but one which would have to be done by professors . . . and one which I thought I could not devote the time required." Seven years after these comments were made, Basso resumed his crusade against the agrarianism of Thomas Jefferson: assuming that Jefferson was well aware of the beginnings of the Industrial Revolution, Basso regretted that the "sage of Monticello" had ignored its progress. He described Jefferson's desire to maintain the agrarian society as undemocratic and myopic.[43] Unlike Jefferson and the Agrarians, but like the group of Chapel Hill sociologists and historians to which Basso did not belong but certainly identified with, he saw industrialization as one of the keys to the South's recuperation.

Basso's fervent anti-Agrarianism and sensitivity to southern issues and problems determined the theme of his *New Republic* criticism of southern literature. He seemed to have been especially resentful of authors' stereotyping of blacks and the black experience. When in his book *John Henry* (1931) Roark Bradford depicted the Negro as a bawdy, humorous, and picturesque figure, Basso reminded Bradford that the Negro's plight involved poverty, hardship, illiteracy, and humiliation. In Basso's view, the black condition could not be trivialized or serve as entertainment, and he regretted that Bradford, whom he knew from New Orleans, had simplified the black situation so much.[44]

In a review of Robert Rylee's *Dark River* (1935), Basso again expressed disappointment with the depiction of blacks. Writing that African Americans were too often stigmatized by the plantation inheri-

43. Basso to Josephson, September 3, 1936, in Josephson Papers, BL; Hamilton Basso, "Farewell and Hail to Thomas Jefferson: The American as Democrat," in Basso, *Mainstream,* 23–43.

44. Hamilton Basso, "Black Beowulf," *New Republic,* September 30, 1931, pp. 186–87.

tance of white superiority, he called for a realistic treatment of the black character, that is, "as a human being in an unfortunate and frequently intolerable environment." Even the story of the African American Angelo Herndon, who was sentenced to twenty years in prison on the basis of a statute that dated back to slavery, could not persuade him. The book merely triggered his hopes for a "deeply felt and deeply experienced book about our American life as it looks through a Negro's eyes."[45]

Basso's genuine concern for a truthful depiction of the black experience and his despair at racism in the South finally contributed to his resolve in the forties to leave the South permanently. His mother's attempts to persuade him to come back to New Orleans were fruitless: like Anson Page of *The View from Pompey's Head*, Basso could not move back, if only it were for hearing that word "nigger" again: "Here it was again, that loathsome word. Here conjured up out of nowhere by an ignorant countryman, were all the things that had caused him to leave Pompey's Head."[46]

Although it is impossible to ascertain to what extent Basso was aware of the intensity of the Southern Renascence, he was a good spokesman for the advancement and recognition of the southern novel. In a book review entitled "Why the Southern Novel?" he tells his readers that the "South is perhaps the most interesting section of the United States today" and the very "stuff" novels are made of. Naturally, he is selling his own trade here, and though he does not mention anywhere that he is a novelist, his diplomacy suggests that he did not want to be too harsh in his judgment of writers like himself. Knowing the damage that critics could do, he was carefully critical and generous with praise. At times, his reviews are ambivalent, revealing a conflict of interest between Basso the critic and Basso the writer. Moreover, since he associated the majority of literary critics with those "little intellectual people," he could not take the profession of the literary critic seriously: "Even a good critic . . . is apt to depend too much on the usual critical formulas, the usual phrases and clichés, simply to get the damned day's work over with. . . . An examination of literary criticism

45. Hamilton Basso, "Some Recent Novels," *New Republic,* August 21, 1935, p. 54; Basso, "Herndon's Story," *New Republic,* March 31, 1937, p. 245.

46. Hamilton Basso, *The View from Pompey's Head* (1954; rpr. London, 1956), 71.

Mountain Muse   83

over the past 100 years would show, I think, that the second-rate people—the Harvey Allens and the Margaret Mitchells—have always been
tapped for Skull and Bones: while the first rate ones go along as 'non-
frat' men until, lo and behold, they are made honorary members—
generally about the age of 60. Every writer, every artist, has to be his
own critic."[47]

Though Basso did not refrain from expressing his aversion if a book
failed to meet his standards, he was merciful and, southern gentleman
that he was, polite. In an editorial letter to a Mr. Whipple, who believed
that criticism was meant to be tough and truthful, Basso disclosed his
critical creed: "I cannot agree . . . that we are privileged to look down
our noses . . . and make patronizing phrases at [writers'] expense. All
of which, I understand, can be waved away by saying that I place too
much importance on politeness—even in criticism."[48]

Inevitably, Basso was most polite when defending his literary
friends, the most noteworthy of whom were Sherwood Anderson and
Thomas Wolfe. Having been one of Anderson's pupils in New Orleans,
he found it difficult to criticize his former mentor, who was steadily on
his way out at the time that Basso was reviewing books for the *New Republic*. Basso remained loyal to his old friend and wrote a flattering review of Anderson's *Puzzled America* (1935). In spite of Gertrude Stein's
praise of the book as "one of the best books that an American has
done," many critics derided and parodied Anderson's art. Basso, however, defended him against the critics who insinuated that it was not
America that was puzzled but Anderson. Instead, Basso praised the
book for its psychological realism and the writer's attempt to see
America through the eyes of commoners. A year later, Anderson published the novel *Kit Brandon* (1936). Again Basso was asked to review
the book, but rather than write a review of the novel, which he thought
contained some of Anderson's best and worst writing, he wrote an ap-
praisal of Anderson's significance as an American author. Calling him
one of "our greatest geniuses of the short story," Basso condemned the
critics who failed to recognize that Caldwell, Faulkner, Hemingway,
and Wolfe, among other writers, were greatly indebted to the *Wines-*

47. Hamilton Basso, "Why the Southern Novel?" *New Republic*, July 22, 1936, p. 331;
Hamilton Basso to Thomas Wolfe, October 20, 1936, in Wisdom Papers, HL.

48. Hamilton Basso, "Mr. Basso vs. Mr. Whipple," *New Republic*, June 30, 1937,
p. 225.

burg author. Concluding that Anderson was still to be reckoned with, he suggested that "it might be wise for us to remember that he was one of the headmasters at school where so many of us learned our ABC's."[49] Basso's politeness and his sense of loyalty and true admiration for writers he considered superior are the hallmarks of his criticism in the *New Republic* as well as in the *New Yorker*, for which he wrote in the forties and fifties.

Finally, his employment with the Yankee *New Republic* was seen by some as a betrayal of his southern roots. His criticism of the South in his novels and *New Republic* articles marked him as a "southern dissident." Cleanth Brooks even hinted that Basso's "rejection" of the South and later exile in the North led to the difficulty of placing and identifying him as a southern writer.[50] One could, however, argue that Basso's enlightened views of the South and his sound politics in the thirties validate his merit as a southern writer today.

When Basso was composing *Cinnamon Seed*, his second novel, he, like other writers of the South at that time, found himself at a crossroads between the past and the present. Was the South a mythical land of moonlight and magnolias, or had the moon waned and the magnolias withered? Was the southern writer to write about the golden antebellum era, or was he obliged to show the poverty-stricken present? In its attempt to answer questions like these, Southern Renascence literature, and *Cinnamon Seed* in particular, exhibits a constant tension between past and present, the Old South and the New South, the agrarian and the industrial way of life, the small town and the big city, nostalgia and disillusionment.

The contrast between Old South myths and New South realities is perhaps illustrated best in Basso's showboat metaphor in *Cinnamon Seed*. Offering a variety of entertainment ranging from musical performances to acrobatics, showboats first appeared in the 1830s and became very popular between 1870 and 1910.[51] However, as the movie in-

49. Hamilton Basso, "Anderson in America," *New Republic,* May 1, 1935, p. 348; Kim Townsend, *Sherwood Anderson: A Biography* (Boston, 1987), 297; Hamilton Basso, "Two Mid-American Novelists," *New Republic,* October 21, 1936, p. 318.

50. Cleanth Brooks, interview with the author, October 15, 1991.

51. Charles R. Wilson, "Showboats," *Encyclopedia of Southern Culture,* ed. Charles Reagan Wilson and William Ferris (Chapel Hill, 1989), 1261.

dustry drew more and more people to the cinema, the popularity of the showboats languished, one of the last boats being the *Cotton Blossom*, which also happens to be the name of the boat in *Cinnamon Seed*. Dekker, the novel's protagonist, has a dim view of the *Cotton Blossom*: repulsed by its vulgar display of sentimentalities and cheap formulas, he thinks showboats are "just grand affairs in musical comedies and books by lady novelists" (*CS*, 230–31).

Interestingly, in 1932 Basso had already written about a showboat performance in the *Sewanee Review*. In fact, a fragment of *Cinnamon Seed* is almost a verbatim copy of the 1932 story, a slight but important difference being that Basso was more explicit in his critique of the South in the *Sewanee Review*. Appalled by the forced picturesqueness of the rustic characters of the showboat play and condemning the entire performance as a grave distortion of reality, he believed that this was an "easy habit to fall into . . . it has become pernicious in so many of the people who have written about the South." As he had maintained in letters to Josephson and Perkins, he reiterated that the South "is not picturesque"; its "good indolent life is gone. It has lost its force and has been robbed of its meaning. It exists only in the past, something to be remembered, something we of the South wish could be restored."[52] To counter southerners' recreation of the Old South in showboat performances and fiction, Basso aimed at a more authentic representation of southern realities in his second novel.

Set in New Orleans and the countryside of Louisiana, *Cinnamon Seed* is an eighty years' chronicle of the Blackheath family. While the novel's "actual time" spans three decades, from the 1900s to the 1930s, the "historical time" goes back to 1850, when the Blackheath patriarch Robert, like Thomas Sutpen in Faulkner's *Absalom, Absalom!* (1936), erected a columned plantation home in the Dixie wilderness. Due to the extended time frame, the novel has a panoramic quality that is reinforced by the narrator's juxtaposition of the fame, fortune, and misfortune of three representative families of the South. The heart of the narrative is taken up by the Blackheaths' story. In the shadow of the Blackheaths is a family of black servants, most notable among them the characters of Horace and Sam. The third family, whose fate is intertwined with that of the Blackheaths and whose rise is inversely propor-

52. Basso, "Cottom Blossom," 385–95.

tional to the fall of Willswood House (the Blackheaths' home), is the Brand family. The focal character of this family is the trashy Harry, who, as Louisiana's governor, senator, and would-be president, is the very image of Huey Long.

The first book opens two days after Dekker's father, Kinloch, committed suicide. Dekker's orphaned state not only highlights his tragic fate, it also complicates his *Bildung*. Unlike the meek Tony, Dekker is rough, impulsive, unpredictable, and rebellious, or as Aunt Olivia characterizes him: "The way he acts is the way your knee acts when you hit it," and "there are two kinds of men in this family: the wild ones and the peaceable ones. The wild ones make life more interesting but the peaceable ones are better to have around. Dekker's one of the wild ones" (CS, 269, 292). Dekker's forthright character saves the novel from the tiresome complications stirred up by the weak-willed Tony. However, because of his wild and shiftless behavior, Dekker is a difficult character to understand.

Believing in ancestral ties, Basso portrays Dekker as someone who identifies with his grandfather Langley and his great-uncle Edward. As mentioned earlier, in several of Basso's novels, fathers play an insignificant role, whereas sons emulate their mythical grandfathers. Merrill Maguire Skaggs, who explored the extent to which Southern Renascence fiction draws on but also departs from southern local color fiction, has written that in reaction to the happy and doting families of local colorists, Southern Renascence writers like Flannery O'Connor and Carson McCullers (and Hamilton Basso) are often preoccupied with the "conflict between two generations of the same family." Indeed, as in most of O'Connor's and McCullers' fiction, nearly all of Basso's fictional children and adolescents do not get along with their "guardian or parent."[53]

After his father's sudden death, Dekker is adopted by Uncle Carter (Kinloch's brother) and his religious wife, Elizabeth, who is a look-alike of Aunt Hermine. Their son John is the opposite of Dekker and, like Carter, a "peaceable" specimen of the Blackheath family. While Dekker has a hard time adapting to the rule-ridden household of his aunt and uncle, his grandfather Langley is responsible for most of the action and atmosphere of Book I. Though his brother Edward died in

---

53. Merrill Maguire Skaggs, *The Folk of Southern Fiction* (Athens, Ga., 1972), 253.

battle, Langley survived the war to live his life in the shadows of the past. Like Beauregard, he finds comfort in a world of reminiscences.

Recollecting the past in tranquil and ponderous flashbacks, Langley remembers how Edward and his faithful servant Jube (Horace's grandfather) rode off to war while Langley was left sulking at the plantation gate because he was too young to be a soldier. In Langley's flashbacks, we meet Peter Brand (Harry's grandfather), the cruel overseer at Willswood. We also encounter Bella, Robert's black mistress and grandmother of Sam. We further obtain a glimpse of the family secrets, which, like the family secrets of Louis Couperus' plantation families, have left an indelible mark on the surviving relatives and hang like a curse over the house.[54] Together with Langley, we witness Edward's brave demise in battle, and upon the former's return home, we find the family patriarch, Robert, in his pine coffin. The war is over, and while the house is enveloped in mourning, the naked Bella performs an orgiastic dance in front of the mesmerized soldiers. Humiliated by her husband's past infidelities, Mrs. Blackheath shoots the dancing woman and Langley, like a true cavalier, takes the blame, but his mother is convicted after Peter Brand testifies in court that he saw Mrs. Blackheath fire the gun. The progenitor's death at the close of the war, the consequences of defeat, and the Blackheath crime seal the family's fate. Conversely, those events occasion the rise of the Brands, who symbolize the new order supplanting the order of the Old South.

The disintegration of the Blackheath family is precipitated by Carter's and Kinloch's move to New Orleans, where they open a law firm. The ailing Langley and his two unmarried daughters, Olivia and Ann, are left to run Willswood, which because of their lack of funds becomes a Faulknerian ruin. The house is in danger of being demolished altogether when plans are made for a highway to cut across the Blackheath property. At the close of the first book, Langley's friend Solomon comments: "Pretty soon the whole river'll be built up from New Orleans to Baton Rouge. Won't be a farm or plantation left. Nothin' but in-dustrial enterprises" (*CS*, 104). As the industrialized South encroaches on several fronts, the Old South is breathing its last: after he learns that Carter has employed Harry Brand, Langley dies, his body slumping on the twilit porch.

54. Louis Couperus (1863–1923) is a Dutch novelist who wrote on planters' experiences in the East Indies.

Langley's death, coinciding appropriately with the end of Book I, is preceded by a curious subplot. Like their grandparents, Ann and Sam are attracted to each other but do not acknowledge this because of the southern taboo against miscegenation. There is another taboo, however, for theirs is an incestuous impulse: not only do Sam and Ann descend from the same grandfather, but as a servant in the feudal household, Sam is essentially looked upon as a member of the Blackheath family. Denying their sexual urge, which in Basso's books always seems to be more alive in the hot and humid environment of the South than in the cold and sterile North, they both make their escape: Ann marries a Minneapolis doctor, and Sam leaves surreptitiously in search of the seemingly brighter horizons of the North. Thus by the end of Book I, Olivia is the only Blackheath left at Willswood. Though she knows that times are changing and Willswood may go under, she perseveres and, like her father, clings to the past.

Book II lacks the imaginative force of the first book. This can largely be ascribed to Langley's absence. When "the Colonel goes out of the book," Perkins told Basso, "it makes a great difference." Robert Coates, who was highly complimentary of the novel, also suggested that Langley's death left a "void."[55] Compared to the lively and atmospheric first book and the action of the third, the second book is a bland intermezzo in which Dekker, like the young Basso, drops out of law school and turns up on Olivia's doorstep to help her run the plantation. John, on the other hand, graduates from Harvard, travels to Europe, gets engaged to the dull Constance Cummings, and finds employment with an advertising agency. In view of Basso's experiences with the advertising world, which he disliked—a dislike that would resurface in *In Their Own Image*—it is not so surprising that Dekker ridicules John's job as a mere "writing of poems for ladies' drawers" (*CS*, 211). While John settles down in what Dekker sees as a despicably sedate lifestyle, Dekker becomes increasingly restless. Reveling in drunken bouts and brawls, his restiveness peaks at John's engagement party: feeling closed in by the phony world of his adoptive family, Dekker leaves to find his true identity.

Book III is filled with (perhaps too much) action. Again we find

---

55. Perkins to Basso, July 18, 1933, in SA; Robert Coates, "Five New Novels," *New Republic*, March 28, 1934, pp. 190–91.

Olivia alone at Willswood, and to emphasize her lonely battle for survival, the narrator confronts her with Harry Brand. As the story unfolds, the Blackheaths lose more and more ground in their confrontations with the Brands, for while Olivia cannot stop Brand from building the highway (just as Huey Long could not be stopped from building highways in Louisiana), Carter cannot deter him from scandalizing the Blackheath firm. But Olivia is not abandoned completely. She is followed around the house by her faithful servant and friend Horace, and like an old married couple, they spend the rest of their days bickering.

At one point Olivia and Horace are joined by Ann's daughter Elinor, who must recuperate from her bronchitis in the warmer South. Although her physical health improves, her mental health deteriorates in the region's Gothic environment, where the impish and dwarfish Dee-Dee, a kind of demon child, sneaks up on the pale Elinor, spies on her through doorways, and peeps in on her through her bedroom window at night.

Sam eventually returns to Willswood, disillusioned with the North's equally racist environment. The victim of more unjust treatment in the South, however, Sam does not find the peace he longs for. At the same time, Dekker, who had strangely disappeared from the story, resurfaces and wanders about the South, taking on a variety of blue-collar jobs in tanneries, mills, and mines. Yet, like Sam, he feels the pull of his roots and finally returns to the family plantation.

At Willswood, Dee-Dee, who likes to torment animals, takes his cruelty a step further and pushes the unsuspecting Elinor in front of Tard Sturkins' onrushing car. Witnessing the scene, Sam leaps for the little girl and saves her life. Unfortunately, his embrace of the shocked child and his kisses are misinterpreted by the "nigger hating" Sturkins, who subsequently beats him up. Dekker comes to Sam's aid, and although Sam recovers, and is thanked profusely by the Blackheaths, he can no longer tolerate the constant exposure to prejudice and hangs himself. Dee-Dee dies, too; fleeing the loft where he is hiding, the strange child falls to his death. In the closing pages of the novel, Horace dies of old age, and though these deaths seem to further the disintegration of the Blackheath household, the continuance of the family line has somehow been secured by Dekker's return. Not only has he returned a "man," but the announcement of the coming of Jonquill Keitt, a girl to whom Dekker has always been attracted, suggests the continuation of Blackheath progeny. The concluding scene leaves the reader with an image of the South that will not go away: "Behind the house Jeff Davis worked the pump, the handle rattling and the water sloshing into the pail, and from the cabins the voices of children rose thin and quarrelling on the sunlit air. They shrilled their quarrel out and then there was only the sing-song of the pump and the glittering afternoon drawing subtly to its close. Splashes of sunlight fell upon the house and from the fields there came the scent of growing cane" (*CS*, 378–79).

Dekker Blackheath is a considerable improvement over Tony Clezac. He is not only more consistently drawn, but he also wins our affection more easily. Whereas Tony is a rather weak and introverted character who is all feeling, Dekker is strong, extroverted, and guided by instinct. And where Tony's revolt is modest and inane, as he silently mocks the Church and quietly tries to live up to the gentlemanly image of his grandfather, Dekker exclaims "To hell with the Bible!" (*CS*, 5) and "To hell with being a gentleman!" (*CS*, 151). Dekker casts aside everything that is associated with the South: he not only flees from his adoptive family but also resents southern religion (as epitomized by his pious aunt Elizabeth), southern gentlemanliness, southern hospitality, southern sentimentality, and southern white trash (as personified by Tard Sturkins). Besides rebelling against his heritage, Dekker, like his creator, scoffs at law and politics. He describes the legal profession as grubbing "around in other people's business and spouting your head off before some pot-bellied judge" (*CS*, 172). He calls political activists (of Josephson's and Cowley's kind) "futile and cowardly" because they merely "run around trying to identify themselves with the working class, declaiming that they belong to the proletariat" (*CS*, 301).

Dekker appears to be a working-class hero who would be on the side of the revolution "if there was a revolution tomorrow" (*CS*, 301), but he does not sympathize with the Communist Party, thinking the organization too exclusive a "club." Also, despite his blue-collar episode, which may strike a proletarian note, *Cinnamon Seed* is *not* a proletarian novel. Notwithstanding Basso's *New Republic* articles on southern mills and strikes, he insisted that this novel was not political, as that would be "a pose" on his part. Basso never subscribed to the proletarian genre, or as he wrote in a letter to Maxwell Perkins: "Once upon a time all perplexed people in novels solved their problems by suicide; now they join the Communist Party. I'm afraid it's just another literary device. And now that I've lived near a mill-village and have come to understand working people a little better I am more impatient with garret revolutionists. A tower is a tower even if it happens to be painted red." Thus, to Basso, Dekker's work in the mills and the tannery was merely to have him "object to the Capitalistic system," and as such, was entirely "incidental" to the novel.[56]

While Dekker may be apolitical, his rebellion and refusal to conform to southern society are rooted in the fact that unlike his forebears, he does not have anything "to believe in [or] something to accept without questioning, just as [Langley and Edward] accepted their Episcopalianism and their God" (*CS*, 208–209). Knowing that the meaning of planters' families has become obsolete in a changing South where men like Harry Brand "run the show" (*CS*, 209), Dekker has to reinvent his own and his family's role and significance in society. Tony experiences the same dilemma when he realizes that he cannot make the same choices and lead the same life as his grandfather did. The orphaned state of the protagonists, as well as the sense that they have fallen between the old order and the new, aggravate their lonely condition. "I have no home," Dekker says. "I am an orphan" (*CS*, 8).

Ironically, in spite of the characters' "homelessness," they need to return home to come to a definition of their identities and roles in society. While Tony's quest for a mature and full identity only starts upon his arrival home, Dekker's quest has been fulfilled by his homecoming: "He was back now. . . . In the end, no matter what you said or did, you always came back. You scrubbed hides, you drove a dinky . . . you sweated and got drunk and gave yourself to the moment, and then you came back. There are some things you cannot escape. What next? Who knew? Perhaps the storm. But for a moment, before it came, here was peace again, peace and beauty, a deep healing sense of peace" (*CS*, 338).

In *Relics and Angels* and *Cinnamon Seed*, the main character's homecoming is inextricably tied up with his ultimate *Bildung* and rapprochement with family and society. Accordingly, as if Dekker's revolt

---

56. Basso to Josephson, February 25, 1933, in Josephson Papers, BL; Basso to Perkins, [*ca.* 1934] and August 2, 1933, in SA.

never took place, in the end he reconciles himself with being a planter, his love for the soil being too much a "part of his being" (*CS*, 175). Basso told Perkins that eventually Dekker "could not get away from the pull of the earth, from the tradition of several generations of planters. And so finally he goes back home. . . . Once home, he understands that there is what we might call an obligation of blood, of history and that is his proper place in life."[57] A sense of place as well as an understanding of the family identity are prerequisites to the protagonist's final maturation and the key to his pursuit of happiness.

Maxwell Perkins was enchanted with the novel's atmosphere but complained that Dekker lacked prominence. Since Basso rounded out characters like Olivia and Langley so much, Dekker was not, in Perkins' view, the main character of the book: "His direction is vague and so is he when he grows up. . . . the story spreads out into pools and shallows and gradually dissipates itself." Dorothy Scarborough, a *New York Times Book Review* critic, made the same point; although she praised *Cinnamon Seed* as an "interesting novel of the new South," she did not think that Dekker was the most important let alone most interesting character in the book.[58]

Perkins' and Scarborough's criticism was justified. In *In Their Own Image* and *Wine of the Country* (1941) too, Basso failed to render the protagonist in such a way as to make him the designated hero. At the same time, one may ascribe *Cinnamon Seed*'s "dissipation," or Dekker's lack of distinction, to its panoramic quality. The problem of the main character is irrelevant if one assumes that Dekker is not the protagonist but that his family, as a whole, acts as the corporate protagonist. As in *Relics and Angels*, *Cinnamon Seed*'s characters derive their ultimate identity from their family. Thus Olivia reflects: "Here, in this earth, was rooted the history of her house. Its story was their story. . . . There they had all lived, gaining meaning from their place and time and leaving behind them, on the earth, some slight impress of themselves. Not until Carter went to New Orleans followed by Kinloch, had the earth ever been deserted; and now save for herself, the desertion was complete" (*CS*, 263). Like Tony, Olivia and Dekker experience the same sense of duty, or

57. Basso to Perkins, August 2, 1933, in SA.

58. Perkins to Basso, July 31, 1933, in SA; Dorothy Scarborough, "A Louisiana Senator," *New York Times Book Review*, February 25, 1935, pp. 8–9.

"obligation of the blood" and the soil; for this reason also Olivia stays and Dekker returns to the family estate. The Blackheaths are exemplary in their manifestation of family solidarity. Not only are the "wild" Blackheaths (Langley, Olivia, and Dekker) the core of the family and the most pertinacious in their preservation of the estate, they also represent the family's continuity: when one character is momentarily offstage, another takes over to either remember the past (Langley), preserve the present (Olivia), or secure the future (Dekker). Robert Coates described the Blackheaths' cohesion as a "kind of pull that exists between relatives, no matter how far apart they may be or how much at odds."[59]

Their extraordinary family identity is strengthened by heredity patterns and the history the family shares. Joseph Millichap has justly argued that the Blackheaths resemble Faulkner's McCaslins in the way in which the family's past relationships reverberate in the present.[60] Like the Blackheaths, in *Go Down, Moses* (1942), the McCaslins inherit the burdens, curses, and relationships of the past. Additionally, *Cinnamon Seed* exhibits a systematic twinning of people's fates; thus the novel opens as well as closes with a suicide (of Kinloch and Sam). Besides the firm tie among Langley, Olivia, and Dekker, there is an equally strong bond among Carter, Ann, and John: as opposed to the "wild" and rebellious members of the family, who stand firm and do not abandon Willswood, they are the "peaceable" ones, who turn aside their obligations to the soil and leave for the city. These patterns also apply interracially, that is, the relationship between Robert and Bella returns in the relations between Sam and Ann, Dee-Dee and Elinor, and more platonically, Horace and Olivia. Similarly, Langley's relationship with Horace mirrors the master-servant relationship of Edward and Jube. Less obvious but certainly more than coincidental is the analogy between Dekker's and Sam's rebellion, their secretive leavetaking, and their unexpected return home. Forever a family unit, the Blackheaths and their servants are one, and as such their fates are wholly intertwined.

To draw attention to the societal transition from Old South to New South, the narrator alludes frequently to the nature of the changing

59. Robert Coates to Hamilton Basso, February 20, 1934, in Basso Papers, BL.

60. Millichap, *Hamilton Basso*, 42–48. Millichap further suggests that it is not unlikely that Faulkner might have been inspired by *Cinnamon Seed*, as "in all possibility Faulkner would have read his friend's first successful novel."

order. While Horace admits to the "Cunnel" that they "ain't much longer for dis wu'ld" (CS, 134), Langley feels lost in the vast "uncertain emptiness that separated two alien but sometimes identical worlds" (CS, 55). Remembering the South's golden age, when the gardens bloomed and the minstrel songs mingled with the tinkling of crystal chandeliers at plantation balls, Langley does not see that in reality Willswood House is, like the Clezac house, in a state of disrepair and decay. Like the Clezac garden, we find that behind the house, "where the formal gardens once were, the trees had grown into a thicket" (CS, 46). Also, symbolizing the advent of the new age, the industrial push is tangible and relentless. As the highway comes closer and closer, Horace and Olivia notice the transformation that the neighboring Bennett plantation underwent after its sale to an oil company. Even warfare becomes an industry. Contrasting the Civil War to the mechanized warfare of World War I, Langley's friend Solomon observes: "Men don't fight men no more. It's machines fightin' machines" (CS, 160). Finally, to emphasize that the antebellum era is a bittersweet memory of things past, the narrator has Langley, like some aged Eugene Gant, look back and mourn the evanescence of time in such plaintive expressions as "Lost and forever gone!" Particularly Wolfian, and gratingly so, is Langley's sentimental "Oh youth! Oh life! Oh time! Oh yesterday!" (CS, 143).

In his sometimes sentimentalized juxtapositions of the plantation past and the industrialized present, Basso does not seem to have been partial to either era. Just as he condemns the many feudalisms of the Old South, so does he insist that modern times and a life in the city do not necessarily guarantee progress or happiness. While the plantation survives as a kind of anachronism, the city is hit hard by the Depression, and John's conversations turn from golf to economics. Also, Carter's law firm, though much more profitable than Willswood, is brought into disrepute because of Brand's dirty politics. Sam does not ensure his happiness in the city either: because of the Depression, he loses his job and returns to the country, where Willswood serves as his safety net.

Finally, Sam's story needs to be highlighted here, for Basso's *New Republic* reviews were especially critical of novelists' portraiture of blacks in the South. Although black characters were never absent from the earliest southern fiction, it was not until the twenties and thirties that the stereotyping of black characters was called into question. Whereas, prior to the twenties, blacks were often seen as plantation "types" (such as the contented slave, the brute nigger, the comic negro, the black mammy, and the tragic mulatto), as the twentieth century progressed, the black type became more human.[61] Although Faulkner has received special credit for his role in this evolution, Basso was very much ahead of his time in his sensitive portrayal of black southerners.

In *Cinnamon Seed* the question of race is first introduced when the young Dekker stumbles upon the hidden lives of the black servants: perturbed by the hysteria of a bayou revival meeting, he runs home and asks his aunt how blacks are different from whites. As someone who has inherited the feudal views of her family, Olivia answers that it is something one must "feel" and something that has been "arranged" (*CS*, 69–70). As can be expected, this response does not satisfy the boy's curiosity, so he approaches Horace with the same question. Horace is equally vague. Having learned to accept the difference, his answer is that "De diffunce am already dere" (*CS*, 70). Overhearing this conversation, Sam objects and tells Dekker that blacks are "an oppressed and exploited people," which elicits Horace's flippant admonition: "One day he's gonter open dat big mouf er his'n onct too often. Den dey's gonter be a diffunce sho-de diffunce 'tween a dead nigger en a live un. Yessuh!" (*CS*, 71).

Whereas Horace's character falls into the category of the docile and happy-go-lucky servant stereotype, Sam's creation defies any such categorization. For a thirties novel, Sam is an unusual black character, presented as a real human being. Also, as a character who inherited the Blackheaths' wild streak, Sam is essentially the opposite of Horace. In contrast to Horace, who as the typical "good Negro" of local color fiction is loyal, agreeable, content, lazy, naïve, and jolly, Sam is rebellious, defiant, unhappy, proud, intelligent, and serious. Nicknamed "Mr. Edjucation" and described as an "uppity black," Sam feels both superior and inferior, and can neither identify with the plantation blacks nor feel comfortable among whites. His mixed blood lies at the root of his dilemma, because, "homeless" like Dekker, he walks the no man's

61. John Bradbury, *Renaissance in the South: A Critical History of the Literature, 1920–1960* (Chapel Hill, 1963), 79; Seymour L. Gross and John E. Hardy (eds.), *Images of the Negro in American Literature* (Chicago, 1966), 10.

land separating the two races. Like Faulkner, Basso took mulattoes as
the quintessential victims of a segregated culture. As Irving Howe has
noted, "Trapped between the demarcated races, the mulatto is an un-
avoidable candidate for the role of the victim" and is therefore often referred to as the "tragic mulatto," a type that already existed in southern fiction of the nineteenth century.[62]

Among other mulattoes in southern fiction, Sam is probably closest
to Joe Christmas in Faulkner's *Light in August* (1932) and Sherman Pew
in Carson McCullers' *Clock Without Hands* (1961). Although Sam is a
softer and more saintlike version of Joe and Sherman, the predicament
of these mulattoes is the same. Despite their recalcitrance and daring,
Sam, Joe, and Sherman are lonely, sad characters who are highly self-
conscious of their color. An embittered man by the end of the novel,
Sam "had tried to establish an identity unconditioned by the color of
his skin, to be not a negro but a man. [Yet] he was still a negro. No matter what happened . . . he would never be able to escape the pigmenta-
tion of his skin" (*CS*, 284). Joe and Sherman cannot escape the pigmen-
tation of their skin either: once whites know that they are of mixed
blood, they pigeonhole them and treat them as blacks. Fellow blacks,
on the other hand, view them as whites, or part white, and therefore do
not accept them either. This schizophrenia of color, or the inability to
find comfort in either the black or the white world, ultimately leads to
the men's sad deaths.

Their similar fate notwithstanding, Sam is also very different from
Joe and Sherman. Whereas the latter two succumb to uncontrolled violence and act out their roles as assertive and aggressive avengers of the
black race, Sam is a painfully passive victim of the white race. Indeed,
one may even wonder if Sam, in all his martyrdom, is not too much a
mirror image of Harriet Beecher Stowe's Uncle Tom. Because Basso
emphasized Sam's heroism and tragic suicide and avoided the controversial topic of miscegenation, *Cinnamon Seed* is a straightforward indictment of racism in the South. The same applies to *Clock Without
Hands*: in that novel, too, the reader cannot ignore the author's plea for
civil rights reform after Sherman is killed by an angry white mob. *Light*

---

62. Irving Howe, "Faulkner and the Negroes," in *Images of the Negro in American Literature*, Gross and Hardy, 213.

in August is less unequivocal, however. Since Christmas is such a controversial character whom neither the narrator nor the reader can fathom, the book's implications are much more complex. This is also what distinguishes Faulkner's treatment of black characters from Basso's. In Faulkner, African American characters are always seen from without, through the eyes of white people; in Basso's novels and in *Cinnamon Seed* in particular, black characters are seen from within. Thus whereas Faulkner uses the epithets "impenetrable" and "inscrutable" to describe mulatto characters like Christmas and Lucas Beauchamp, Basso places himself inside Sam's character. And while Faulkner and to a lesser extent McCullers seem to imply that there will always be a rift between the black and white worlds because the white man will never fully understand the black man, Basso does not appear to have such reservations and simply functions as a spokesman for the Negro. The question remains whether Basso succeeds, for despite his good intentions, his vision is one-sided as well as ambivalent. Sam may be human and real, but Horace never rises above the level of stereotype.

Nonetheless, critics praised *Cinnamon Seed* for its unusual and realistic treatment of blacks. Perkins told Basso that they were "presented differently" from what he had "ever known before." Indeed, in *The Negro in American Culture* (1956), Margaret Butcher singled out Basso, William March, and Robert Rylee as writers who "picked up the challenge of the South in a third generation defiance of its sacred taboos, especially its sex mores and the subject of the Negro, [writing] not so much in specific desire for retributive justice for the Negro as out of loyalty to realism's basic credo."[63]

The reviews hailed Basso as a "gifted young writer who deserves wide recognition" and significantly (from a Southern Renascence point of view), as one of the "rising young" penmen who were "going to create something uncommonly first-rate out of the supposedly barren soil of Southern letters." Not without flaws, one being the problem of the protagonist and the other Basso's crowding of the plot, *Cinnamon Seed* is a considerable improvement over *Relics and Angels*. Not for nothing

---

63. Perkins to Basso, April 2, 1934, in SA; Margaret Just Butcher, *The Negro in American Culture* (1956; rpr. New York, 1971), 139.

did James E. Rocks call the book the "author's most enjoyable and satisfying novel," and Joseph Millichap described it as one of Basso's
"most interesting and best written works."[64]

Of Basso's southern novels, *Cinnamon Seed* is perhaps the best example of a Southern Renascence work. Some of the Renascence motifs
summed up by John Bradbury in *Renaissance in the South: A Critical History of the Literature, 1920–1960* (1963)—the guilty relationship with the
slave past, disintegration and decay after defeat, the past functioning as
a framework for the present, the black experience, the contrast between
the city and the country, and the transition from the Old South to the
New South—are present in the novel. In addition, like Basso's first
novel, *Cinnamon Seed* can be categorized as a social novel of manners: it
examines not only the life and behavior of a certain southern class but
also the consequences of a new order replacing the old one. Above all,
it is a novel that aims at southern realism, and though occasionally the
author gets carried away with the charms of the past, the book's plantation material has not been used to glorify the antebellum era but to
show the reader that that era is incongruous with modern times. Like
Glasgow, Faulkner, Welty, and other Southern Renascence writers,
Basso did not borrow characters, plots, conventions, and stereotypes
from nineteenth-century southern romance writers and local colorists
to perpetuate this popular tradition but to transcend it. Finally, *Cinnamon Seed* may be seen as the fictional realization of what Allen Tate described as the "backward glance" that gave us "the Southern Renaissance, a literature conscious of the past in the present": as a novel that
has the "anamnestic" setting of Willswood as its focal point, the book
is the prosaic embodiment of a present that is conscious of and derives
its meanings from the past. As Basso told Perkins when he conceived
his plan for the novel: "It's about the South but about the South, I think
and hope, in a different way—seen through the flux and flow of people's lives."[65]

---

64. Scarborough, "A Louisiana Senator," 8–9; Albert Goldstein, "Mr. Basso, Mr.
Mencken and Uncle Tom," *Southwest Review*, XX (1935), 11–12; James E. Rocks, "Hamilton Basso and the World View from Pompey's Head," *South Atlantic Quarterly*, LXXI
(1972), 333; Millichap, *Hamilton Basso*, 48.

65. Skaggs, *The Folk of Southern Fiction*, 221–34; Allen Tate, "The New Provincialism," in Tate, *Collected Essays* (1945; rpr. Denver, 1959), 292; Basso to Perkins, July 11,
1933, in SA.

* * *

In December 1933 Basso was going over the proofs of *Cinnamon Seed*.
At this point he was still struggling financially. Humbly, he asked Perkins for his December stipend because the engine of his old Ford "fell
plumb out and we had to invest in a new one."[66] At the time the novel
was published, the Bassos had exchanged the rugged mountains of
North Carolina for the horse country of South Carolina. Spending the
spring of 1934 in "hoity-toity" Aiken, Basso admitted that after the
many inconveniences of Pisgah Forest, it was "good . . . to experience
again the decadent luxuries of high-balls, soft beds, dressing for dinner, and to know, that when bedtime came, you didn't have to put
chains on your Ford or walk 1/4 mile skyward on a slippery path."

From Aiken, Basso wrote Perkins about *Cinnamon Seed*'s reception,
singling out reviewers' lines about certain characters: Herschel Brickell's "I cannot recall from a fairly wide reading in Southern literature a
better-done Negro than Horace"; Edward Laroque Tinker's "Olivia is
the outstanding character. Never showing her real affection, she bul-
lied her men folk fiercely for their own good, but wisely knowing the
limit of their endurance, left them alone when she knew she must";
and Dorothy Scarborough's "The most exciting person in the book is a
mountebank politician who calls himself the 'Kingfrog' of the pool. He
seems incredibly alive in his attitudinizing and blatant crookedness.
The book is worth reading for this figure alone." He suggested to Perkins that the novel should be marketed as a "book of living people"
rather than "another book about a Southern plantation."[67]

In May 1934 the couple returned to their cabin in what Basso called
a "grand part of the world": "All the dogwood is out and the flame
azalea and there are millions of violets in the woods. I went fishing yesterday with two of my mountaineer friends, way back in the mountains
to a waterfall that drops over a sheer cliff of rock and thunders into a
gorge." After a beautiful spring, a cold summer followed. Thanking Josephson for sending them a copy of his *Robber Barons: The Great American Capitalists, 1861–1901* (1934), Basso told his friend: "We have been
passing the evenings by reading it aloud to each other before the
fire—I hope the picture pleases you; your wise and eloquent words

66. Basso to Perkins, December 6, 1933, in SA.
67. Basso to Perkins, March 2, 1934, in SA.

sounding in our little mountain house with the fire hissing and the rain in the leaves."[68]

Josephson's book, together with the ever-encroaching Depression and Basso's observations with regard to the prosperity of Aiken versus the poverty of southern mill villages and mountain towns, formed the inspiration for his next novel, *In Their Own Image*. "I have started another [novel]," Basso wrote Josephson from Aiken. "[It] will deal, fictionally with the grandsons and granddaughters of the Robber Barons you have fixed once and for all. The crisis, it seems to me, has been seen too much from the bottom. A view from the top, from the privileged classes, so timid and bewildered and frightened should be of some value. [Aiken] is a very curious part of the world—great wealth and great poverty, the two utmost extremes of American life." Later that spring, when trying to cope with the bad sales of *Cinnamon Seed*, Basso was hopeful for the success of *In Their Own Image*, for he wanted to "get the entire scale of American life . . . merely by putting down . . . what happens in this part of the world . . . millionaires in Aiken, mill people six miles away, great wealth, great poverty, the fear of the rich . . . and the growing unrest of the poor."[69]

While plagued by minor illnesses such as colds and headaches, Basso was gravely disappointed by the public's reception of *Cinnamon Seed* and wondered if his high hopes were perhaps "just another witch-fire gleam in the night." Cheered on by Josephson, he wished for his friend's company: "I wish very much just now, with a whip-poor-will calling outside and my kerosene lamp burning and branches scraping in the wind, that I could see you and talk with you. I get very lonely sometimes." Although Basso did not have his intellectual peers close by and therefore felt isolated, he did socialize with poor North Carolinians, discussing the Depression with them: "We talk for hours but things have been this way with them for so long they cannot envision any change. . . . If they are fond of you they will do anything they can to help you, they have absolutely no hate or bitterness and so I am drawn to them."[70] Basso's genuine sympathy for the mountain people

68. Basso to Perkins, May 8, 1934, in SA; Basso to Josephson, June 13, 1934, in Josephson Papers, BL.

69. Basso to Josephson, March 9, April 28, 1934, in Josephson Papers, BL.

70. Basso to Josephson, April 28, 1934, in Josephson Papers, BL.

he lived with and the mill villagers he interviewed for the *New Republic* no doubt deepened his scorn for the Aiken millionaires he satirized in *In Their Own Image*.

When writing *In Their Own Image*, then still entitled *The Centaurs*, Basso told Perkins that the book was to be "pitched . . . in a different key," declaring that "I cannot go on, as some of my friends do, rewriting the same book over and over."[71] Dreading that he was going to be pigeonholed as a "southern writer," Basso had not yet realized that the South would remain the best material for his novelistic potential. Whenever Basso relied on anything other than a Dixie setting—for example, in parts of *In Their Own Image* and *Wine of the Country*, in *The Greenroom* (1949), and in his last novel, *A Touch of the Dragon* (1964)—his work lacked the depth, passion, and atmosphere that all his southern novels possess.

Basso certainly sensed his own weaknesses and was at this point still very much in doubt about his work. Having finished the first one hundred pages of his novel, he was filled with trepidation: "The other day, when I went to town to have the batch of manuscript I sent to you [Perkins] sealed, I thought of the outline it contained and liked it so little that I took it out and tore it up. It rattled around like a bag of bones and I was worried that it would spoil the effect of the manuscript. . . . I could get nothing of the reality and the feeling I wanted the book to have." A few months later, he already seemed to have lost interest in the book. Announcing to Perkins that he wanted to take two years off to write his Tolstoy biography and take up Russian as well as try for a Guggenheim fellowship, Basso became convinced that he needed to move to New York City for a while: "I felt too, that I didn't want to write another book immediately—having composed three of them in three years—and want to lie fallow for awhile and take a crack at writing for the magazines. I did not have enough money of course, to just idle around New York and so I am going to join the staff of the *New Republic*.[72] No doubt, *In Their Own Image*'s poor reception influenced Basso's decision.

* * *

71. Basso to Perkins, May 25, 1934, in SA.
72. Basso to Perkins, May 28, September 8, 1934, in SA.

Basso's third novel elicited Howard Mumford Jones's criticism that "Mr. Basso's novel" was simply "very brittle and very bad."[73] However, we should not dismiss the novel out of hand, as Jones did, despite its shaky plots, cardboard characters, lack of a protagonist, ineffective suspense, occasional melodrama, and strange motivations of some of its characters. *In Their Own Image* is nevertheless worth looking at in the wider context of Basso's political journalism for the *New Republic* and his epistolary battles with Malcolm Cowley and Matthew Josephson. Also, being a two-dimensional rather than a three-dimensional work, an allegory rather than a novel, *In Their Own Image* should not so much be appraised from an aesthetic point of view as from the standpoint of its ideas.

Inspired by Basso's visits to southern mills and his stay in Aiken, *In Their Own Image* was to bring out the contrasts between the haves of polo-playing Aiken and the have-nots of the nearby mill village, Berrytown. Unfortunately, most of the novel's action is given over to the frivolous pastimes of the idle rich. The book opens with the arrival of Pierson James, whose successful advertising launched the fame and fortune of his hostess, the "Mayonnaise Queen," Emma Troy. Her "Aiken cottage," which bears great resemblance to Biltmore, the Vanderbilt mansion in Asheville, houses a number of guests, among them two caricatured Europeans who rail against what they see as the many absurdities of American culture.

A social climber, Emma tries to arrange a marriage between her sympathetic but unhappy daughter Virginia and the Americanophobic Italian count Aldo Piedmontese. Weary of her mother's matchmaking, Virginia is frightened to enter a marriage with a man she does not love and elopes with a commoner, Tommy. Besides Virginia, there is Emma's son Freddie who, as a grotesque example of well-to-do indifference, is described as a "heavy, lumbering, dull-witted dog" (*IT*, 196). To bring out his pathetic side even more, Basso places him in a marriage with Benita Sturme, who, like Carmen, derives great pleasure from seducing and abandoning lovers. In an early plan for the novel, Basso named Benita "Roxanne" and wanted her story to be central to the novel. But because her nymphomania might have been too much

73. Howard Mumford Jones, "Social Notes on the South," *Virginia Quarterly Review*, XI (1935), 452–57.

for the straitlaced Perkins, she became one of the book's many minor characters. As Basso wrote with the typical circumspect deliberations of a writer who had to persuade his editor, "This will not be a 'scandalous' book as I have no stomach for that sort of thing. The girl's sexual adventures will not be given any unnecessary importance. They will not be played down but they will also not be played up. I want them to be artistically real rather than realistically real . . . without turning my back on realism in any way. What I am trying to say . . . is that the book is not to be a book about screwing. Screwing will have its place, just as it has its place in life, but it will not be the end and aim of the book. I am more interested in helping these people to become alive."[74]

One of Benita's "crawling" and "drooling" lovers is the painter Kurt Beach. To satisfy his materialism, Beach has prostituted his art to the whims of the rich. Wishing he could be a portrait painter like Sargent, he ends up as a second-rate Stubbs. Bored with painting horses and remorseful over his selling out, he is utterly frustrated yet cannot bring himself to return to "the clean exhilarating air of art" (*IT*, 76). Although he tries to take up portrait painting again, planning to paint the portraits of "the middle class Small Town," Beach's arrival in Berrytown is viewed with suspicion, and afraid to trespass, he flees back into the arms of his wealthy patronesses.

Conversely, Michael Langford, also a painter but a native of the mill village, is intrigued with the glamor of Aiken. Painting the various Aiken estates, Langford is seen as an intruder too. Falling victim to the Red Scare paranoia of the rich, he is killed by one of Emma's detectives. Berrytown and Aiken are worlds apart, and the incident seems to illustrate, in a rather black and white fashion, that the chasm between America's very poor and very rich can never be bridged.

John Pine is a third painter in the novel and, as Millichap has suggested, has no relation to the plot at all but is simply "trotted in whenever Basso needs a forceful spokesman for one of his own ideas."[75] Pine's observations are interesting because they echo Basso's views on the rich, art, and the South. But his comments are chafing: his editorializing is obtrusive, repetitive, and really belongs in the columns of the *New Republic*.

74. Hamilton Basso, "Roxanne" (Typescript in SA), n.p.
75. Millichap, *Hamilton Basso*, 50.

After Michael's death, the season is over and the party disperses. The two Europeans depart out of fear of more killings and James is headed for a marriage with Emma, who, through Virginia's leap for happiness, comes to see the folly of her struggle for high life. According to Millichap, this ending resembles the conclusion of "many a 1930s film comedy where the social-climbing wife receives her comeuppance and realizes the error of her ways."[76] To give the plot an extra twist and the story a redundant climax, Benita is caught cuckolding her husband, who finds her in bed with a prizefighter. The incident is a residue of the Roxanne outline, and Basso may have thought that it was too good an episode to waste. Nevertheless, the event has clearly been pasted in and hence seems forced and purposeless to the novel as a whole.

Basso's delineation of Aiken society life, a world that is vaguely reminiscent of Fitzgerald's dramas of the nouveaux riches, is mainly intended as a satirical indictment of the vain lives of the rich and famous. In contrast to the mill village, which forms a bleak locale of poverty, unemployment, and social unrest, Aiken is a decadent scene of empty materialism and hedonism. In order to convey the artificiality of the latter, the narrator resorts repeatedly to the metaphor of the theater: the butler looks like a butler out of a play, and the different characters are perceived as actors and actresses who dutifully deliver their lines.

According to one of John Pine's many theories, the theatricality of Aiken has been "manufactured" by the rich as a means to shut out Berrytown. Sheltered by their wealth, the elite use their money to evade the real world: "The greatest value of money to these people is that it enables them to purchase an escape from reality. They wall themselves in with money the way a fort is walled with stone—a series of fortifications all designed to keep them protected from reality" (*IT*, 144). Living in their own cushioned "reality" or, rather, living "in their own image," the rich create a cocoon that renders them oblivious to the problems of the outside world.

But there is more to Pine's theory. Basso, who by 1935 had started reading the Behaviorists, has Pine further expound that the moneyed classes, by locking themselves out of reality, will ultimately be unable

76. *Ibid.*, 55.

to distinguish between illusion and reality. Pine calls this a "schizo-phrenic" state of mind and sees it as detrimental to the rich's overall "conditioning." Knowing deep down that "the rich live in a manufac-tured, unreal world" (*IT*, 204) in which true art cannot flourish, Kurt tries to break out of that mold, but his failure to do so shows that he has been conditioned too much already. Langford's failure to break through in the other direction finally proves Pine's point that it "is just as hard for the rich to escape from their class as it is for the poor to es-cape from theirs" (*IT*, 143).

Like Basso, who valued authenticity in literature, Pine believes that the true artist should not shun reality but immerse himself in it. This means that, like a quintessential "go-and-see-America" artist of the Depression era, Pine does not paint "a single goddamned mammy or a colonel or a house with white columns" but "good honest American stuff, stuff with guts to it," like "cotton gins, nigger cabins, mill work-ers, poor whites [and] those brick chimneys that remain standing when a house burns down" (*IT*, 139). Conversing with Beach, who is a south-erner, Pine claims that the South is not represented by "what your granddaddies did in the Civil War" but by the "modern South." Most southerners, however, Pine continues, talk as if "the modern South does not exist," that is, southerners have been "so busy affirming the past" that they have "forgotten all about the present" (*IT*, 174). Of course, this is a well-known argument of Basso's. Moreover, Pine's the-ory of the rich's "unreality" versus the poor's reality underscores Bas-so's belief that it is in the South especially, where people are already so accustomed to ignoring reality, that the rich can get away more easily with their negation of the truth.

Pine does not only function as a character who vents Basso's objec-tions to the extremes of capitalism and the South. As an artist, he also voices the novelist's artistic creed. While the premise of Pine's aesthet-ics comes down to his preference of reality to make-believe, he also re-veals that art should not merely equal realism but should reject the eso-teric and the political. Accordingly, Basso's denunciation of Cowley's panegyric of Auden's poetry may come to mind when we hear Pine mutter that he does not like Picasso because he "intellectualized all the guts out of painting" (*IT*, 138). In the same way, Basso's remark that his art was not drawn from books but had been inspired by life, experi-ence, and people lies at the core of Pine's argument that art "had to be rooted in a man's place and time. The only important art" is art that springs from "a deep awareness of life. It was experience absorbed by a man of great talent and returned to the world in a form that only he might impress upon it" (*IT,* 188). Similarly, the debates that Langford has with his union friend, Timothy, remind one of Basso's discussions with Josephson. While Tim tries to "radicalize" Michael, the latter re- fuses—like Basso—to "turn his art into an instrument of class war- fare" (*IT,* 102).

In Their Own Image did not greatly contribute to Basso's develop- ment. The work seems to have been written in haste and is badly con- ceived. The author's preachy and ardent arguments about capitalism, art, and the South may be interesting but are too nakedly present in the novel and make the characters look pale and lifeless. Colored by issues of the day, the novel is a mediocre mixture of social satire and proletar- ian art. Because of Basso's inexperience with either of these genres, the book is shallow and never manages to grip the reader. In contrast to *In Their Own Image,* Basso's next novels, *Courthouse Square* and *Days Before Lent* would establish his reputation as a southern writer more securely.

The Bassos did not, as they intended, stay in New York City for a year but for a mere few months. In the winter of 1934 they were back in their mountain cabin, but after enduring two "successive blizzards" and a "shattered plumbing system," they escaped to Aiken once more, driving over the mountains on a road that was "nothing but ice, skid- ding crazily into a bank once [and] taking nine hours to go 160 miles." In February 1935, Basso returned to New York. Though he had prom- ised himself to stay away from novel writing for a while, in a letter of February 27 he asked Perkins for an advance because he was saving for a trip to the West Indies, "not for any romantic notions but because I need an island, and a knowledge of what life on an island is like, for the book I want to write. The book . . . is to be a very thoughtful and se- rious one—the most ambitious thing really, I have set out to write. I want to pour into it all the things I know and think and feel. I want to say my say about this city [New York] of confusion confounded and to write a story about a man and woman who are in love and who both seek their proper place on the earth."[77]

77. Basso to Perkins, January 1, February 27, 1935, in SA.

The Bassos never made it to the West Indies but returned to the mountains that summer and moved into a different and somewhat more comfortable cabin in Pisgah Forest. Unpacking boxes, Basso noticed the quietude after "the granite and noise of New York" and started to write immediately. Though the failure of his last novel had discouraged him, he was excited by his new ideas and told Perkins that in his next novel he was going to use the flashback more extensively and strive for what he called "the unity of ultimate emotion": "I was thinking this afternoon that when a man dies, and we think of him, or if we read his name on a stone, we get a feeling . . . of his entire life: at least I do. And so I think it should be with a novel; and it is that feeling, the sense of knowing and understanding that come with the reading of a name, that I want to get into my book." In the same letter, he tried to persuade Perkins to come for a visit: "I beg you again to quit that awful New York place and come down here for a while. I can't promise you surcease from care or anxieties, for I have learned that no matter where I go I always find myself, but I can promise you . . . the privilege of being alone. We won't bother you, I can let you have a room to work in and, under no circumstances, will we go Southern and plague you to death with hospitality."[78]

In a subsequent letter to Perkins, Basso conveyed the same enthusiasm for country life and invited the editor again: "I still insist that you ought to come down here . . . just to look at the world from a distance. . . . It all goes back to the idea . . . that the truth of anything is not its own hard kernel . . . but at its periphery where it impinges on all the rest of life. . . . So you had better come down here. It makes for health, industry, understanding; and it sharpens one's desire to do fine work and to replenish the earth; and arrogance, in the presence of these blue ranges, is impossible."[79]

Once more, Basso was made aware that he needed isolation to be a writer. Like Thoreau, whose Walden habitat detached him from the intellectual community of his day, Basso's remote residence involved a great degree of personal, artistic, and intellectual independence. "It's no use, pals," he writes in a letter of August 1935, "This is where I like it most and where I feel I ought to be. Sometimes I miss New York, but

78. Basso to Perkins, July 4, 1935, in SA.
79. Basso to Perkins, July 24, 1935, in SA.

... The intellectuals sort of got me down and I like farmers better anyway. Farmers may be barbarians of the intellect but intellectuals, all those empty pretentious little children of the arts and the revolution, are barbarians of the soul; so long they have lived in their dank and sunless garrets that I used to think sometimes they had fungus on their minds." Climbing out of what he called his "early apprenticeship" and beginning "ambitious projects" such as the composition of his new novel, Basso confessed that the peace and quiet of the mountains greatly stimulated his writing. Typically, he added, "I never want to compete with anybody for anything."[80]

80. Basso to Josephson, August 7, 1935, in Josephson Papers, BL.

Basso as he appeared in the
1926 Tulane University yearbook
Photograph courtesy author

407 Royal Street, site of the *Double Dealer*
literary gatherings in the twenties
Courtesy Raymond H. Weill

Basso "dancing the Charleston with the Muse,"
a caricature drawn by William Spratling for
Sherwood Anderson and Other Famous Creoles (1926)

Basso's friend and one-time mentor, Sherwood Anderson
Palladiotype by Alfred Stieglitz, 1923, 24.2 × 19.2 cm,
The Alfred Stieglitz Collection, 1949.726,
photograph © 1998 The Art Institute
of Chicago, all rights reserved.

Basso's good friend Thomas Wolfe
Photograph courtesy Aldo Magi

Maxwell Perkins, famed editor of
Wolfe, Fitzgerald, and Basso
Photograph courtesy Thomas Wolfe Collection,
Pack Memorial Public Library, Asheville, N.C.

Just after Thomas Wolfe's funeral service. Basso is second from the left.

Photograph courtesy Thomas Wolfe Collection,
Pack Memorial Public Library, Asheville, N.C.

Basso in 1946, on vacation with his family in Arizona

Photograph courtesy Etolia S. Basso (photographer unknown)

Basso at his desk, 1959. This photo was taken upon
publication of *The Light Infantry Ball*.
Photograph by George Cserna, courtesy Etolia S. Basso

4

Southern
Soul Searching

Amid the much-needed isolation of Pisgah Forest, Basso made sure to keep in touch with his literary friends. In 1937 he wrote Thomas Wolfe:

> I manage to rock along, hitting my daily single, sometimes scampering like hell and stretching it into a two-base knock. It's just that this particular game is going to last for at least 62 innings and I know that a few bobbles, letting the ball roll between my legs or giving a base on balls, will end me up on the short end. Such is literature, eh me boy? What a whore the old girl is—and what a golden whore! She'll sleep with anybody from Shakespeare down on to the newest boy wonder and knowing that, fully aware of what a bitch she is, we still are willing to tear out our hearts, even our guts, and lay them at her feet. Only, as you say, to have her kick us in the pants. But what's the out? There is no out, that's the answer. You've got to live your own life and you can't fake (like the New York esthetes) and pretend something you aren't.[1]

The first meeting between Basso and Wolfe, in the spring of 1935, was accidental and took place in Scribner's offices. As southern novelists,

---

1. Hamilton Basso to Thomas Wolfe, 1937, in Wisdom Collection, HL.

the two had quite a few things in common, among them their close relationship with Scribner's celebrated editor, Maxwell Perkins, their love-hate relationship with the South, their passion for Tolstoy, their individualism, and their ambition to one day write the Great American Novel.

On June 11, 1935, Basso initiated their correspondence, asking whether Wolfe would submit a short story to the *New Republic*. Wolfe, discernibly flattered, responded positively and promised the impossible, namely that he would stick to the proposed word limit. During the rest of 1935 Basso and Wolfe corresponded regularly: Basso asked Wolfe where he spent time, and Wolfe sent Basso postcards from Europe with news of his growing popularity in Germany. In a warm letter of October 12, 1935, Basso for the first time writes of his admiration for Wolfe. Praising *Look Homeward, Angel* for its sense of space and its heroic scale ("you are carving heroic friezes on the face of the Rocky Mountains"), he contrasted it to his own concern for small-town detail.[2]

The same letter mentions F. Scott Fitzgerald, then staying in Asheville close to Zelda, who was hospitalized at the time. Since both Fitzgerald and Wolfe resided in and around Asheville in the summers of 1936 and 1937, Perkins thought that Basso was in an excellent position to keep an eye on two of Scribner's more unruly authors. Referring to the shared Scribner's ties, Basso told Perkins repeatedly that if he had "any sense of responsibility to the firm," he would come down to the area and have "a round-up of Scribner people." Of the three writers, Fitzgerald was in the worst shape, nearing a nervous breakdown. On various occasions, Perkins asked both Basso and (indirectly) Wolfe's relatives to visit the depressed Fitzgerald. Thus Wolfe told his brother Fred in a postscript: "There is a poor, desperate, unhappy man staying at the Grove Park Inn. . . . Perkins thought if Mama went to see him and talked to him, it might do some good—to tell him that at the age of forty he is at his prime and nothing to worry about if he will just take hold again and begin to work. His name, I forget to say, is F. Scott Fitzgerald."[3] Basso visited Fitzgerald too, but as the latter seemed "hell-

2. Basso to Wolfe, October 12, 1935, in Wisdom Collection, HL.
3. Hamilton Basso to Maxwell Perkins, May 17, 1937, August 3, 1935, in Basso Papers, BL; Thomas Wolfe to Fred Wolfe, October 5, 1936, in *The Letters of Thomas Wolfe*, ed. Elizabeth Nowell (New York, 1956), 542.

bent on professional suicide," he found it difficult to pull him out of his low spirits, which sank even lower after Hemingway vilified him in *Esquire*. However much Basso pitied Fitzgerald, he also thought that Fitzgerald behaved like a pampered child. Wolfe, on the other hand, who had in Basso's opinion valid reasons for feeling distressed—over the lawsuits and the worsening relationship with in loco parentis Perkins—exhibited less of a "sophomoric attitude."

Until Wolfe's death, Basso's formal criticism of his work was rather two-faced: although he believed that Wolfe had managed to transcend his regional background by rebelling against "the isolation in which [Wolfe] was vacuumized as a boy," he felt that Wolfe had remained a provincial at heart. Not afraid to acknowledge he was a "hick" himself compared to his more cosmopolitan friends Malcolm Cowley and F. Scott Fitzgerald, Basso identified with Wolfe's parochialism; in fact, he joked once that Wolfe did not put more "thinking" into his books because he was affected by a "real humbleness, along with the provincial's feelings . . . that he wasn't in the same class with the real bright boys." Basso further speculated that Wolfe was never attracted to the ideas of the Agrarians because he thought he did not "have enough sense." Although Basso knew that this remark was largely meant as a joke, he thought it "revealing. . . . I've heard him bellow in torment because he wasn't as 'smart' as some of his critics." After Wolfe actually met the Agrarians, he displayed the same—and perhaps tongue in cheek—modesty: "I spent a very pleasant evening with the Warrens, the Tates, the Brooks and Mr. Ransom. In fact, I did almost everything except become a Southern Agrarian. I suppose I don't understand enough about that."[4]

Given Wolfe's parochialism, Basso was particularly impressed that he had nonetheless been able to break out of Asheville. Walking through Asheville himself, Basso had often wondered "how such a walled-in place produced a writer so deeply conscious, so very disturbed by the vastness of America." It was because of Wolfe's ability to surpass regionalism and "think big," Basso believed, that his books had a widespread appeal. Seeing Eugene Gant as a kind of Everyman

4. Hamilton Basso, "Thomas Wolfe: A Portrait," *New Republic*, June 24, 1936, pp. 199–200; Basso to Matthew Josephson, July 3, 1937, in Josephson Papers, BL; Thomas Wolfe to Dixton Wecter, March 3, 1937, in *The Letters of Thomas Wolfe*, ed. Nowell, 615.

whose autobiography carried "something of the autobiographies of us all," he argued that Wolfe's power lay in the "re-creation of a place and characters understandable, in the light of their own knowledge and experience, to readers all over the Western world." In the same article, which was especially intended as an invocation of the muses of critical appreciation, Basso associated Wolfe's panoramic view with his height. In a book review he had already propounded this theory, writing that Wolfe's "mountain-top of six foot six" was not only "strange and lonely," its view was unique and knew no equal in the landscape of American letters. In a letter to Wolfe's sister, Mabel Wolfe Wheaton, Basso used the same grandiose imagery to describe what he called Wolfe's "windyness": "Sure he was windy sometimes. But he was windy because he had to huff and puff . . . to blow that house down. . . . He saw the essential meaning of life as being contained in a lot of big, thick walls—hidden from view. He wanted to open up the view. . . . So he had to push down the walls. Hence windyness sometimes—huffing, puffing, blowing as hard as he could: *anything* to get these walls down. And when he succeeded—well, he opened up views that had never been opened before. That is his greatness."[5]

Though Wolfe's vantage point was exceptional, Basso thought his friend's grandiloquence both a strength and a weakness. Like many of his fellow critics, Basso regretted Wolfe's lack of discipline, and comparing the novel with a barrel in which the novelist throws his hay, Basso believed that Wolfe's barrel was lost, causing the hay to sprawl in all directions: "If only it were possible to make [Wolfe] realize the distinction between looseness of form, pliability, etc., and literary anarchy." In a similar vein, Basso wrote that a novelist can never convey the full 100 percent: "The reader, if you are 90% successful, can supply the other 10% himself. I think perhaps that is Thomas Wolfe's only serious defect as a writer. Over-zealousness, trying to get it down 100%." If Wolfe could only curb his Whitmanesque urges, he had every potential to become a great writer.[6]

Basso's reviews were generally complimentary, and because they appeared at a time when Wolfe was receiving a negative press, the lat-

5. Basso, "Thomas Wolfe: A Portrait," 201; Hamilton Basso, "Mountain View," *New Republic*, January 1, 1936, p. 232; Hamilton Basso to Mabel Wolfe Wheaton, September 27, 1940, in North Carolina Collection, WL.

6. Basso to Perkins, July 28, 1937, May, 27, 1936, in SA.

ter was very grateful for Basso's critical support. To thank Basso for "Thomas Wolfe: A Portrait," Wolfe wrote the following:

> The whole thing [the portrait] has warmed me up more than I can possibly tell you, and if I was fired with the ambition to "learn 'em" before, that piece of yours has set off a bonfire . . . I do think that I learned something valuable from the piece, in addition to the happiness it gave me. I think you hit the nail on the head with what you said about the railroad trains in my books and how the feeling of space is probably derived from the childhood of a man who grew up in the confinement of a mountain town . . . my whole childhood was haunted by the ringing of train bells at night, the sound of whistles fading away somewhere along the French Broad River, the sound of a train going away down the river towards Knoxville and the West.[7]

In the same year that this was written, Basso published his fourth novel, *Courthouse Square*. In it, departing trains, riding and whistling through the night, are emblematic of the main character's sentiments. Returning to his southern hometown, David Barondess feels imprisoned and cut off from the rest of the world, the town having turned into a cultural swamp. Thus the train in the distance comes to symbolize escape and the only contact with the external world. Clearly, Wolfe's fiction served as an intertext here.

The year 1936 saw the friendship of the two men deepen. "Thomas Wolfe: A Portrait" may have certainly contributed to this effect, Wolfe being acutely sensitive to both criticism and praise. While Basso continued to live in the North Carolina mountains and struggled with *Courthouse Square*, sometimes working on a single page for a couple of days, Wolfe returned to Germany. The authors' letters of this period deal with literature, writing, and dissatisfaction with the critics whom Wolfe described as "scavengers," "filth purveyors," and worse than "Adolf Hitler's Nazi thugs." Basso vented his disgruntlement with the critics too and argued that good criticism, at its best practiced by writers themselves, is simply a matter of the right "gut-feeling . . . it finally boils down to something like this: How does your belly feel about it?" To prove his point, Basso added that Wolfe's "The Web of Earth" gave

---

7. Wolfe to Basso, June 24, 1936, in *The Letters of Thomas Wolfe*, ed. Nowell, 531.

him a "good belly-feeling." All this should be seen in the light of *Courthouse Square*'s release; while Basso told Perkins that this was the novel he had promised himself he would write some day, the critical and public reception of the book was only lukewarm.[8]

Meanwhile, Wolfe's relationship with Perkins had begun to deteriorate. Pressured by the publication of his new novel and critics' innuendo that he could not compose a book without Perkins' aid, Wolfe decided to leave Scribner's. To convey his troubled feelings, he wrote a twenty-eight-page letter that is a moving and insightful account of the intimate relationship he and Perkins had had. In the letter he broke off all relations with editor and publisher. Wolfe mailed this long letter in January 1937 but had already finished it in December 1936 when Basso visited him in his New York apartment. Clearly upset with the Perkins entanglement, he could not be appeased by Basso, who thought that Wolfe should talk things over with Perkins. But Wolfe could not be dissuaded, and by the end of the afternoon, when Basso was ready to leave, Wolfe "went to one of those packing boxes of his, pulled out a sheaf of second sheets, got a pencil and wrote 'To my friend, Hamilton Basso: Dear Ham—I've gone upon the record here— this is not perhaps the whole story—but in a general way it says some things I felt had to be said. I am leaving this copy of the letter in your care, and, if anything should happen to me, I leave it to your discretion what should be done with it.' " With this gesture, Wolfe gave the copy of the now-famous letter to Basso, who, with Perkins, was the only one to receive the document. In a letter to Mabel Wolfe Wheaton, Basso inflated this incident: "Tom had this dark suspicion he was going to die and, about a year or so before it happened, he wrote a postscript on the bottom of a long letter which said, in effect,—no, in those exact words—if anything happens to be [*sic*], please see that the record is straight."[9]

Wolfe's tempestuous relationship with Perkins made Basso aware of how "tractable" an author he had been himself; complaining about Perkins' failure to respond to his letters, Basso joked:

8. Wolfe to Basso, October 14, 1936, *ibid.*, 547; Basso to Wolfe, October 20, 1936, in Wisdom Collection, HL; Basso to Perkins, June 26, 1936, in SA.

9. Hamilton Basso to Elizabeth Nowell, August 14, 1949, in Basso Papers, BL; Basso to Wheaton, September 27, 1940, in North Carolina Collection, WL.

I don't get in your hair nearly enough. I come down here, write my books in comparative silence, never get in anybody's way. Something more than that, obviously, is necessary—something more—what shall I say?—Wolfian perhaps. The dark streets of midnight, dawn over Brooklyn, wild cries of exultation and despair. Or, on the other hand, it might be something Ernestian: coming in over the mountains with just the right emotion, the tannic taste of wine from Iberian goatskins. . . . Or again, the method might be that of our contemporary Scott: hob-nailed boots stamping on the floor, a girl's face peering out of the shadows, somewhere in the soft snow a phonograph playing If You Know Suzy; Like I Know Suzy. It will interest you to know, therefore, that I have left my wife and home and am departing with a Cherokee Indian girl for the Cocos Islands—where, God help me, I will never write another word.[10]

Thirteen years after Wolfe handed Basso his long letter, Elizabeth Nowell, his short story editor and agent, was collecting Wolfe's letters and found references to the long letter to Perkins yet could not trace the actual document. Learning, however, that Wolfe would sometimes hand out extra copies of important manuscripts and papers to a close friend, she wrote Basso and inquired whether he was perhaps the "mysterious friend" that Wolfe entrusted his papers to. Basso answered that he indeed possessed the letter. With his usual self-effacement, he claimed no credit for being, as he most likely was, Wolfe's "mysterious friend." With a fine sense for discretion Basso was insulted when Nowell subsequently suggested that he publish the letter before she did: "What's got into you anyway? Did you think for one moment that I would want to hoard Tom's bones in order to grind them into literary flour for myself; or that I would be inclined to race you or anybody to the public prints; or that, if the letter Tom gave me turned out to be the missing, mysterious document, it wouldn't be yours for the asking? At ease, lady, at ease!" Basso was in no mood to rush and publish the letter that Wolfe had slipped into his hands so confidentially. Called upon by Nowell, however, he felt he ought to reveal the letter, only "to see that Tom gets a proper, final hearing."[11]

10. Basso to Perkins, September 24, 1936, in SA.
11. Basso to Nowell, April 12, 27, 1949, in Basso Papers, BL.

In reply, Nowell apologized for her brash suggestion and tried to allay Basso's irritation with one of her fond memories of him: "You are a lovely guy, and I always think of you the way you were when you came up to Tom's apartment one night and he was sitting in that big Tudor chair and you felt so good you spun around and swiped your arm above his head. So I hope you feel like that all the time, and my false delicacy or whatever got me all snarled up, didn't make you stop for even a few minutes." Eventually, Nowell did not have to resort to Basso's copy of the letter; she found the original among Perkins' papers. Still, she asked Basso to check the editorial notes, whose accuracy he was very concerned about: "I know I am seeming overpunctilious, but there is something so awfully personal about letters, involving, as in this case, so many people, that I think they ought to be handled with care."[12]

In the winter of 1936 Basso reported more trials with cabin living: the frozen pipes and the perpetual empty belly of the oven made him lament that "everything that needs to be done around the place I must do myself. It is good to be able to do it, I like the feeling of being absolutely dependent upon myself, but I feel, sometimes, pretty lost and lonely down here." His loneliness was coming to an end, however, for in 1937 Thomas Wolfe decided to return home after years of exile in the North and abroad. For the summer, he had rented a cabin at Oteen, North Carolina, in the vicinity of the Bassos' cabin at Brevard. Perkins had forewarned Basso that Wolfe was on his way down. His remark that Wolfe had said that "he was going back to his native mountains to die" sounds strangely foreboding in the light of his death one summer later. To welcome Wolfe at Oteen, Basso wrote him a letter whose envelope held the legendary note: "Postmaster: Will you be good enough to hold this until the arrival of the addressee whose presence will be made known, probably, by an earthquake or some other violent upheaval." The letter itself is written in a different vein, closing off with "well i gess i better sine off now but if you dont rite me about getting together i am er going to be rite sore. don't git any gum in youre hair. with kindest regards from your ole fren and himble and obedint servant you big bussird you." The intimate and playful tone is indicative

12. Nowell to Basso, April 28, 1949, Basso to Nowell, May 2, 1949, in Basso Papers, BL.

of their friendship, and the letter would be a harbinger of more times spent together.[13]

Shortly after Wolfe arrived, he and his family paid the Bassos a surprise visit. They had first shown up at the Grove Park Inn to pay their respects to Fitzgerald. Fitzgerald must not have been too pleased with his visitors; he recommended they go see the Bassos and sent them away with a bottle of gin. Etolia Basso remembers the get-together vividly: the Wolfes stayed until well into the evening, but the only food she had to appease their giant appetites was the meager leftovers of a chocolate cake. Basso recalled the afternoon in a letter to Matthew Josephson: "If you think this book [*Of Time and the River*] howls, you ought to be around his family, en masse. He brought them over here to spend an afternoon, a whole crowd of Wolfes and Pentlands, and they were so exactly like they are in the book, it got more and more fantastic until finally I thought maybe I was a character in a book too and I tell you right now it is a very funny feeling to feel like characters in one of Thomas Wolfe's books."[14]

Later that summer, Basso spent a weekend with Wolfe in Oteen. According to Basso, the weekend was "wild," not "riotous" but "just wild" in the pattern "in which Tom spent all his days." Reporting back to Perkins that he still had the "lingering echoes of Tom's oratory" in his ears, he noted that his friend really enjoyed being a local celebrity. Joe P. McLeod, who lived "a little more than a stone's throw down" from where the Bassos lived, remembered how, in the summer of 1937, Wolfe and Basso passed by one day when he was tending his garden; he looked up and noticed "Tom Wolfe and Hamilton Basso. . . . They walked down to the river, stood about a bit, still talking hard as they could. Then they walked back toward Partridge Hill. I didn't call out. They were busy talking." It was a summer of content for Basso, who, often troubled by loneliness, now felt he had found a friend with whom he could share the mountains, his observations upon the South, and his writing.[15]

Wolfe, however, felt enclosed by the mountains again and decided

13. Basso to Perkins, December 23, 1936; Perkins to Basso, July 6, 1937, in SA; Basso to Wolfe, July 3, 1937, in Wisdom Collection, HL.

14. Basso to Josephson, July 3, 1937, in Josephson Papers, BL.

15. Basso to Perkins, August 1937, in SA; Lathrop, "Thomas Wolfe and Partridge Hill," 29.

to move on. Leaving Oteen, he visited the Bassos once more and entrusted them with the manuscript of "The Party at Jack's." Wolfe wanted to hear Basso's comments upon this story but never responded to Basso's well-intended remarks. Moreover, at this time Wolfe seems to have been overworked, which made him extremely sensitive to criticism of any kind. His subsequent visit to Sherwood Anderson in Marion, Virginia, did not improve his condition. Anderson, who, according to Basso, had "a streak of malice" in him, apparently said something mean to Wolfe, which, coupled with Basso's comments on "The Party at Jack's," shattered Wolfe's confidence even more. From a letter never sent to Basso but handed to him by Mabel Wolfe Wheaton at Wolfe's funeral, Basso remembered the following: "Dear Ham: So you have a chip on your shoulder and want me to knock it off. All right—I will—I have just performed a similar operation on the Squire of Marion. . . . I thought you were my friend." "In addition," Basso remembered in 1949, "Tom said that he understood I was getting ready to do a job on him—by which I gathered he meant what is called a literary attack—and he accused me of not any longer being his friend."[16] Cut loose from Perkins' guardianship, Wolfe felt as if the whole world had turned against him. Wolfe's antagonism probably brought Perkins and Basso closer together. As loyal, patient, and forgiving friends of Wolfe, they got along well with each other and would console each other when Wolfe had one of his bouts of suspicion.

Wolfe's last letter to Basso is dated September 9, 1937, and is a mere businesslike scribble, asking Basso to send on all his manuscripts to Elizabeth Nowell. Before Basso set sail for Europe, he sent Wolfe a note, confirming that he had sent the manuscripts to Nowell and hoping he would see Wolfe before he left: "If I don't—so long and good luck. I'll certainly see you when we get back." Basso never saw Wolfe again. Despite his repeated attempts to renew their friendship, Wolfe sent him only a postcard depicting Old Faithful in Yellowstone Park. He called it "Portrait of the author at the 2,000,000 million [*sic*] word point," and Basso admitted that the spouting geyser "sort of looks like Tom, too."[17]

In August 1938, Perkins broke the news of Wolfe's pneumonia and

---

16. Basso to Nowell, April 27, 1949, in Basso Papers, BL.

17. Basso to Wolfe, September 19, 1937, in North Carolina Collection, WL; Basso to Nowell, April 14, 1949, in Basso Papers, BL.

asked Basso if he could visit the Wolfe family to find out more. This was immediately followed by Perkins' news of Wolfe's famous last scribble: "Had a very nice letter from Tom, written in a rather feeble hand, he was not supposed to write and had a relapse afterwards and even when I last heard from Mrs. Nowell, was running some fever. But I guess he is out of danger now." Wolfe died shortly afterward, and when Basso learned of his friend's death, he fell silent and went for a long walk in the woods. "I have never known anything to affect [Ham] as this," Toto Basso wrote to Wolfe's sister, Mabel.[18]

An interesting detail is that after Wolfe's death, Basso was apparently sent out by Perkins to get Wolfe's papers. Relying on Basso's tact, he may have thought that Basso would be the right person to "negotiate" with the Wolfe family. Basso would ultimately fictionalize this experience in *The Greenroom* and *The View from Pompey's Head*: in both novels the main character is sent by his employer to confront a famous but extremely difficult and inaccessible author (and author's family). However, Basso's real efforts must have been in vain, as Perkins writes: "I had written Mrs. Wolfe, but I had feared difficulties. Everyone in that family seems to hold on to whatever there is of any kind, whether valuable or otherwise. Tom had that trait himself."[19]

Both Perkins and Basso were pallbearers at Wolfe's funeral in Asheville. Basso recalled the funeral in a 1940 letter to Perkins and remembered how he and the Scribner's editor had had a melancholy conversation "on the portico of an ugly hotel, in the ugly town of Asheville." At the time, Perkins had asked Basso whether he thought Wolfe had "carried out his plan." In the letter, Basso answers that question with a yes, Wolfe's "plan" involving a "running, endless autobiography." However, whether Wolfe had reached the peak of his potential, he hesitated to confirm. For the first time, he doubted whether Wolfe would have become a great writer at all: being too much a "prisoner of his own personality," and writing from what Basso referred to as the "window" of his terrible egotism, Wolfe never managed to escape from the chains of his ego: "he *was* the earth's center. He says so, time and time again, in page after page. And this, for all his sincere ambi-

18. Perkins to Basso, August 2, 1938, SA; Etolia S. Basso to Mabel Wolfe Wheaton, [*ca.* 1938], in North Carolina Collection, WL.

19. Perkins to Basso, October 10, 1938, in SA.

tions, all his dismal despair at times, he enjoyed. He wanted to know all things, see all things, be all things—but out of the compelling thirst he had, to slake the throat of his own being." Mentioning Tolstoy and Shakespeare but also Abraham Lincoln and Thomas Jefferson as examples of men who broke away from their egocentricity, Basso claimed that Wolfe simply could not remove himself from his own center and "immerse himself in other people."[20] To Basso's mind, this was the key to Wolfe's perfection and imperfection.

Basso remained very concerned about Wolfe's legacy. When John Terry launched his abortive research for a Wolfe biography and approached Basso, who had been recommended by Perkins as one of the "celebrities" that Wolfe knew, he was not amused: "This cultism gravels me exceedingly and I think it would have made Tom sick." Basso also wrote Mabel, "I have a horror of these little people who are swarming in his wake. All these damnable little essays, pieces, surveys, criticisms by people Tom totally disliked." In rebuttal, he was reluctant to give away any material when Nowell was editing Wolfe's letters. His reservations seem to have been engendered by his desire to tell the truth about Wolfe and, where necessary, set the record straight. Or as he told Mabel: "As far as I can prevent it, [Wolfe] won't disappear into myth, or fable or nonsense." In Basso's last article, "Thomas Wolfe: A Summing Up," he came to the aid of his dead friend once more by countering some of the assumptions critics were making. He also refuted Harper's claims that "Wolfe's last two books marked a new enterprise" and that "they were finished before he died." Having seen most of the manuscripts when Wolfe was in Oteen, Basso knew which pieces Wolfe had written a few months before his death and which he had written as early as 1934. He also knew that Wolfe had not finished his work at all, a fact that made Richard Kennedy observe that thanks to Basso, there was for the first time "complaint that the publisher was not dealing fairly with the public or with Wolfe."[21]

The tone of "Thomas Wolfe: A Summing Up" is rather defensive. Whereas in his earlier Wolfe portrait, Basso had objected to the writer's

---

20. Basso to Perkins, September 7, 1940, in SA.

21. Basso to Perkins, August 22, 1940, in SA; Basso to Wheaton, September 27, 1940, in North Carolina Collection, WL; Basso, "Thomas Wolfe: A Summing Up," *New Republic,* September 23, 1940, pp. 422–23; Richard Kennedy, *The Window of Memory: The Literary Career of Thomas Wolfe* (Chapel Hill, 1962), 410.

tendency to embellish, in this last article on Wolfe, he argued that "the flaws in his writing do not particularly matter." Convinced that Wolfe would never have become a disciplined writer but would have been "forever loose and sprawling and sometimes windy enough to blow your hat off," Basso asserted that when Wolfe did get a hold of his material he was "magnificent in a way that few American writers ever have been." In a letter to Perkins, he explained that he had written the article because Harper's suggestions would "inevitably confuse anyone who might someday or other, want to do a serious book about Wolfe."[22]

Basso was even willing to write a book himself, "just to get things straight." He never did but remained a favorite candidate for any Wolfe project. When *Life* wanted to devote an article to Wolfe, both Elizabeth Nowell and Edward Aswell suggested Hamilton Basso. Nowell even exclaimed to Edward Aswell that he "would be the Grade A Blue Ribbon choice! More than anyone!" She recommended Basso so strongly not only because he had known Perkins and Wolfe equally intimately but also because he was a "Real Writer and a Name since Pompey's Head." Earlier on, in 1946, Mabel Wolfe Wheaton had also suggested that Basso should write a book on her brother, because she felt that she was too poor a writer to do it herself.[23]

Basso's importance as a friend of Wolfe's has been insufficiently noticed. The letters the two writers exchanged carry the proof of friendship in them; they reveal tender feelings, camaraderie, inside and intimate jokes, frustration with the critics, and mutual admiration. Thus, on receiving a copy of *Courthouse Square*, Wolfe told Basso: "I read a first rate review of it in the book section of the New York Times last Sunday. I was delighted. . . . I see we were likened unto each other, which may be a tough break for you but which pleased me greatly." While we should recognize the relevance of Basso's *New Republic* criticism on Wolfe, it is regrettable that he never wrote a Wolfe study. Perhaps this was because Basso had become too close a friend, for he confessed to Mabel: "Among all these writing people I know, he was my

22. Basso, "Thomas Wolfe: A Summing Up," 423; Basso to Perkins, September 18, 1940, in SA.

23. Elizabeth Nowell to Edward Aswell, 1955, in *In the Shadow of the Giant; Thomas Wolfe: Correspondence of Edward C. Aswell and Elizabeth Nowell, 1949–1958*, ed. Mary Aswell Doll and Clara Stites (Athens, Ga., 1988), 196; Mabel Wolfe Wheaton to Basso, August 6, 1946, in Basso Papers, BL.

best friend." Basso would finally admit that it was "hard to write about him. . . . The things I have to say . . . will never, never be said. If Wolfe's defect lay in saying too much, mine perhaps, lies in saying too little."[24]

Not much can be said about Basso's other illustrious friend, F. Scott Fitzgerald, partly because Basso and Fitzgerald were not as close. Also, the few letters that Fitzgerald sent to Basso were lost in a flood that inundated the Bassos' cellar. What we do have is Basso's correspondence with Perkins at the time Fitzgerald was suffering from a nervous breakdown and worsening alcoholism. Despite several attempts to cheer up the *Gatsby* author, Basso had little confidence in his painstaking efforts. After one of his visits to Fitzgerald (who, according to Etolia Basso, liked to invite strangers and servants of the Grove Park Inn to his table so that he did not have to dine alone), Basso told Perkins: "I felt—and still feel—that, if he wants to abandon fiction and write only about himself, a straightaway autobiography would be a darned interesting, even exciting, book. I didn't get very far with the idea. He countered with some crazy idea about writing the story of his life 'as it might have been—if he had won the Princeton-Yale game in the last quarter, if the Great Gatsby had sold 1,000,000 copies'—I don't know Max. I'd do anything in the world I could but I'm afraid I'm not much help. I think I'm pretty much of a hick as far as Scott is concerned—I haven't lived the international life he has."[25]

Perkins was annoyed and said that it would be "nonsensical of him to write that pseudobiography where he made a touchdown against Yale etc. He has got to stop that sort of nonsense . . . and be serious and do something important." Basso's tact, as well as the realization that he was not close enough to Fitzgerald, stopped him from conveying Perkins' message. Further evidence of Basso's kid-gloves handling of Fitzgerald can be found in a letter of February 13, 1936. Writing from New Orleans, Basso tells Fitzgerald of a wonderful dream he had had: "You had published a new book, or I was reading one of the old ones, and there was that feeling of pleasure and delight that comes from reading a perfect page—every word and accent right, every image there, the

24. Wolfe to Basso, October 28, 1936, in Basso Papers, BL; Basso to Wheaton, September 27, 1940, in North Carolina Collection, WL; Basso to Perkins, September 7, 1940, in SA.

25. Basso to Perkins, October 6, 1936, in SA.

lovely evocation of mood—and while reading, you yourself in the background somewhere, the tone of your voice etc."[26]

Basso admired Fitzgerald greatly and would often favor his talent over that of another famous contemporary, Ernest Hemingway. Describing Hemingway as a "bully-boy" caught up in a "lost generation act," and as "too old a man to keep on having wet dreams," Basso preferred Fitzgerald because he was more of a "moral writer": "I thought that Scott was a moral writer and Hemingway wasn't (I don't believe that fellow in The Bell, not in the last chapter). And I'm not asking for preachments or evasiveness. (There is no preachment or evasiveness in Gatsby and yet you find the morality of that book matched against Scott's personal morality: something he's never been given credit for, being a bad boy)."[27]

Basso's last letter to Fitzgerald was written one month before he departed for Europe; having sold *Courthouse Square* to the movies for the then-grand sum of five thousand dollars, he had been persuaded by Toto to go abroad for a year. In the letter, Basso refers to the debate Wolfe and Fitzgerald had had over the question of whether a writer should be putting things in or leaving things out: "I saw Tom . . . last weekend and heard about the furious literary controversy you two are conducting. As an innocent and deeply interested by-stander, may I urge you not to take Tom . . . too seriously. He is somewhat worried that you will—but no word of this, of course, to him." Concluding, Basso said a last farewell and stated his regret that they had never really tried to become better friends. From a professional and personal point of view, Basso and Fitzgerald were incompatible. However, their sympathy for each other seems to have been genuine: at one point Fitzgerald told Basso that he liked *Courthouse Square* "enormously" and wanted to discuss it "in person." Basso would remember Fitzgerald fondly as well as melancholically when he learned of his untimely death in 1940: "It was dreadful about Scott; even more than Tom in a way. There was always some shadow of the red black man about Tom, or so it seems now, but even when I last saw Scott—all bashed up and broken though he was—there was still a quality of life and laughter

26. Perkins to Basso, October 9, 1936, in SA; Basso to F. Scott Fitzgerald, February 13, 1936, in SA.

27. Basso to Perkins, October 11, 1939, July 8, 1941, in SA; Basso to Cowley, January 9, 1951, in Cowley papers, NL.

about him; even though there was the suggestion, now and then, that he was looking beyond the moment and into the past—into the frustrated promise of a lot of glamorous dreams. So that's two down, out of men I have known fairly well, and it looks like we turn out fairly young. Good old Scott, good old Tom."[28] Basso's sadness was heartfelt. He valued his friendships with Wolfe and Fitzgerald tremendously, and his association with these important writers can be seen as a significant episode in his career: both Wolfe and Fitzgerald left their traces in Basso's fiction.

While Basso was composing *Courthouse Square*, social reform of the South was much on his mind. Not wanting to conform to what he called the "decay novels" of the South and rebelling against the Fugitives who ran "back into the past and write poems . . . about the Civil War," Basso decided to treat the South like a "psychiatric patient": "It has an extreme case of introversion. It must be taught to look away from the past into the present. It must be made aware of the modern world." It is for this reason also that C. Hugh Holman has called Basso, together with T. S. Stribling, one of the few southern novelists who have "tried to construct great connected records of social change." *Courthouse Square* is such a record or, rather, a call for social improvement.[29]

Like *Relics and Angels*, *Courthouse Square* opens with the return of the native. Disenchanted with Greenwich Village and "still conscious of his New York clothes" (*CTS*, 3), David Barondess steps on to the dusty town square of Macedon and finds that nothing has changed. David, however, has. Having left the town as an adolescent, he returns a man. Like George Webber in Wolfe's *You Can't Go Home Again*, David has become a successful novelist. But like George's writings, David's work on the South is not held in high esteem by his fellow townsmen.

David's return is not merely an escape from the banalities of New York intellectual life. What really triggered his flight was a severe marital crisis. Already strained because of a northern-southern "culture

28. Basso to Fitzgerald, August 21, 1937, in SA; Fitzgerald to Basso, October 23, 1936, in Basso Papers, BL; Basso to Perkins, December 29, 1940, in SA.
29. Basso to Josephson, February 29, 1936, in Josephson Papers, BL; C. Hugh Holman, "The Novel in the South," in *A Time of Harvest: American Literature, 1910–1960*, ed. Robert E. Spiller (New York, 1962), 87.

lag," David's marriage finally breaks up when his pregnant wife, Letitia, slips on an icy sidewalk and subsequently miscarries—an accident based on the death of Edmund Wilson's wife, Margaret Canby, who tripped on some steps and fractured her skull. After a sad parting in Central Park, Letitia leaves for Central America, and David returns home. His homecoming is both an attempt to come to terms with his grief and the fulfillment of his wish to write a book about his grandfather, Edward, one of a few southerners who fought in the Union army.

The Barondess family, whose name not only has an aristocratic ring but also contains the letters B-A-S-S-O, is an impoverished version of the Blackheath family: "One understands, from the house and the gardens about it, that the people who lived here originally were not wealthy but only moderately well-to-do: and that the fortunes of their descendants have suffered a considerable decline" (*CTS*, 11). Though the Barondesses have come down in social status, the people in town think they put on airs and therefore gossip about them as being "queer" (*CTS*, 48).

The reason for the Barondesses' ostracism goes back to the family patriarch, who, like the patriarchs in two of Basso's previous novels, determines the family identity and behavioral ethics for his progeny. Thus Edward's sympathies for the black southerner are inherited by his son, John, and his grandson, David. While John is a retired judge who made himself unpopular by refusing to allow his courtroom to be the setting in which racial prejudice and family feuds were played out, David embraces the family identity too, when, in the end, he courageously saves a mulatto townsman from a lynch mob. Living on "Abolition Hill," a name that may be somewhat too obvious, the Barondesses are social outcasts because of their racial libertarianism.

Just as Dekker's story in *Cinnamon Seed* runs parallel with that of Sam's, so is David's story tied up with that of Alcide Fauget. With his education and mulatto background, Fauget may well be seen as Sam's fictional brother. Like the Barondesses, Fauget is liable to become a pariah; that is, coming from out of town and being academically trained, Fauget runs the risk of being stigmatized as an "uppity black." However, his self-effacing behavior and diligent service as the town's druggist turn him into an unobtrusive member of the Macedon community. What Fauget's fellow citizens are unaware of is that he is really the son of the town's Confederate hero, Cincinnatus Legendre, whose statue is in the town square (the courthouse square of the book title). Following in his father's footsteps, though considerably quieter in his heroism, Fauget wants to buy the derelict Legendre plantation mansion, renovate it, and turn it into a Negro hospital. When John Barondess gives Fauget the necessary legal advice, one of the Barondess servants overhears the conversation and the news is leaked to the local newspaperman and aspiring novelist Pick Eustis. Always envious of David's success as a novelist, Eustis distorts the news and announces that Fauget, helped by the Barondess family, wants to buy the house to live in it. Tongues start wagging, and in no time the rumor spreads that Fauget is an "uppity nigger" after all. A mob is raised by the town bigot and, after lynching three blacks, proceeds to Fauget's house. When David intervenes, Fauget manages a narrow escape, but David falls into the hands of the hostile crowd.

Being nursed back to health by his aunt Celia, who closely resembles *Cinnamon Seed*'s Olivia, David has feverish visions of preying buzzards, scenes of his country childhood, his life in New York City, and, curiously, "mountain snow" (*CTS*, 367). He survives to find his estranged yet loving wife by his bedside. The ending is sentimental and "smacks of the movies, particularly the 'woman's picture' of that decade, wherein wives nobly sacrificed themselves for noble husbands." Basso's poor handling of romance and female characters debilitate and date his novels. At the same time, the happy ending of *Courthouse Square* was encouraged by Maxwell Perkins, who preferred conclusive and commercial endings to open and tragic ones. In a letter of July 3, 1936, Perkins thought the original ending too "inconclusive" "as to what happens to everybody." This bothered Basso enough to go up to New York, discuss it, and rewrite the final pages of the book. Going over the proofs a few months later, Basso acknowledged the following: "I don't suppose I have to tell you how glad I am that you liked the ending. It put me through the mill, I can tell you that, and I knew only too well that, in large part, the book stood or fell by it. I feel also, when I was in New York, that you were sort of dubious—not sure that I could carry it off—and I am simple enough to feel good because you liked it finally."[30]

30. Millichap, "Hamilton Basso," 48; Basso to Perkins, September 2, 1936, in SA.

David shares some fundamental characteristics with Basso's earlier protagonists. Like Tony, he is sensitive and suffers from *Weltschmerz* and loneliness. Like the rebellious Dekker, he is "in arms against life" (*CTS*, 368), and like Tony and Dekker too, David is orphaned: although we meet his father, John Barondess is so absent-minded and caught up in a world of bad memories that he seems more dead than alive. When David tries to have a conversation with him upon his homecoming, he feels as if there is a "pane of glass" between them (*CTS*, 58), in a scene reminiscent of Tony's awkward reunion with his sister Laurine.

David's attempts to get through to his father do not succeed. When, toward the novel's end, David breaks the news of Eustis' slander and wants his father to respond, John seems unperturbed. "He is even beyond hurt. . . . He is not alive at all," David concludes (*CTS*, 233). While David's father is mentally absent, his mother is physically absent. She died when he was still quite young. *Relics and Angels, Cinnamon Seed, Courthouse Square* (and *Days Before Lent*) reveal that Basso's fiction of the thirties, like Faulkner's fiction of the same decade, offers "no white mothers who are central to the action . . . the mother is often literally or psychologically absent."[31] Instead, Basso's heroes are surrounded by spinsterish aunts (Hermine, Olivia, Elizabeth, Ann, and Celia) who are undersexed and fail to fulfill a nurturing role. Whereas Faulkner tries to compensate for the mother's absence by placing the protagonist in the care of a black mammy, the Basso character is deprived of a nurturing figure, and thus bound to be lonesome in childhood and adult life alike.

David's loneliness is accentuated by an overall sense of rootlessness. Regardless of his forced attempts to fit in with Greenwich Village's artistic life, he finally rejects New York's bohemia, partly because he is repulsed by its intellectual pretense and partly because he fears that he is too much of a "hick" to ever fit in. (Curiously, though *Courthouse Square* is most critical of New York intellectuals, the book was dedicated to Malcolm Cowley and Matthew Josephson.) However, upon his return home—and much like Basso's return to New Orleans in the twenties—David learns that while he thought he would never belong in New York City, he has also outgrown the small-town ways of

31. Richard King, *A Southern Renaissance: The Cultural Awakening of the American South, 1930–1955* (Oxford, N.Y., 1980), 80.

Macedon. This gives rise to a sense of double exile, which Eugene Gant in *Look Homeward, Angel* experiences in an equally poignant way.

Ironically, while Eugene has to leave his hometown in order to find himself, Basso's characters return to their cities of birth to come to terms with themselves. And whereas in Wolfe's oeuvre the protagonist sustains the revolt from the village as his reluctant homecomings prove that it is indeed impossible to go home again, Basso's usually focuses on the theme that critics have termed the "return of the native." In other respects, Basso's small-town feelings are quite similar to Wolfe's. Basso's and Wolfe's small towns are identical in their isolated setting, which has been reinforced by the outward-bound trains that whistle in the distance at night, and both David and Eugene are galled by the backwardness of the towns: condemned to poverty, torpidity, and decay, Macedon "was just like Mencken said. The Sahara of the Bozart" (*CTS*, 73). David thinks that his hometown suffers from a "timelag," a kind of "cultural amnesia" that causes it to retain "the symbols and concepts of a culture, when actually, that culture no longer exists" (*CTS*, 200). But he also realizes that the remnants of that very culture are part of the South's beauty and mystique. In this way, his homecoming brings about a blending of the grotesque and picturesque, a revelation of the South's vices and virtues. Thus, when David sees a forsaken Negro church on a red hill, he muses: "This was the way he thought of it, mistreated by men and mauled by mules, lost in the backwash of time—and yet lovely with a loveliness he could neither outlive nor forget. It was like malaria in his blood" (*CTS*, 246).

Although his homecoming brings with it an awareness of "the unreality of the South's beauty," David also realizes that there lurks violence, intolerance, and hate underneath that "goddamned romantic" veneer (*CTS*, 54). As an estranged southerner, he is torn between his affection for the land and his disgust with the South's failings. However, whereas Eugene is just as aware of the South's divisions and goes on the run, David stays put and contemplates the South's problems. Also, as David has been away, he sees the region's predicament more objectively; when he explains to his southern friends that the region's problems should no longer be blamed on the Civil War and Reconstruction, Pick accuses David of "going Yankee on" them (*CTS*, 155). David's ambivalence brings to light his fundamental loneliness, for he tells Pick: "If you think that I can get any fun out of being on the other side of the fence, in conflict with my own kind of people—my kin, my friends, persons I like and respect—you are greatly mistaken" (*CTS*, 155). At the same time, when one of his New York friends suggests that he should go back if he is unhappy in the North, David replies: "I don't know exactly where back is" (*CTS*, 27).

David finally does go back, and where Eugene becomes his own man by fleeing his hometown and family, David finds his responsibility in life by returning to and rebelling against his town and thus confirms his own and his family's identity. The Barondesses' fate, David's father observes, is "a central tragedy, part of the inheritance of" the house (*CTS*, 20). Just as John Barondess realizes that he must remain true to his father's ideals and subvert the town's intolerance in his courtroom, so does David, like his father and grandfather, achieve "a brave and noble thing" by standing up to the town's bigotry and violence (*CTS*, 85). The Barondesses are like the Sartorises in Faulkner's *The Unvanquished* (1938): they "are, exist completely, in their own uniqueness only as members of a particular family functioning in social stewardship within a particular community and place."[32] Or to quote one of David's southern friends, home and family are "props" to one's identity. Similarly, David's urge to go home stems from a tribal longing to be among his own kind: it is a "kind of atavistic throwback, a stone-age hangover—the feeling of being warm and secure in your own allotted cave, with the fire dispelling the black threat of the unknown and the other members of your tribe all around you, while outside the wolves and vengeful banshees howl hungry in the snow" (*CTS*, 201).

In *Courthouse Square* and *Look Homeward, Angel* the theory of the family identity is affirmed, but whereas Eugene is a romantic rebel whose revolt is psychological and solipsistic because he only gives in to his own needs and desires, David is a reformer whose revolt has social and familial implications. Where Eugene escapes from his family in an act of rebellion, David returns to his family in an act of reconciliation. Also, where George Webber, the grown-up Eugene, returns home to be convinced that one cannot go home again, David shows that one *can* go home again if only one is willing to face the South's problems. To extend the comparison, while Wolfe may be considered a romantic novel-

32. Bradford, *Generations of the Faithful Heart*, 30.

ist because he bases his writings on the highly sensitive inner lives of his characters, Basso is a social realist whose novelistic ground is not so much the hero's private life as his public responsibilities. And while Wolfe has received great credit for, and has indeed become the banner man of, the theme of the southerner's conflict with his hometown, Basso examined the paradox between the southerner's sense of place and displacement more often, more deeply, and less solipsistically.

Courthouse Square is the central novel of Basso's homecoming topos. It not only exemplifies the theme that most of his novels return to, but also sheds light on the author's personal feelings about going home. David may be the most autobiographical of Basso's protagonists; when Basso outlined David's character to Perkins, he drew a self-portrait: "He is sick of the talk, the petty gossip, the little children of the Revolution. He is a humane man, who finds it hard to hate, and the elevation of hate to the fountain-head of a new religion, Communism, the fact that many of his friends have, contrary to their old and basic tolerance, adopted the new religion depresses him greatly. . . . He is able finally to reach the simple conclusion that it is only by identifying himself with humanity, to love not a party or a class but all humanity, to be humane and tolerant and honest, that he can function as a man. It means putting love in the place of hate; tolerance in the place of intolerance; hope in the place of despair."[33]

Basso's 1936 novel established his reputation as a social (and southern) realist. Impelled by his social conscience, Basso believed that fiction was more powerful than history or fact in its ability to "illuminate." Later in life, in his speech "Readers and Writers," he told his audience that "facts are deceptive" and "fiction is truth." By way of illustration, he propounded that the truth of the battle of Gettysburg could never be known or recreated, because we were not present at the battle and consequently lack "total vision." In fiction, however, "total vision is possible. . . . Impious though it may sound, the novelist can play God. Nothing is hidden from him, nothing is concealed. He can approach as close to the truth as his genius permits."[34] Basso was also convinced that fiction was sometimes "better" than fact because, un-

33. Basso to Perkins, [*ca.* 1935], in SA.
34. Hamilton Basso, "Readers and Writers," June 13, 1957 (Typescript in Basso Papers), n.p.

like fact, it inevitably encapsulated the slant and morality of its creator. This also explains the didactic concerns of Basso's writing, which, when telling about the South, may have been especially appropriate. Not only was the South of the thirties a region that had much to learn in terms of civil rights and industrial progress, the public needed to learn much about the South as well; misrepresented by plantation romances and stigmatized by its postbellum backwardness, the South deserved very little credit in the eyes of northerners and other non-southerners. Writers like Basso, and most Southern Renascence writers in general, shared the ambition to debunk and demystify some of the worst stereotypes of the South and its inhabitants.

Courthouse Square should be praised for its authentic picture of middle-class southern life. While the works of Erskine Caldwell and William Faulkner are radical departures from the antebellum school, presenting a vision of the South that is often extreme and grotesque, Basso did not want to see the region "in terms of [these] polarities—aristocrats versus poor whites—" but together with fellow southerners like Howard Odum, Ellen Glasgow, and others, he intended to show a middle-class South whose "very existence . . . had been hitherto 'ignored' by writers of the region."[35]

Although Basso did not want *Courthouse Square* to be classified as a "Southern novel," writing to Perkins that the novel's "crisis may be Southern because of its relation to the Negro, but it may be transposed, I believe with minor differences, to any part of the country," the book is unmistakably material of the Southern Renascence.[36] Apart from its main theme, the southerner in conflict with his hometown, the novel is an indictment of the South's denial of civil rights to blacks. Not only does the protagonist become the target of racist violence, but his father presides over a court case that is quite similar to the Scottsboro case. In fact, John Barondess is the kind of judge that the Scottsboro trial should have had. In a passage that is a virtual rewriting of the Scottsboro article that Basso did for the *New Republic*, we read how "John hated intolerance and prejudice . . . but it was an attitude he understood. It was the South again, the history and psychology of the South, the old incu-

35. Daniel J. Singal, *The War Within: From Victorian to Modernist Thought in the South, 1919–1945* (Chapel Hill, 1982), 288–89.

36. Basso to Perkins, April 4, 1936, in SA.

bus of slavery yet lying across the land—punishment for the sins of the fathers being imposed even unto the third and fourth generation. It was the same of the Old South . . . transmuted into the defiance and resentment and prejudice of the new. It was the isolation, the distrust of strangers and new ideas and outside things" (*CTS*, 43).

More so than in any of Basso's other novels, the South is a recurrent topic in both John's and David's discussions. While they criticize both the region's backwardness and its reluctance to let go of the past, they do not realize that they have fallen victim to southern anamnesis themselves: like the region they inhabit, John and David will not and cannot forget. Memory being an important agent in the book and the flashback its main device, David and his father are both vexed by their fixation with the past. Unable to shake bad memories, John resembles Langley Blackheath, for he finds "the images of memory" "sharper and more definite" than the people who surround him in reality (*CTS*, 20). David has bad memories too, and "wishes it were possible to somehow end the past, not to be plagued by it, to drown it as you drown unwanted puppies in a stream" (*CTS*, 139). Conscious of the past in the present, he wishes "memory did not have its hooks in him. . . . Not to remember. Not ever to remember again." Yet in the anamnestic setting of the South it is impossible to forget (*CTS*, 203–205). This is what David learns when, at the close of the novel, he declares that it "was very important to remember. Memory was a part of life, to remember was to live, and he did not want to die" (*CTS*, 365).

In its preoccupation with the South as a setting for artistic potential, *Courthouse Square* is clearly written on the wave of the Southern Renascence. Aware of Mencken's criticism, David attacks the old plantation legends for producing a "hundred third rate romantics" but not one "first rate artist" (*CTS*, 57). Elsewhere, David wonders why nobody ever painted the "real thing" of the South: "The South was begging to be painted, crying out for somebody with a hot, sun-obsessed palette like Van Gogh. . . . It needed a man of genius, with excitement and sincerity and passion, and it had been turned over instead to a lot of pygmy people with pastel minds" (*CTS*, 207). Pick Eustis is equally concerned to lay down the reality of the South: "I tried to do something different. I'm tired of all these books about degenerates. There are a lot of decent people in the South" (*CTS*, 154).

Upon its publication the novel was certainly noted as an innovative and progressive work about the South. Lyle Saxon believed that the book placed its writer "among the significant writers of the South," and Jonathan Daniels thought that Basso had proved he was "typical" of that breed of writers whom he called "awakened young Southerners." Matthew Josephson, clearly unaffected by Basso's critique of intellectuals, was of the opinion that his southern friend took "more courageous ground than the 'agrarians' . . . by and large you are striking strong blows so far as the South is concerned—for the good cause, for the old Enlightenment and for true humanism. All of which is terribly necessary." Again, Basso objected to the southern label of the book: "I am beginning to chafe a little in this Southern straight-jacket. It is natural, I suppose, in a country as large as ours, for writers to be put into the handy provincial pigeonholes but I am determined to break out of it: and I will, in my next book, just you wait and see."[37]

A general point of criticism came from reviewers who thought that the novel was too moralistic and therefore failed to qualify as a "lasting" novel.[38] There is some validity in this objection, especially if David's endless theorizing about the South is taken into account. Nevertheless, for those interested in the Southern Renascence, *Courthouse Square* is a work that may tell more about the South than Faulkner's extraordinary if less accessible art or Wolfe's tiresome jeremiads.

Courthouse Square may in fact be read as a strong precursor of Harper Lee's *To Kill a Mockingbird* (1960): both novels are narrated from the viewpoint of a progressive family in a conservative small town; in both books the father of the protagonist uses his legal profession to fight racism and the protagonist is raised without a mother; and in both novels we encounter a white-trash mentality, the power of gossip, and the ease with which mobs can be raised. Why Lee's book became an instant best-seller and *Courthouse Square* was never reprinted can be explained by the fact that *To Kill a Mockingbird* was written at the time of the civil rights movement in the South. The lack of attention to *Courthouse Square* may have been due to the book's very progressiveness: with the issues it raised, the novel was obviously written ahead of

37. Lyle Saxon, "Uneasy Blood in Their Veins," *New York Herald Tribune Book Review*, November 1, 1936, p. 8; Jonathan Daniels, "Native's Return," *Saturday Review of Literature*, November 7, 1936, pp. 11–12; Josephson to Basso, October 28, 1936, in Josephson Papers, BL; Basso to Perkins, November 4, 1936, in SA.

38. Mark Van Doren, Review of Hamilton Basso's *Courthouse Square*, in *Southern Review*, III (1937), 171.

its time. Today this is part of the novel's strength. *Courthouse Square*'s merit lies in its exploration of the southerner's ambiguous relationship with his hometown, its analysis of southern small-town psychology, its sensitivity to black civil rights, and its realistic portrayal of the southern middle class. As the fourth of Basso's eleven novels, *Courthouse Square* constitutes the apogee of the writer's early work and his first claim to maturity as a writer of serious fiction.

Basso himself considered the novel a turning point in his literary career. Declaring that he would be reluctant to write another book if it flopped, he told Perkins that "Courthouse Square is goddamned good and if it doesn't poke its head above the flood of novels, I'll eat it page by page." At the same time, there was always room for self-doubt. Describing the writing process as "walking across the Niagara Falls on a tightrope with a bucket of water in each hand and one on your head," Basso often felt like a fly in the spider's web of his own work.[39]

After finishing *Courthouse Square*, Basso felt somewhat "lost" and tried to distract himself by "doing manual labor all day," that is, getting in the wood supply for the winter and putting a new roof on the garage: "All this I enjoy but I enjoy literary peonage also." During one of his chores Basso fell in a tub of whitewash and broke a few ribs; to Lyle Saxon he wrote that he was in great pain both physically and mentally as he anxiously awaited the reviews. In debt with Scribner's and insecure about his future as a novelist, he agonized over the fact that his literary pursuits did not pay off. Nevertheless, he defended his last novel to Matthew Josephson, who, upon a second reading of the book, believed that David Barondess' critique of New York intellectuals was unfair. "I distorted [bohemian life in New York City] for a purpose," Basso writes in a letter of November 7, 1936:

It does become distorted when your nerves are frazzled and there are those little book reviewers and one-poem poets and all those swarms of words. . . . I was not saying that the life of Macedon was any better: or urging a departure back to small towns. No . . . There is no place like our metropolis to charge a run-down battery. . . . But once the battery is charged, go off and do your own work. . . . And you must not be too harsh with me if I like mountaineers and farmers better than I like literary ca-

39. Basso to Perkins, November 4, 1935, May 27, 1936, in SA.

reerists and frauds—because after all, my best friends, the ones I trust and admire are all "intellectuals." But not the kind I was blowing off about in my book.[40]

Spending part of the winter of 1936 in New York City, Basso was mostly found at his *New Republic* desk, where he reviewed books and wrote with great sensitivity of the threat of Fascism at home (in the guise of radio-priest Father Coughlin and the newspaper magnate William Randolph Hearst) and called on the visiting Cardinal Pacelli to do something about what he called the "new Dark Ages." Writing with his own Catholic upbringing and background in mind, he confessed that though he had "drifted away" from the Church, he remembered with fondness his friend, the bayou priest Father John, whose humanity and "absolute good will" epitomized, to his mind, the light in the dark: "He is the most Christlike man I ever knew—even when he is in a blind with his old shotgun waiting for the ducks to come in, or winking at the loose talk of the fishermen, or getting to feel good on orange wine." Fearing that the Catholic Church would side with the Fascists (as the Spanish Catholics had already done), Basso used the example of Father John—a figure he would also use in his next novel, *Days Before Lent* (1939)—and argued that the world needed a new unity of faith, not necessarily a religious faith, but Father John's "faith in the hope and future of man: a faith . . . that men can join together and work together for a better and more humane world." Basso became more profoundly perturbed by Fascism when he visited Europe the next year.[41]

The visit to Europe was, according to Basso, not intended to make progress on his new novel: "I have never been to Europe and now that I have a little money I want to blow it before everything there blows up. If I do any writing, OK. I have been working steadily now for four months, as much as fifteen hours a day, besides taking care of my garden and the place. By the end of September I will have been at it for six months . . . and I would like to knock off for two or three months and just let the stew keep on boiling without trying to take any out of it."[42]

40. Basso to Josephson, October 3, 1936, in Josephson Papers, BL; Basso to Lyle Saxon, October 27, 1936, in Saxon Papers, HT; Basso to Josephson, November 7, 1936, in Josephson Papers, BL.

41. Hamilton Basso, "Cardinal Pacelli and Father John," *New Republic*, October 28, 1936, pp. 343–45.

42. Basso to Cowley, August 12, 1937, in Cowley Papers, NL.

In another undated letter to Malcolm Cowley, Basso repeated this sentiment, saying that he hoped to spend the winter in Corsica, not to write but to see the place "before it blows up."

Later on that year, Basso wrote from France that the European trip had come as a welcome change after an exhausting summer: "The suicide of my wife's mother and all that followed is just beginning to be dispersed and then there was the cancer scare about Toto which called for one of those things called 'exploration' operations and on top of that a mysterious malady which was finally found to be anemia. It all took a good bit out of me." In addition to these personal problems, Basso's writing of his next novel went excruciatingly slowly or, as he told Perkins in a letter of August 22, 1937: "I'm so full of things that I want to get down—and at the end of a 12 hour day all I have to show for is two typewritten pages." He was desperate to "come through" for his editor, for after all the years with Scribner's without success, Basso realized that "one of the firm pillars" of his life was the "knowledge" that Perkins was his friend.[43]

The Bassos left for Europe from Baltimore on September 30, 1937. Two weeks later, they were roaming the streets of London, a city that Basso called the "capital of imperialism." Like a true innocent, Basso noticed how Londoners were somehow "different . . . they have a hell of a time trying to understand me. They speak English." In a letter to Malcolm Cowley, Basso criticized the British for their hypocrisy and a "conscious moral rectitude" that he experienced as a "pain" in his "extremely moral neck." France agreed more with Basso. Though he admitted that he still did not like big cities ("so much of humanity living in an artificial climate"), he praised Paris as the "city of them all," the Parisians being "so successful in the arts of peace and love. . . . They are Epicurus, living for the moment, in the moment—unlike the Americans who are always wanting to 'return' so that we can start being happy." Enjoying the sights and visiting the museums (where Da Vinci's *Virgin on the Rocks* got him "by the throat"), Basso quietly wondered how his "mountains, those barren backwoods of mine" would "seem after this."[44]

Although Basso had vowed to Cowley that he would take some

43. Basso to Perkins, December 7, August 22, 1937, in SA.

44. Basso to Perkins, October 15, 1937, in SA; Basso to Cowley, November 15, 1937, in Cowley Papers, NL; Basso to Perkins, October 28, 1937, in SA.

time off, he confessed to Perkins: "If only I did not have that albatross of a book hanging around my neck—always banging against my chest, keeping me from really diving into all the things I'd like to dive in." Basso was an extremely conscientious writer, and the change of scene could not really distract him from thoughts about *Days Before Lent*. During the winter of 1937 and early spring of 1938, the Bassos stayed in St. Paul de Vence. They had found the thirteenth-century city in the Maritime Alps by accident: having taken the bus from Nice on their way to Vienna, they got out for lunch at Vence and never made it to Vienna; after having had a delicious meal at L'Auberge de la Colombe d'Or, they noticed that the walls of the inn were covered with paintings by French Impressionists. The innkeeper, Francis, turned out to be an unusual patron of the arts: he and his father allowed artists to stay for free, and in return the artists, and painters in particular, would leave one of their works. When Francis learned that Basso was an *écrivain* looking for lodging, he rented the couple a capacious studio for $250 a month, including meals. "This auberge," Basso wrote, "is so absolutely right that it reminds you of a set for a musical comedy."[45]

The inn would be immortalized in *The Greenroom*, Basso's only novel set on European soil (as well as in "A Candle for the Marquis," one of his unpublished and suspenseful Vence stories). As *The Greenroom* reveals, the inn saw many intriguing visitors. Thus Toto Basso remembers asking one of the French guests what kind of solitaire he was playing. The old gentleman promised her he would teach her, just as his grandfather had taught him, having learned the game when holding up a candle for the game of solitaire Napoleon Bonaparte used to play in his battlefield tent.[46]

Although Basso did not speak a word of French, he loved to mix with the locals, whom he would occasionally join for a game of *boules*. Describing his relaxed life in the south of France to Lyle Saxon, Basso heard back from his old New Orleans friend that he could just imagine Basso "with arms folded, scowling out over the Mediterranean or Sweet Waters or Asia, or whatever the hell it is one gazes out upon. I'll bet anything that you go completely native with a fierce mustache—your first step to becoming a brigand." Basso was very happy indeed, or as he told Perkins, "I feel rested and have forgotten I have nerves

45. Basso to Perkins, October 28, December 7, 1937, in SA.
46. Etolia S. Basso, conversation with the author, June 1995.

and am very happy here." This also inspired him to work. In the auberge he did much of his writing for *Days Before Lent* as well as some
journalism on the side: "I have done a semi-journalistic piece which I
think is pretty good. You know how I am—interested in damn near everything that touches my time."[47]

The piece Basso referred to is a *New Republic* article on Thomas
Mann, which, like Basso's unpublished "A Candle for the Marquis," is
written against the background of the impending war. Though Basso
had dreaded undertaking his European travel because of the imminent
war, he found, like his American protagonist in "A Candle for the
Marquis," that the French "speak of the War the way Americans speak
of Death. You know it is coming and you know there is nothing you
can do about it; yet it always seems far enough away, no matter how
imminent, to be spoken of with a certain detachment."[48] The threat of
war could no longer be ignored by the Bassos once they visited Italy in
the early spring of 1938.

Although Basso had been looking forward to finding himself in the
country of his forebears, he was gravely disappointed by the country's
docile support for Il Duce. He attended one of Mussolini's rallies, and
the event reminded him of the gatherings of the New Orleans childhood gang, the Elysian Fields: "If you belonged to the Elysian Fields as
I did not, you had certain rights and privileges: just like the military
and the bureaucracy here. The boys in the gang, to identify themselves,
used to print an EF in a circle on their forearms. In Italy that encircled
EF has been glorified into the whole dazzling array of Fascist uni-
forms." As Basso walked away from the rally in disgust, he was overwhelmed by an uncanny foreboding of things to come. Ill at ease and
ready to leave, he sensed the same menacing atmosphere in Florence's cold and damp weather: "It's hard to tell about this cold. . . . It is
a slow crawling cold of dampness and fog . . . slowly, little by little, it
creeps into you. It is like the way the fog from the Mississippi creeps
into the waterfront streets in the early hours of morning. In the end
you are cold all over. Your body aches for the sun . . . for the American
sun."[49]

47. Saxon to Basso, August 2, 1937, in Basso Papers, HT; Basso to Perkins, December
7, 1937, in SA.

48. Hamilton Basso, "A Candle for the Marquis" (Typescript in Basso Papers, HT).

49. Basso, "Italian Notebook," 147–49.

It is not so surprising that in these ominous years before the outbreak of World War II, Basso reviewed Thomas Mann's *Avertissement à l'Europe* (1938) for the *New Republic*.[50] He had once encountered the exiled Mann at a New York dinner party, but too shy to approach, he had picked up his hat and left. In print, however, he would not leave Mann alone, identifying with his political standpoint in the *New Republic* piece but discarding Mann's Joseph novels (1933–43) as the dullest books he had ever read and deprecating his *Dr. Faustus* (1947) in *New Yorker* reviews. Mann himself was rather miffed at Basso and called the 1948 *New Yorker* review the "low point" of all the Faustus reviews. If, however, he had read Basso's sensitive *New Republic* article, Mann might not have had such a bad opinion of Basso.

Both Basso's 1938 review and Mann's *Avertissement* warned against the barbaric nature of Fascism. To prevent this barbarism and Nazi "mass drunkenness" from spreading, Mann called on the artist to serve as the conscience of the nation. Without becoming a politician or a propagandist, the artist had to embrace a New Humanism that would alert and warn people of the dangers of Fascism. Like Mann, Basso was of the opinion that artists, and writers in particular, should neither be uninterested in world affairs nor partisan to either left- or right-wing politics, but should be adequately informed and have their feet firmly planted in society so that in times of trouble they could speak out and condemn the evils of political extremism. Possibly, Basso's and Mann's belief that the artist should not be an elitist but should have a certain public responsibility derives from their rejection of the elitism of their day—the high-minded aestheticism of the Agrarians and, in Mann's case, the aestheticism of the *l'art pour l'art* movement. Basso's debate with Matthew Josephson regarding the role of the intellectual also comes to mind, and it is not surprising that Basso revealed to Josephson that the Mann article could be read as a personal message: "It contains, at any rate, much of what I would say to you," Basso told Josephson in a letter of February 3, 1937.

Mann's mention of mass madness from which the artist has to dissociate himself must have struck a chord in Basso, who used the idea for *Days Before Lent*. Resorting to Pavlovian and behaviorist theory,

---

50. Hamilton Basso, "Thomas Mann and a New Humanism," *New Republic*, March 9, 1938, pp. 120–23.

Basso made the distinction between so-called "unsurprisables" (people who surrender their individuality to the mass madness and drunkenness of a Mardi Gras parade) and "surprisables" (free individuals who are not conditioned by the masses but make up their own minds). In other words, as the ultimate savior of society, Mann's New Humanist is close to what Basso defined as the surprisable individual. Surrounded by too many unsurprisables in Europe, the Bassos finally found the threat of war too much to bear, and after a short visit to Rome, which Basso described as a "somewhat dowdy but charming provincial lady suddenly introduced to international society," the couple sought the safer shores of America.[51] By April 1938, they were back in Pisgah Forest, in time to attend Thomas Wolfe's funeral.

In letters to Cowley, Josephson, and Perkins, Basso argued that Europe did not "change" his world but "illuminated a world already pretty well formed." The expatriate adventure, so common an experience among Basso's contemporaries, came late for him and was rather different from the experiences of his friends. Whereas Josephson, Cowley, and Wolfe had lived in Paris and London as impressionable young men, Basso, an established writer by 1938, avoided Paris and chose the southern French countryside instead. Typically, he preferred the country to the city, domesticity to the life of the garreteer, and quietude to the social and artistic scene. Although Cowley and Josephson had given him the names and addresses of artists and writers in Paris, he never contacted any of them. In fact, throughout his life Basso would suggest that the expatriate drive of the lost generation was overrated; in an article on H. G. Wells he even argued that the "lostness" of the Victorian writer in the modern world was more genuine than that of the "Dada bohemians of the Left Bank who were lost until it was no more fun, or too expensive, and then came home."[52]

Back in Pisgah Forest, Basso missed the company of Wolfe and Fitzgerald and told Cowley in an undated letter that the summer of 1938 was long, lonely, and uneventful: apart from falling into the river when he went fishing nothing happened, and in order to escape another cold and lonesome winter, the Bassos stayed from November 1938 to Febru-

51. Basso to Cowley, February 4, 1938, in Cowley Papers, NL.
52. Basso to Josephson, February 3, 1938, in Josephson papers, BL; Basso, "The Fate of H. G. Wells," *New Republic*, December 13, 1939, p. 234.

ary 1939 in Beaufort, South Carolina, a less pretentious alternative to
Aiken. The stay in Beaufort came as a much-needed vacation; Basso
hinted in a letter to Josephson that he was "beset, not only by the ugli-
ness of the times, but also much personal worry—including what
could have been a breakdown on my part and the threat of a severe illness to Toto."[53]

Having discovered Beaufort as early as 1933, the Bassos had been
immediately smitten with the place. To Basso, the small coastal town
was "unquestionably the most alluring and charming place [which]
exists in its entirety, unchanged from the time 'befo de war.' There are
birds everywhere, squirrels scamper in the streets (unpaved, save one,
the street that follows the bay). . . . And so beautifully backward is the
place that we had to hunt for a gas-station." He would recommend the
town to his New York friends as a pleasant southern getaway and believed that the "sandy cove" of Beaufort was the "sort of place I am
happiest in, where I can get to know the people and the 'feel' of the
country, and I go fishing with Gullahs in batos [*bateaux*], and talk duck-
shooting with small-town lawyers, pharmacists etc." Beaufort,
together with Savannah, Charleston, and New Orleans, was an authentic reminder of the Old South and formed the inspirational basis for the
fictional town of Pompey's Head. But before he invented Pompey's
Head, Basso went home to New Orleans once more in *Days Before
Lent*.[54]

Though extremely useful as an atmospheric setting, in *Days Before Lent*
New Orleans is clearly no longer the locale of *Double Dealer* coziness or
childhood capers. Although the protagonist, Jason Kent, a thirty-year-
old bacteriologist, has had a Quarter childhood that is practically interchangeable with that of his creator, New Orleans is presented as a city
that has lost some of its mystique. This can be ascribed to Basso's
changing feelings about the Crescent City: every time he revisited the
city of his birth, he would be disillusioned with how much it had
changed. In *Days Before Lent*, the city is cheapened by tourism, decay,
and an overall museumlike quality. The Mississippi River, once the ar-

    53. Basso to Josephson, November 30, 1938, in Josephson Papers, BL.
    54. Hamilton Basso to Roy Schwarz, January 10, 1933, in Etolia S. Basso files; Basso
to Josephson, February 20, 1939, in Josephson Papers, BL.

tery of the United States, has lost a good deal of its glamor too, or as Jason contemplates on one of his many river rambles: "Only a few of the steamboats were still afloat . . . trailing behind them a wake of melancholy as mournful as the old Confederate soldiers who sold repainted golf balls in the park" (*DBL*, 110).

The story's title refers to the time frame of the novel: before Lent, which is the fasting period after the Mardi Gras festival, Jason has to decide whether he wants to pursue medical research or choose the more mundane life of a general practitioner. The one would involve adventure abroad, with Jason accompanying his mentor, the bacteriologist Jonathan Hunt; the other would lead to the more ordinary destiny of medical practice at home and marriage to his true love, Susanna.

Although the central action of the novel revolves around Jason's difficult choice, the reader is introduced, by means of flashbacks and the protagonist's encounters with other New Orleanians, to characters whose lives run parallel to and are connected with Jason's life. As it happens, Jason's pursuit of the right profession—or to put it in terms of his mythical namesake, his quest for the golden fleece—is interwoven with a search for a father. The Telemachus theme is a relevant subtheme in view of Basso's many "orphaned" protagonists. But more so than Basso's earlier main characters, Jason relates to various father figures. First there is his biological father, Peter Kent. For an educated man, Kent's interests are curiously working class. Having failed to become a prizefighter, Kent trains and dotes on the talented fighter Joe Piavi. Jason, on the other hand, is not a fighter but a thinker and thus does not have the special relationship that Joe has with his father. As he explains to Susanna, he could not call his old man "father" or "dad," for these terms would imply "a relationship" he never had (*DBL*, 37). Like David Barondess, Jason would like to be closer to his father but ultimately fails to have a satisfactory relationship with his single parent. The absence of the mother figure, which seems almost customary in the Basso novel by now, enhances these feelings of failure. Out of frustration, Jason seeks solace from various surrogate-father figures.

Dr. Jonathan Hunt is Jason's intellectual father. In contrast to the book's Faustian scientist, Ernest Muller, Hunt represents science with a human face. Called a "skeptic" but never a "cynic" (*DBL*, 14), Hunt is Jason's mentor both in bacteriology and in life. A third father figure is based on a revered figure out of Basso's childhood who would also serve as a source of inspiration for a *New Republic* article entitled "Cardinal Pacelli and Father John."[55] In *Days Before Lent* he goes by the same name and functions as the protagonist's spiritual father; in spite of Jason's anticlericalism and atheism, he admires Father John as an example of "tolerance, humanity, kindness and goodwill" (*DBL*, 126). Like the socialist priest Norman Thomas, whom Basso looked up to, Father John leaves his parish to do relief work for the poor in the bayous. He dies when an epidemic of the infectious tropical disease kala-azar breaks out, and Jason gives him an overdose of medicine: because Jason is only slightly familiar with kala-azar and vaguely remembers the cure from Hunt's textbooks, he has to experiment with the dosage. Although Jason is hailed as a medical hero who prevented the epidemic from spreading, he suffers from guilt over Father John's death.

A fourth father figure, Dr. Gomez, helps him cope with this problem. An exiled revolutionary from a fictional Latin American country, the doctor offers Jason his practice when he decides to return to his homeland. Gomez sees Jason "as a son," gives him fatherly advice, and has long philosophical discussions with him. Gomez's offer finally shows Jason a way out of his dilemma: whereas previously his choice was between research abroad and a job at an insecticide plant in New Orleans, now Jason can practice medicine and thus still be engaged in the medical profession without becoming a "scientific monk" (*DBL*, 275).

Besides these father figures, who help Jason out of what he calls his "Hamletness" (*DBL*, 25), the protagonist is surrounded by peers who have problems of their own. One is Joe Piavi. Since his fame has waned and his coach has died (like Dekker's father, Kent senior killed himself), he is given to bouts of alcoholism and smokes marijuana. Bound for trouble, Joe shoots a mafia boss, and when he tries to find Jason for help, he runs into Danny O'Neill, a flashy newspaperman who thinks he can squeeze a good story out of the "wanted" Joe. When they leave Jason's apartment, they are both shot in the back by avenging gangsters. Joe's death gives rise to an epiphany, in which Jason finally comes to understand the "nature of his bond with Joe," that is, the

55. Basso, "Cardinal Pacelli and Father John," 343–45. Lambasting Pacelli's Fascist sentiments, Basso contrasted the cardinal with the inspiring example from his childhood, Father John.

bond with his father, his family, and "the world he cherished most, the world of man against the world of ideas, the open world of humanity as against the closed world of the laboratory" (*DBL*, 351). At the same time, Jason's friend, the Catholic priest Victor Carducci, has a moment of revelation: after the archbishop vetoes his housing project for the poor because it smacks of Communism, Victor decides to abandon his social work and devote himself fully to the Church. While Jason comes to the conclusion that his place is in society, Victor withdraws from society.

Apart from his father figures, Jason also has a number of "brothers." Joe is what Joseph Millichap calls Jason's "dark, violent brother," representing the life of the streets. Victor, on the other hand, is his spiritual brother. Jason's third "brother" is the playwright Tyrrell Surtees, and though Millichap describes him as a "sort of Tennessee Williams version of a decadent Southern playwright," Surtees is intended to be "one of the lost generation" (*DBL*, 247) and is apparently modeled on Harry Crosby and F. Scott Fitzgerald. When Malcolm Cowley asked Basso whether Surtees had been based on Fitzgerald, Basso answered in a letter of July 17, 1939: "To answer your minor questions: Yes, Tyrrell Surtees *was* suggested by Scott Fitzgerald (I sincerely hope this won't be considered a *portrait* of Scott. I would be very ashamed and distressed if I was the cause of hurting his feelings. Perhaps I did take him too seriously: Surtees I mean: as in fact, I take Scott. And there is a kind of theatrical quality in Scott that I tried to get) . . . But besides Scott, Surtees had some of Harry Crosby in him too."[56]

The resemblance to Fitzgerald is especially striking. For instance, just as Basso felt inferior and provincial when visiting Fitzgerald in Asheville, Jason thinks "his own history" "commonplace and dull" compared to Surtees' "great success, the legends that had grown up about him, his romantic marriage [and] even the tragedy that had overtaken his wife" (*DBL*, 33). Also, the narrator's description of Surtees' writing clearly resonates with Fitzgerald's: "Tyrrell's incisiveness never cut very deep . . . the emphasis was always upon foliage rather than root, but in all his work . . . there was a muffled beat of tragedy: gaining in effectiveness because it was never permitted to rise above an

---

56. Millichap, "Hamilton Basso," 70, 72; Basso to Cowley, July 17, 1939, in Cowley Papers, NL.

undertone: the muted insinuation that all the bright glitter of these lives was simply the sparkle of mica in shifting treacherous sands. And time—this black depression—had shown he was right" (*DBL*, 81). Like Fitzgerald in 1936 and 1937, Surtees is on the verge of a nervous breakdown and despite Jason's attempts, which greatly resemble Basso's, to cheer up the playwright, Surtees knows "the party is over" and the world "is done for" (*DBL*, 209). On Mardi Gras day, he circles over the parade in a silver plane and finally makes a suicidal dive into the Gulf. His last thoughts are filled with a bitter (and particularly Bassoesque) justification of his art: "But the world, eventually, would come to realize that he had beaten this phony crop of 'social consciousness' boys to the gun by years. . . . Yet the critics, simply because he did not believe in thumping a drum, because he thought the function of art was higher than the function of propaganda—oh what the hell!" (*DBL*, 319). Surtees' condemnation of proletarian art does not only bring to mind John Pine's and Basso's preference of art over politics; the idea that Surtees might have been more representative of his generation than any of his contemporaries also derives from Basso's conviction that Fitzgerald "rather than Hemingway or anybody else was the intellectual conscience of his generation."[57]

More so than in his previous novels, Basso based some of his characters on people he knew. Jason's girlfriend, Susanna, resembles Etolia Basso, and one of the minor characters, B. Wallace Winter, is an alter ego of William ("Willie") B. Wisdom. Etolia Basso confirmed that the description of Winter fit her recollection of Wisdom. She further remarked that her husband disliked the New Orleans socialite initially, an animosity that he toned down when Wisdom became such a diligent caretaker of the Thomas Wolfe estate after the author's death in 1938.[58] Interestingly, the contact between Wisdom and Wolfe had been brought about by Basso. When Wolfe planned his visit to New Orleans, Basso had written down Wisdom's name in case Wolfe wanted to attend a New Orleans ball. However, since Basso himself was not fond of Wisdom, the Winter character is caricatured. Described as being "lifted from his clerkship in an uncle's brokerage office to the realm of the

---

57. Basso to Cowley, November 8, 1941, in Cowley Papers, NL. In the same letter, Basso argues, "It's the Gatsby book, rather than the Sun Also Rises, that's the distillation of our time. As for Dos Passos, the other contender, it seems to me that it's just badly written obviousness that gets nowhere and says nothing."

58. Etolia S. Basso, interview with the author, November 6, 1993.

glamorous, the wealthy [and] the socially secure," Winter is a social climber and a dilettante who, with his "two front teeth protruding from his fishlike mouth," looks down on the Mardi Gras crowd; seeing the mob as a threat "not to what he was but to what he hoped to be: a person of wealth, position, powerful and influential," Winter aspires to his ancestor's fame, which "had gained him entrance . . . into local society" (*DBL*, 254, 311–12). Obsessed with caste and ancestry, Winter is guilty of southern Shintoism, a phenomenon that Basso saw as one of the detrimental inheritances of antebellum society.

With the exception of Susanna, *Days Before Lent* has an all-male cast. In his depiction of men and women, Basso was clearly more at ease with male characters than with their female counterparts. As in the earlier novels, the romance element—the relationship between Jason and Susanna—is overly sentimentalized. Basso's delineation of women as inferior creatures who adjust their behavior and life to the whims of men becomes offensive when Jason utters phrases like it "is impossible for a woman to understand how a man feels when he feels like that" (*DBL*, 157).

If we ignore the sexism and the penny-novel romance, *Days Before Lent* is an intelligent book; it was endorsed as such by public and critics alike. Listed among the *New Republic* "One Hundred Notable Books of 1939," it won the Southern Authors Award of 1940 and was adapted for a film, *Holiday for Sinners*, whose title was much abhorred by Basso. Referring to "Hamilton Basso's brilliant new novel" as "intelligent Southern realism," Alfred Kazin commended Basso as one of those "young Southern novelists who have not only heard of Appomattox, but are quite willing to forget it." Equally complimentary, Evelyn Scott observed that with this novel, Basso departed from Faulkner and Wolfe in his preoccupation with "genuine intellect rooted in actuality." Clearly, Basso had tried to break away from standard southern themes. Admittedly, the New Orleans setting and the celebration of Mardi Gras classify the book as southern, yet the novel's theme is not intrinsically southern. Also, compared to Dekker and David, who had, according to Lyle Saxon, "uneasy" southern blood in their veins, Jason lacks their inflammable temper and is almost too philosophical to be a southern hero.[59]

59. Alfred Kazin, "Intelligent Southern Realism," *New York Times Book Review*, August 6, 1939, p. 5; Evelyn Scott, "Doctor's Choice," *Saturday Review of Literature*, August 5, 1939, p. 7; Saxon, "Uneasy Blood in Their Veins," 8.

Having the face of a "dreamer," Jason has more in common with Tony than with either Dekker or David (*DBL*, 16). Like Tony, Jason is attracted to the life of the mind. They are both bacteriologists, and they are both stimulated by their intellectual fathers, Hunt and Mullendorf. But more so than Tony, Jason is not merely intelligent and sensitive but tries to channel his sensitivity into a philosophy based on scientific principle: rejecting Freud, Basso resorts to Pavlov, whose theories he employs to explain his own behavior and that of others. Jason wants to "take Pavlov's discoveries out of the realm of information, out of print and make them more an immediate and meaningful part of his own life" (*DBL*, 47). Jason's use of objective science to explain human behavior and life mirrors Basso's own groping: after his emotional debates with Josephson, Cowley, and other intellectuals, Basso experienced a longing for something definitive, a theory or philosophy that would explain and justify the intellectual turmoil of the thirties. While Cowley, Josephson, and others had leaned on Marx, Basso had, throughout the thirties, relied on his own instincts, or what he called his "gut feeling." However, by the end of the thirties, when he was composing *Days Before Lent*, he may have felt that gut feeling was not enough, and to fend off the constant theorizing of Josephson and Cowley, he devised his own philosophy as a means of self-defense. "I am ashamed of how ignorant we are," Basso writes to Cowley:

—an ignorance that leads us into all kinds of sloppy thinking, wrong conclusions. . . . It does make you angry . . . to see a man like Edmund Wilson . . . tie himself into dialectic knots and revealing large gaps in his mind where science is concerned.

The whole piece [i.e., one of Wilson's articles] seemed to have no relation to anything but an abstract game of chess—or better, counting the hairs on an imaginary bald man's head.

Well, I'm trying to hack my way through all this confusion. It seems to me that as a man grows older all the complexity—almost the bewilderment—of his youth, the undirected, uncomprehended quest for learning etc., gets resolved into a few simple beliefs.[60]

The "few simple beliefs" Basso refers to are also the fundamentals of Jason's theory.

60. Basso to Cowley, n.d., in Cowley Papers, NL.

The novel opens with a long discussion on the question of whether fear motivates people to act in certain ways. Though Maxwell Perkins dreaded that "all this scientific talk" would discourage the reader, it sets the tone of the book; while preparing the reader for Jason's continual rationalizations, it immediately highlights the behaviorist concept of man's submission to social conditioning.[61] "Society, life," Jason tells Susanna, "does the same thing to most people that Pavlov did to his dogs, only more so" (*DBL*, 27). Elaborating on John Pine's belief that people are confined and conditioned by their own enclosures, their own realities, Jason argues that people "grow up in cages—suburbanite cages, country club cages, Maine-in-the-summer-Florida-in-the-winter cages—and since they are all given more or less the same stimuli at more or less the same time (paralleling Pavlov's method) they all end up like a lot of buttons stamped by the same machine. They live alike, dress alike, play alike, hope alike, fear alike and above all, think alike" (*DBL*, 27). Because these people lose control over their free will and turn into mere automatons of desire and fear, Jason calls them "unsurprisables." The happy few who manage to escape their cages of conditioning, having preserved their own freedom and will power, are called "surprisables." The truly admirable characters—Father John, Hunt, Jason's father, and Dr. Gomez—are all surprisables, and as can be expected, Jason's destiny lies among these individuals.

Like a true quester, Jason learns from the various (surprisable) "sages" around him and is faced with choices that he must decline in order to reach his final goal. One of the choices is religion, which, as in *Relics and Angels*, has an overarching presence in the book. Because of this, various critics interpreted the novel as a turning point in Basso's perceptions about the Catholic faith. Malcolm Cowley even suspected that Basso was reconsidering his old faith; piqued by one of the characters' observation that Communism and Fascism were "wolves from the same litter [and] the great enemies to human liberty," Cowley challenged Basso by saying that he would rather "kiss Stalin's toe than Pacelli's." Basso was very upset with Cowley's innuendo and covered his

61. Perkins to Basso, June 2, 1937, in SA: Basso defended Jason's fondness for rationalizations: "I have been reading the best of all writers lately, by the name of William Shakespeare, and I believe it can be learned from him that the traffic will bear a lot of contemplative stuff, as long as there is the promise of action to come—a duel, a murder, a stabbing in the night" (Basso to Perkins, June 8, 1937, in SA).

friend's letter with exclamations pertaining to what he called Cowley's "blind faith" in the Soviet state. Like Cowley, though, James E. Rocks wrote that *Days Before Lent* reveals the "essential religious cast of Basso's mind." However, on a close reading of the novel, Basso's supposed "conversion" to the Catholic Church cannot be inferred. Not only did Basso fervently deny Cowley's claim but shortly before finishing the book, he had attacked the Roman Catholic Church courageously and categorically in two *New Republic* articles. The novel itself further evinces that Jason's attitude toward the Church and organized religion in general is that of an apostate rather than a devotee.[62]

Like Tony and Basso himself, Jason is raised a Catholic, but as he grows older, he becomes "increasingly careless" about his faith (*DBL*, 128). Nonetheless, at times of confusion and doubt, he is drawn to the Church, as it embodies a sanctuary of order in a world of disorder. While Jason remains critical of the Church throughout the novel and will not even enter the cathedral when looking for some sort of "psychic catharsis" (*DBL*, 59), he supports Basso's (biological) argument that religion is a basic human instinct (which is especially dominant in the character of Victor). In the end, Jason embraces both Dr. Gomez and Victor as two spiritual and admirable extremes, one whose "anti-Catholicism had resolved itself into moral integrity" (*DBL*, 97) and the other whose devout Catholicism only strengthened his moral integrity. Conceivably, Basso's religious ambivalence was inspired by George Santayana, who was equally skeptical but who claimed that the Church was a shrine of "instinct and reason," and as such invaluable in its ability to comfort man and help him organize his life.[63]

Curiously, although Jason rejects religious doctrine, his ultimate philosophy contains the basic tenets of Christianity. Thus he learns from Hunt that while in science "the principle of doubt" is a prerequi-

62. Cowley to Basso, July 11, 1939, in Basso Papers, BL; Rocks, "Hamilton Basso and the World View from Pompey's Head," 336; Basso, "Cardinal Pacelli and Father John," 343–45; "The Catholic Church in Politics," 202–203.

63. Basso to Cowley, July 17, 1939, in Cowley Papers, NL; Basso to Perkins, January 6, 1938, in SA; George Santayana, "Magic, Sacrifice and Prayer," in *The Philosophy of Santayana: Selections from the Works of George Santayana*, ed. Irwin Edman (New York, 1936), 149. It is not clear what Basso may have actually borrowed from Santayana, but he was familiar with the American philosopher, whom he mentioned and admired in *Mainstream* and in his correspondence.

site to "discover the relative, non-absolute truth," in life the "principle of human interrelationship" is most important: "the forging of a bond—a living human bond—with other beings. The more ties [Jason] had with other men . . . the richer and more fruitful his living experience" (*DBL*, 90). As Jason learns to distinguish and choose between science and life, medical research and practice, and between man on the periphery of society and man in society, he understands that a career as a general practitioner involves love and fellowship. Like Basso, who, in a letter of April 21, 1938, told Josephson that he could not "breathe in the rarified atmosphere" of *New Republic* intellectuals because it gave him "mental nosebleed," Jason is finally more intrigued with "ordinary everyday life": "It was this life that interested Jason most. Essentially anti-intellectual, disbelieving in the absoluteness of mental values, trusting instinct and common sense more than he trusted any system of philosophy . . . the Higher Life was not for him. He could not breathe in that rarefied atmosphere. He had mental nosebleed" (*DBL*, 46). Elsewhere, he lauds fellowship: "A man was a man [if] he inhabited the earth [and] lived with other men" (*DBL*, 86). To validate this view, Basso summons Hunt, who, as a kind of Greek chorus in the last chapter, brings this point home to the reader once more. Starting out by saying that "Hunt was no churchman," the narrator has Hunt make a scientific equation that leads to the somewhat abstruse (and Santayanesque) conclusion that "Wisdom = widely integrated knowledge plus a tolerant, loving-kindly attitude: a skilled cortical analyzer plus a humanized, cultured autonomic. Granted wisdom, the Religious Instinct, drawn by the magnetism of Order, might conceivably move in the right direction" (*DBL*, 370–71). With a "balloon-puncturing expression on his face," Hunt then leans back in his chair and says, "So that's the answer. . . . That's what it adds up to. My village pastor taught me that when I was six years old" (*DBL*, 371).

Jason's revelations further illustrate Basso's belief that the life of the mind is not enough, "the most learned" not only being "the most confused" but also being "pathetically bogged down in the marshes of the Higher Life, searching for absolutes, Truth, Beauty and the Ideal Future" (*DBL*, 46). To Basso's mind, the learned man, the intellectual, should not sequester himself from life, for true wisdom does not lie in study or the laboratory but in life itself. *Days Before Lent* is a manifesto of the author's pragmatic views, and Jason's final embrace of the "surprisable" philosophy is really an expression of Basso's intellectual individualism. Unfortunately, as critics were unaware of his correspondence with Cowley and Josephson, the novel has not previously been seen as an explanation of ideas Basso dwelt on in the thirties.

Enlightened by Hunt's semi-scientific formulas at the end of the novel, the reader has been made aware of contrary notions that can all be reduced to the surprisable-unsurprisable opposition. While the surprisable human being escapes from the cage of conditioning and represents intellectual independence, life, humanitarianism, tolerance, love, instinct, and emotion, the unsurprisable human being is imprisoned in the cage of conditioning and robbed of his independence, freedom, and capacity to enjoy life. In broad general terms, the surprisable versus the unsurprisable symbolizes the contrast between independent man in society and man enslaved by society.

Jason's surprisable ideal is the pursuit of happiness, which all Basso protagonists embrace: though always independent, they all try to achieve harmony with their environment, or rather, they all attempt to become responsible and altruistic members of society. Thus Jason's thirst for knowledge should not only be interpreted as an appetite for science but as his desire for a better understanding of "the manifold complexities of the life about him," which would lead him "to establish, if possible, a fairly harmonious relationship with his place and his time" (*DBL*, 46). Although Jason's philanthropy may be more pronounced, because he finally opts for the altruistic profession of the medical doctor, the desire for personal and social fulfillment also lies at the root of Tony's, Dekker's, and David's pursuits. Since these protagonists clearly undergo a spiritual growth or conversion of sorts, which in Tony's and Dekker's situation involves a large part of their personal development and in David's and Jason's case a definition of their role in society, Basso's thirties novel can be classified as an *Erziehungsroman* in which character development, or the "education" of the hero, is central.

Although the southern motifs that are usually part of Basso's strength are not as markedly present, *Days Before Lent* is an intriguing novel and is indisputably one of Basso's better books. The novel clearly incorporates the culmination of a formula that was already present in *Relics and Angels*. Tony, Dekker, David, and Jason are typical Basso protagonists: on their way home, or contemplating their departure from home, these characters strive for a surprisable life of independence, tolerance, humanity, and altruism. Trying to reconcile themselves with certain demands of society and aspiring to be in harmony with their environment, they are determined individualists who have a tendency to rebel and seek justice for people who are less well off than they. Although Basso was highly circumspect in using autobiographic detail, it is clear that Tony, Dekker, David, and Jason are spokesmen for their creator and represent the various stages that Basso went through as a thinker, writer, and human being.

Having sent off *Days Before Lent* to Perkins in the summer of 1938, Basso was fatigued and close to another breakdown; Perkins' telegram, however, which praised the manuscript as "magnificent," "beautifully done," and "unusual," mended Basso's spirit to the extent that he was "riding back to the wars" again. Nevertheless, he found it hard to settle down again in his writerly routine and reclusive lifestyle. Thomas Wolfe had been dead for a year, and Fitzgerald was in Hollywood. Moreover, after his European sojourn, the South looked particularly bleak and dull. In letter after letter Basso told Cowley that he wanted "out." In a letter to Perkins he wrote that he had begun to feel like Seneca in exile: "Without identifying myself with that rather unattractive and dubious character it was inevitable, then, that I should start thinking about another book—which I have." When Toto became pregnant, Basso's desire to leave became more definite. Having a low opinion of southern education, he told Cowley that "the people you like to play with are not always the people you like to think with."[64]

When Keith Hamilton was born in March 1940, Basso was strangely reticent about the boy's arrival. In a letter of March 18, Maxwell Perkins asked Basso why he was in Asheville: "Isn't it because of a baby, and haven't you had one? I was told it was a boy by Zippy [Perkins' daughter and a friend of the Bassos] on the phone yesterday. I hope it is true and all goes well. I wish you would tell me about this." Basso wrote Perkins the next month, saying that the cold of April sent him out, "wood-chopping and wood-carrying to keep the boy's ears from freezing off."[65]

64. Perkins to Basso (telegram), July 6, 1938; Basso to Perkins, July 8, 1938, June 15, 1939, in SA; Basso to Cowley, May 30, June 16, August 28, 1939, in Cowley papers, NL.

65. Perkins to Basso, March 18, 1940, in SA; Basso to Perkins, April 14, 1940, in SA.

Basso had already started the writing for *Wine of the Country*, which was then entitled "The Noonday Bride" after one of the main characters, or, as the author explained, "this New England girl who is taken South and whose various reactions to the place cause all these complications, and the title comes from a line in Milton's *Samson Agonistes*, 'O dark! Amid the blaze of noon irrevocably dark!'" To give himself a "fresh look at the locale" of his new novel, Basso traveled to New Orleans to give a talk to the city's librarians: "I hate this lecturing," he told Perkins, "but I can't pass up the cash." Progress on the new novel went painstakingly slow because of the "emotional and physical fact of the boy." Toto forbade her husband to use his loud typewriter when the baby was sleeping, and when he was not asleep, people like Mabel Wolfe dropped by: "I like Mabel Wolfe fine, when she's not hitting the bottle that is," Basso wrote. "Yet right now, when I'm working my head off trying to get us settled here, I simply couldn't have one of those five-to-eight-hour sessions."[66]

Having few relatives on either side of the family, the Bassos asked Perkins to be their son's godfather at his christening in August. According to Basso, this would involve no obligations or responsibilities, "except this—to give him a chance, when he's old enough, to understand that slant of yours, your 'way,' that has meant so much to me during the past ten years. That's all." Attending the christening was Thomas Wolfe's mother, who was much disgruntled that the Bassos had not named their newborn after Tom.[67]

The Bassos' decision to leave became a little easier when a paper mill was established at Brevard. As the stench of sulphur swept over the mountains, Basso deplored how the quaint old mountain community had changed so rapidly into a dull, industrial small town. To get away, he accepted an invitation to lecture at Mount Holyoke in South Hadley, Massachusetts. Basso liked New England; to his surprise he found that the New Englander, just like the southerner, "is apt to be a haunted house—it's a good thing. Midwesterners are *not* haunted houses and look at them!"[68] Ellen, the mad character in *Wine of the Country*, was obviously created during the Bassos' stay in South Hadley.

66. Basso to Perkins, April 14, June 1940, in SA.
67. Basso to Perkins, May 5, July 20, 1940, in SA.
68. Basso to Perkins, June 3, 1940, in SA.

Excited about the novel, Basso sent Perkins the first six chapters, which were told in what the author called a much more "straightforward manner" than *Days Before Lent*. When Perkins replied that the chapters were "extraordinarily promising" in a letter of July 18, Basso repeated that he wanted to write this book "truly" and "without literary tricks or affectations." He further added that he was optimistic but that Perkins' job still amounted to cheering him up whenever he was "stuck in one of those awful Louisiana swamps of depression."[69]

When the family returned to Pisgah Forest in the late summer of 1940, Basso's loneliness became unbearable. In a woebegone letter of August 13, 1940, he tells Josephson: "It's a wet, soppy, drippy mountain day with fog on the ridges and gurgles in the drain and the world is in a rotten wretched shape and what the situation calls for is to be with one's friends instead of being a thousand miles away." At the same time, Basso realized that he needed seclusion in order to write. Owning up that he would "rather hunt turkeys and play poker and tell stories than write any day," Basso knew that he had to "enclose" himself in the mountains to get pen to paper. Getting out of the mountains, however, he felt "like a woodchuck coming out of his hole," wanting to "see everybody" and "talk and talk and talk and *talk*."[70]

In search of a more enlightened place to live, the Bassos moved to Charlottesville in October 1940. They picked the Virginia college town because Basso thought of writing a book on Thomas Jefferson, a plan that was abandoned when he found out that Dumas Malone was already working on a life of Jefferson. "So that clears that up," Basso told Perkins, "and I'm proceeding as planned with my little book [i.e., *Wine of the Country*]." The first impressions of Charlottesville were favorable. Describing the town as "pleasant," Basso told Josephson how his fellow townsmen, most of them academics, had "suddenly found out there is something called liberalism in the world, which they are for, but sometimes I think it is the way a sixty-five year old man would be for women if he discovered them for the first time at that age."[71] Basso was given a study in the university library; he worked there from nine to five and thus made more progress on his novel than when he was

---

69. Basso to Perkins, July 6, 20, 1940, in SA.

70. Basso to Josephson, August 13, October 15, December 23, 1940, in Josephson Papers, BL.

71. Basso to Perkins, November 6, 1940, in SA.

writing in the mountain cabin that he had shared with his wife and baby son.

But soon his mood changed. By November the word "pleasant" had turned into "pleasantly dull." While Basso appreciated the "decent library" and "much convenience for Toto who has lived for so long in the backest back-woods," he told Perkins that the academics got "in his hair." This must not have come as a surprise: after all, how could Basso envision a congenial way of life among the puffed-up intellectuals he so despised? Describing the academic establishment as "men teaching Swift whom Swift would have hated" and "Poe-worshippers who if they had lived in his time would have hounded him to death," Basso confessed that if he had to live "in the center of that sort of thing, I'd go nuts."[72] His disdain for academics would be used in his next novel, in which Tait, a self-critical professor, scorns scholars who confuse knowledge with real experience: "Name some of the academics you know—one classroom after the other. How can they be expected to know anything about the way life is lived?" (*W*, 285).

Basso also complained about Charlottesville's worship of "an England that does not exist: you know, the great landed estate country house England that died with the last war. There is, too, a kind of un-Southern stiffness: a paradoxical lack of social grace by people socially inclined: but in the wrong way: calling, dinner parties, that sort of thing. Stiff. The sort of stiffness I expected to find in New England but didn't." He cited Toto, who compared Charlottesville to "that place in the Atlantic where all eels go to breed—only here they breed professional Southerners."[73]

While the progress on *Wine of the Country* was slower than expected, Basso tried to sell his short fiction to various magazines. A rejection by the *New Yorker* put him in one of his darker moods: "I've worked my heart out to get established as a serious writer—and now what happens? The very fact of my seriousness is held against me. . . . What the hell, Max, what the hell! It would be amusing if I didn't have a family to support. . . . It's the same old story and once I write a best-seller all will be well. Best-seller or no, I'll still teach the icky bastards what to

72. Basso to Cowley, November 20, 1940, in Cowley Papers, NL; Basso to Perkins, November 6, 1940, in SA.
73. Basso to Perkins, November 6, 1940, in SA; Basso to Cowley, November 20, 1940, in Cowley Papers, NL.

like. That's a promise." By Christmas, Basso was still not out of the doldrums. Unable to work, he worried about Toto, who had failed to recover fully after Keith's delivery: "I'm getting a little angry over having to pay these doctors' bills without her showing much improvement." In addition, Charlottesville irritated him. Escaping to Aiken, where the family had been offered "the whole wing of a great big lovely old house," Basso needed to get away from "these damned stiff tea-parties I'm hounded into." Accusing Charlottesville academics of being "pompous frauds," Basso lamented that the only "authentic" and "natural" people were the blacks: "They are fine. And I hope, for Virginia's sake, that it's not all like this. And please don't tell me it's what you are that counts, not where you are. You can't even be what you are in this hole without being regarded with a certain amount of suspicion." When they returned from Aiken in January, Basso was ready to leave again, calling Charlottesville a "stinkpot" of smug faculty members. For a short interval they moved to South Hadley, where Basso finished his research for *Mainstream* and Toto compiled *The World from Jackson Square: A New Orleans Reader* (1948). Leaving the South behind, the Bassos had decided to settle in New England for good or, as Basso told Perkins in a letter of November 6, 1940, "real New England, out of the artist belt."[74]

74. Basso to Perkins, December 3, 29, 1940, in SA; Basso to Cowley, January 12, 1941, in Cowley Papers, NL.

5

The Middle Years

Inspired by the New England scenery of South Hadley, Basso did not open his sixth novel, *Wine of the Country*, with a dusty southern square and the statue of a Confederate soldier but showed his reader the snowy common of the college town of Chadhurst. Like Basso's previous protagonists, Tait Ravenwill is an intelligent and handsome young southerner who finds himself at the beginning of a promising academic career in anthropology. At the book's opening, he hurries his way across the common to meet with fellow anthropologist Dr. Prescott, a widower who lives with his three adult daughters, Catherine, Elizabeth, and Jean, and his niece Ellen.

Of these female characters, Catherine and Ellen are given the most attention. Catherine is a sensible young woman who has a string of beaux she finds too dull to marry; Ellen is recuperating from a broken engagement. Unlike the happy-go-lucky Elizabeth and Jean, Ellen is a melancholy figure: her mother died when she was quite young and her father, a diplomat, drowned himself when she was nineteen. Ellen is not only another "orphaned" character but because of her father's different postings abroad, she also experiences a sense of homelessness, a sentiment she shares with her literary brothers Tony, Dekker, and David. Ellen's melancholic demeanor both mystifies and attracts Tait, and soon the two are married after a sentimental courtship in the New England snow. Catherine, who is of course very happy for her cousin, is also a trifle envious: though she tries to hide her infatuation with Tait, it flares up time and again and does not go unnoticed by him.

After the wedding, the couple leave for Tait's southern hometown, Three Crow Corners, where Tait hopes to finish his book before he starts teaching again at Falmouth. But as is customary in Basso's novels, a homecoming is never without complications. Ellen cannot adjust to southern ways, her emotional problems stemming from a collision of northern and southern culture, and Tait abandons his manuscript, unable to harmonize the life of the mind with life on the farm. He finally gives up his research altogether, writes a letter of resignation to his university, and, like Dekker, tries to save the family farm from going under.

Meanwhile, Ellen suffers from bouts of depression, is repulsed by the violence of southern pastimes, and aggravates her own unhappiness and bitterness by jealousy: suspecting her husband of having an affair with one of the local belles, Ellen finally discovers the mutual affection between Tait and Catherine and runs into a swamp, where she wanders around until she dies. Tait's brother Ned also dies in the swamps when his obsession with the deer Old Red culminates in bloody death for both the hunter and his prey. After these tragedies, Tait returns to his book and, like a true Jeffersonian, finds a balance between his agricultural and intellectual pursuits. Catherine returns home to take care of her father, and although the book seems headed for an open ending, the reader's curiosity is satisfied by the correspondence between Tait and Catherine and what appears to be the promise of a future marriage.

Tait and Ellen are the successors of David and Letitia in *Courthouse Square*. In that novel there is a similar clash of cultures, and where David and Letitia leave off, Tait and Ellen take over. Though we never get to see Letitia's full reaction to the South because she only arrives in Macedon at the end of the novel, we may well imagine that if she were to settle in the South, she might develop an aversion similar to Ellen's. Another antecedent of *Wine of the Country* is a short story, "The Headhunters."[1] Though never published, this story appears to have been the seedbed for Basso's novel; it relates the fate of a northern woman who

---

1. Hamilton Basso, "The Headhunters" (Typescript in Basso Papers, HT).

divorces her southern husband because she cannot get used to the savage ideal that southern society espouses.

Notwithstanding Ellen's mounting conflict with southern culture, which is poignant and real, *Wine of the Country* has a number of flaws, first among them the problem of the protagonist, a previously observed Basso weakness. Although one expects Tait to be the protagonist because he has so much in common with Dekker, David, and Jason, he is hardly the center of the reader's consciousness. Seen from without rather than from within, Tait's importance is diminished by the attention that Catherine and Ellen receive. At the same time, they are not protagonists either, even though it can be said that due to Ellen's mental crisis, the reader becomes most intimate with her. Basso's female characters are usually marginal creatures who are merely there to serve and sacrifice themselves for the male hero; *Wine of the Country* is one of the few novels in which a woman plays a leading role. But despite this emphasis, Basso's handling of the female characters is not successful: Ellen and Catherine are dull, sentimental, and painfully pressed to fulfill the roles of the exemplary wife and daughter. Unlike their intellectual husband and father, they view philosophical questions as matters "above" their "mental station," their only ambition in life concerning *"la vie domestique"* (*W*, 8, 293]. The men in the book have equally conventional expectations with regard to the role of women; while Tait argues that women's fulfillment comes from marriage, Dr. Prescott believes that a career interferes with "certain biological drives a woman has" (*W*, 143, 293).

Meeting Ellen for the first time, one is too readily prepared for the tragedy that is going to ensue. There are a number of references to the streak of madness that runs in the Prescott family. In addition, Ellen has such mood swings that the outcome of her depression and madness seems a foregone conclusion. Once she moves south, her already unstable condition deteriorates rapidly. Telling Tait that the hot weather does "things to her head," she is overcome by the "sense of being set down, without proper warning, in the midst of an old and hot and twisted mystery of the earth she could not understand" (*W*, 166, 204). Like *Cinnamon Seed*'s little Elinor, who is apprehensive of Dixie's Gothic environment, Ellen feels she has entered a realm of dreams she cannot comprehend: "The fantasy possessed her, suddenly, that she had passed beyond reality. Her mind was unable to accept, refused to accept, the information transmitted by her senses—the hypnotic movement of the moss, the tangled dankness of the earth, the heavy bars of yellow sunshine. It was, if not a dream, like being in a dream; a world beyond world's end, sleeping unfinished in the womb of time" (*W,* 205–206).

In the end, the dream turns to nightmare when Ellen sees her way out of the South blocked by Tait's resignation from his university job. Feeling like an "outlander" and a "stalk of alien corn," she cannot get accustomed to southerners and their ways (*W,* 207, 213). An important turning point in the novel is the dove-shoot; the crippled and bleeding doves that fall from the sky are an apt metaphor for Ellen's condition, and when Tait grabs a dove and cracks its neck on the butt of his gun, the analogy is complete. The cockfight that follows further heightens Ellen's emotional conflict: "It was a twisted and confused emotion compounded of dread and alienation and all the things that marked, like rushing milestones, the progress of the estrangement. . . . And so she stood there, caught in the web of her love for him . . . and that which was not hate or repugnance or even dislike, merely not-love, doomed to helplessness like a stray nightbird trapped in a beam of hypnotic light" (*W,* 277). Once the "cock had died [and] in his dying, a subtler thing had also perished," Ellen feels hopelessly trapped, and like Esther in Sylvia Plath's *The Bell Jar* (1963), she experiences the night as "a great black bell without a tongue, swinging mutely across the world, descending lower and lower and dropping at last to imprison her" (*W,* 319–20). Ellen finally goes mad, her wild and hysterical laughter ringing eerily through the empty house.

Basso's psychological realism is highly convincing. Ellen's madness appears to be based on the insanity of a few of her literary sisters: Ellen reads and identifies with the heroine of Tolstoy's *Anna Karenina* (1877).[2] Like Anna Karenina and Flaubert's Emma Bovary, Ellen tends toward extreme pessimism and idealism, suffers from melancholy, and finds herself in a marriage gone awry. Like Anna and Emma too, Ellen breaks down once reality fails to match her fairy-tale expectations. As characters whose fate has already been determined on page one, these heroines lack free will, and unable to change the course of their lives,

---

2. Catherine, on the other hand, is reading *War and Peace* and admires her counterpart, the faithful and enduring Natasha.

they slide into a dreadful depression that ends in suicide. In view of Basso's faith in the power of heredity and the corporate identity of the family, Ellen's decline and fall are a clear demonstration of the author's affinity with the naturalist school.

As his last name indicates, Tait Ravenwill has a will and a mind of his own. Having the machismo of Dekker, the temper of David, and the intellect of Jason, he is the mixed product of Basso's love of life and love of mind. Tait's homecoming, which entails a return to his rural roots and a confrontation with the essentially anti-intellectual environment of the South (his fellow southerners mockingly call him "Professor"), resembles Tony's homecoming in its triggering of a vocational dilemma. As Tait becomes absorbed in the world's problems, he feels the many deficiencies of his ivory tower life: "The world of academicians was a closed garden where the sounds of the larger world's tumult came only in muffled echoes, faint and far away" (*W,* 144).

Naturally, Tait's growing resentment with academe can be seen partly as the expression of Basso's anti-intellectual feelings, which resurfaced when he was living in Charlottesville. One clearly hears the author's voice coming through when Tait accuses both intellectuals and artists of being "noisy prophets . . . amateur politicians . . . party hacks [and] cocktail high priests who know all about ordering other people's lives while messing up their own, the children of fashion veering like weather vanes in the wind, the bright boys, the brighter girls, the cliquists, the critics, the you-pat-me-and-I'll-pat-you's, the whole kit and kaboodle" (*W,* 285).

At the same time, as a student of Pavlov, Tait also knows that "he was still bound, by habit, inclination, by years of conditioning, to the intellectual's life" (*W,* 215). In the end, however, he realizes that he is a farmer at heart when, at a turkey shoot, he is reminded of his blissful country childhood. He acknowledges, like Dekker and David, that his sense of home, on the farm, is more congenial than a life away from home, at the university: "What he wanted was to stay here where he belonged, here where he had some living roots" (*W,* 309–10). Basso's protagonists always come home in more ways than one, the concept of home standing for both the homestead and ultimate fulfillment in life.

Tait's cultural pessimism, shared by Dr. Prescott, seems particularly prominent in the novel. Their gloomy outlook on life is no doubt fueled by Basso's own thoughts about the Spanish Civil War and the outbreak of World War II. As with the Depression, Basso was inclined toward pessimism as well as a sense of resignation. "I'll take this war and what it brings," Basso writes in 1939. "I'll not run away from it a single moment of my time, but I'm going to keep on trying to do my work. So that's the essay on 'Ham Basso and the War.' If it has faults, forgive them." Maxwell Perkins, on the other hand, seemed sincerely worried about the war, and Basso would poke fun at him: "Or have you simply crawled off into a cave of silence to brood over the war? If so, you'd better crawl out again. The old ship we've all been living in is cracking down to its bottommost timber: and there's rough, very rough weather ahead." Basso's apparent cynicism may well have derived from a kind of southern survival instinct; was it not the South after all that, despite a crushing defeat in the Civil War and years of Reconstruction, survived and lived on? Basso would draw that very analogy in a letter to Perkins: "It was a terrible thing that happened to these Southern people in the Civil War and the mere fact that there are so many 'Southerners' proves that a lot of them lived through it. I'm not saying that they lived through it *happily*—old Admiral Simms wasn't happy, and Beauregard wasn't, and I doubt if Lee was either. But Simms and Beauregard checked out, in effect. They cashed in their chips and withdrew from the game. Other people, however . . . didn't. They went on farming, working, begetting children—and in the very long view of things, I believe they were right—and that Simms and old Bory were wrong."[3]

Aside from quiet resignation, Basso exhibited patriotism and faith in the destiny of America. "I am not going to be hysterical," Basso tells Perkins in a letter of July 1, 1940. "I believe, more than ever, in the spirit of this big island of ours. Mysticism, if you like, but as deep a belief as I have." More sentimentally, he had mused a year earlier: "When you drive across this big, raw ugly America of ours, this 'right sizable piece of country' that old M. Twain wrote about—when you see these hard, weather-beaten men doing the fall plowing, when you pass the fodderstacks in the fields and the hay drying, when you listen to their rough, uneducated American speech—well, what you get then is the feeling that any danger to this country, any threat to the idealistic things this continent has come to represent, is latent in our own native earth and

3. Basso to Perkins, October 11, 1, 1939, in SA.

in our own difficulties—not in anything like the return of Asia to Europe."[4]

Unlike a great many Americans, Basso rooted for intervention. As early as 1939, he saw the overthrow of the Finns by Stalin's army as the trigger for American involvement. Portraying the American people as a "warm-hearted people with a tradition of pulling for the underdog" and as "suckers for crusades," he argued that the United States had a moral obligation "to support a conflict waged against . . . barbarous philosophies." However, one should not exaggerate Basso's activist stand; overall he showed an air of indifference, feeling that history was not determined by the masses but by the individuals who were in power: "The Germany of today is the Germany of Adolph Hitler . . . at the moment it is a reflection . . . of the character of that fantastic madman . . . Russia, likewise, is the Russia of Stalin . . . and the U.S., despite its innumerable contradictions, is the U.S. of FDR . . . the character of a state at a given time is largely a reflection of the character of those who possess the qualifications and privileges of action at that time . . . It is for this reason also that one, as citizen, should not become overly worried or run off to Spain to fight the fascists."[5]

Like Maxwell Perkins, who worried about Hemingway's departure for Spain, Dr. Prescott sees the Spanish Civil War as a faddish attraction for the young, who, having lost the spiritual prop of religion, go off to war in search of something that might replace religion. As in *Relics and Angels* and *Days Before Lent*, where religion is viewed as a principle of order in a time of disorder, Prescott argues that man "as soon as [he] is cut adrift from his customary moorings—as soon as he finds himself, like his early ancestors, tossing about on a great sea of doubt and uncertainty—he must of necessity find a new system of faith and practice to replace the one he has lost" (*W,* 106). In addition, like Basso, who by 1940 tired of the Marxism of his friends, Prescott deplores that the young find their new religion in Marx: "He [*i.e.,* the young man] finds a new faith in Marxism. Jehovah comes out of Heaven and takes up residence in the Kremlin. The College of Cardinals . . . becomes this thing he calls the Central Executive Committee. Heaven, a land of milk and honey and three automobiles for every family, is still somewhere

4. Basso to Perkins, October 11, 1939, in SA.
5. Basso to Perkins, December 4, 1939, in SA.

in the future . . . Hell has resolved itself into the 'dust-heap of history.' Purgatory is that limbo in which mortals must remain until they have proven themselves worthy of admission to that most celestial band known as 'the party' " (*W,* 106).

Although Tait's and Prescott's ideas are interesting, they have little to do with the novel's plot and distract rather than illuminate. Basso's tendency to editorialize reached its peak in *Wine of the Country.* Whereas in *Days Before Lent* Jason's axioms form a theoretical underpinning of his character and behavior, in *Wine of the Country,* Prescott's and Tait's philosophizing becomes wearisome and redundant. From a letter by one of Perkins' assistant editors, who praised the novel for being "packed [with] pertinent and provocative thoughts," we know that Basso considered himself a "novelist of ideas" and therefore may have deemed it legitimate to interject his narrative with the issues that were on his mind.[6] When he was composing the novel, he strained to integrate the novel's ideas with its action: complaining to Perkins that he did not know how to "keep ideas moving so that the action is not interfered with," Basso wrote that it was "damn tough, [for] you never know how much playing with ideas the reader can stand. It would always vary with the reader and if you reduce it to the lowest common denominator, you end up by saying oh to hell with ideas, let's shoot a gun or anything to make a noise. Which would be a knife in the heart of the thing you want to do. And my real job . . . is to show how ideas influence action: how every action . . . is the extension of an idea."[7] Regrettably, in *Wine of the Country* ideas and action do not complement, let alone reinforce, each other.

In spite of the novel's weaknesses, the book is absorbing for its portrayal of the South. Whereas the New England section is slow and dull, once the novel moves south, it picks up pace and becomes more attractive. Perkins even thought that once Tait and Ellen arrived in the South,

---

6. The letter reads: "I can't find words to tell you how good it is, and how difficult it is to find the right words to use in describing it. What you said one evening a long while ago about being one of the few 'novelists of ideas' now writing is absolutely and completely borne out by WC. Not only have you packed the story full of pertinent and provocative thoughts but, without any sugar coating, you have cloaked the ideas so gorgeously with story and characterizations that any reader . . . will love every word of it" (William Weber to Hamilton Basso, March 31, 1941, in Basso Papers, BL).

7. Basso to Perkins, August 26, 1940, in SA.

the story "moved too fast." Clearly, the South was and would always be Basso's fictional domain. Linking climate to literary style, Basso told Van Wyck Brooks that unlike the writing of Brooks's New England "chums," Thoreau and Emerson, southern writing was a "kind of reflection, in words and rhythm, of the rank tangle of vegetation that in the hot months stretches down from Virginia to the Gulf."[8] That same style (and landscape) springs to life in the southern section of *Wine of the Country*: as soon as the novel moves south, the reader is made to feel the oppressive heat, the mosquito-infested humidity, and the unruly vegetation of Dixie's marshes.

By having a New England outsider respond to the South, *Wine of the Country* is different from the other novels in which a critical southerner reflects on his native region. Consequently, the South is no longer a setting of ambivalence but a realm of mere negative connotations. Elaborating on the opposition between New England and the South, the narrator implies that whereas New England represents snow, cold, ice, serenity, and peace of mind, the South stands for heat, humidity, restlessness, the stirring of roots, and the stirring of the soul (i.e., madness). Not only is the South's scenery set off against the New England landscape(s), but the contrast reverberates also in Tait versus Ellen, the savage versus the civilized, Gullah and voodoo ritual versus empirical science, heat versus cold, instinct versus intellect, the grotesque versus normality, drama versus reality, and the country versus the city. To Ellen's mind, the South is a place of the grotesque, of hairy spiders in the bathtub and of people whose songs betray "a certain darkness of the blood; giving voice to the vast loneliness that lay like sorrow across the land; the loneliness of marsh and swamp and sky and sea" (*W*, 238). Perhaps one should take into account that *Wine of the Country* was written when, having left the South permanently, Basso had dissociated himself from the region of his birth and therefore summoned up negative rather than positive feelings. Remaining a strangely mythical land, the South would be forever held in the clutches of its own anachronisms: "The fables were less fabulous now (the balls, the young lovers born to doom, the pistol-shots beneath the moss) and the lost mythological world assumed a ghostly reality it never had before. This was a

8. Perkins to Basso, April 1, 1941, in Basso Papers, BL; Basso to Van Wyck Brooks, August 22, 1949, in Brooks Papers, PP.

stage and perforce, a drama had to be devised to fit into its frame. Anything less extravagant, anything less heroic than the death of a people, the loss of a cause, would not have sufficed" (*W*, 330).

In later years, Basso came to condemn the South more harshly and adopted the outsider's rather than the insider's view. On a train ride south in 1947, he wrote to Perkins that he had begun to feel like an "alien" in the South and shared Ellen's belief that the South had somehow missed out on the "civilizing" process: "My own conviction, after long thought, is that if it weren't for . . . certain radial influences from other parts of the country, this whole section would return to its aboriginal state in less than 5 years."[9] Whereas in his thirties novels Basso was still of two minds about the South, in his works of the forties the South became an oppressive backdrop of grotesque situations and characters. The use of the grotesque is in fact a hallmark of southern novels of the forties. As the cultural optimism and high aesthetic ideals of the Agrarians were fading, writers like Truman Capote, James Dickey, Carson McCullers, Flannery O'Connor, and Walker Percy resorted to a darker vein.

Although Perkins applauded *Wine of the Country* and Clarence Ikerd thought that it was "possibly the best" book Basso "ever wrote," the novel is flawed, and it found a negative reception in the reviews. From letters exchanged between Basso and Perkins, it is clear that both of them hoped that the novel might signify a final breakthrough, putting Basso on the map as a more "established" writer of American fiction. Or as Perkins told Basso in a letter of 1941: "Time is really important with an author. He cannot at best write a great many books, and we are mighty anxious to see you get firmly established with a real success."[10]

Unlike *Days Before Lent*, which was widely and favorably reviewed, *Wine of the Country* was largely ignored by the New York press. To vent his frustration, Basso blamed Scribner's for marketing the book inadequately. In a letter of October 15, 1941, an incensed Basso wrote to Charles Scribner: "But what happens to it in New York: and to the book, mind you, that everyone except Herschel Brickell says is my best.

9. Basso to Perkins, summer 1941, in SA; Basso to Etolia S. Basso, January 28, 1947, in Basso Papers, BL.
10. Ikerd, "Hamilton Basso," 90; Perkins to Basso, February 5, 1941, in SA.

None of the daily reviewers touch it. The Tribune gives it to a hack. The Times turns it over to Brickell, notoriously incompetent on every score, and buries it with 'other fiction.' It has been neglected, in New York, more than any book I ever wrote except perhaps, that unfortunate novel about Aiken [i.e., *In Their Own Image*] . . . it was clearly indicated that my future at Scribner's, with you and Max, depended largely on the sale of this book. Do you wonder that I want it to have every chance: are you surprised when I get profoundly discouraged when it falls into the hands of a reviewer incapable of even understanding what I am trying to say?"[11] This letter was soon followed by another in which Basso hinted that he had been approached by another publisher, to which Perkins promptly responded by offering $150 a month for the new novel. By December 1941, a change of publishers was no longer on Basso's mind. Well under way with his new novel, Basso announced to Perkins that his next work would be an altogether different book.

Already irritable because of the bad reception of *Wine of the Country*, Basso became more and more disenchanted with the *New Republic*. Telling Cowley that the magazine was going from "bad to worse—which means a pretty bad worse since I never thought it very good in the last year or so," he became convinced that the intellectuals of the thirties had accomplished nothing and that "the only truth is fiction. . . . And it's people I'm interested in—people alone. The wealth and variety they've given my life—peasants in France, courthouse politicians, mountaineers, sharecroppers, diplomats, men who paint pictures and men who write books."[12]

As he considered leaving the *New Republic*, Basso became worried about his source of income. His freelance income of $35 for the *New Yorker*'s "Book Notes" and "Talk of the Town" columns was not enough, so in 1942 he started working for *Time*: having applied for the job with "what he thought was an outrageous parody of the news magazine's style," the editors were amused and signed him on. According to Ikerd, Basso soon left the magazine because he did not like "the way Henry Luce dictated the editorial slant of the magazine nor

11. Basso to Charles Scribner, October 15, 1941, in SA.
12. Basso to Cowley, November 8, April 7, January 12, 1941, in Cowley Papers, NL.

the particular line Luce took on many issues. He was also dissatisfied
. . . with the anonymous group method of writing."[13]

Still struggling with his craft, Basso became very insecure about his
writing. As 1941 drew to a close he was overcome by a midcareer crisis:
"In four more years I'll be forty. I look across the room at the shelf that
holds my books: and what's there? How good is it; what is it worth?
One thing I know—it isn't as good as I want it to be, as good as I hope
to make it in the future. Maybe this last book [*Wine of the Country*] is as
'slick' etc. as they say it is—I don't know but I do know it was honestly
done. . . . If only there was some way of knowing where I may have
gone wrong, where I haven't measured up. God knows it is in me: how
to get out? I'm still going to try—that's the most important thing of all
again."[14]

Although Keith's birth in 1940 had been a source of joy, the early
forties were trying years from a marital point of view as well: the Bassos' finances were strained, and Toto complained about her husband's
absence and his wish to join the army. "The pressure of this war is always on me," Basso told Perkins in 1942, "and I feel it necessary to do
something, but I can't truthfully see the wisdom in serving God and
Country by being bored to death." Earlier that year, when he was close
to finishing *Mainstream*, he considered becoming a war correspondent:
"I think I'll do another trick at journalism, going abroad if I can—I feel
so goddamn out of things and there seems to be no way of getting in,
not until I'm drafted. I looked into this 'fighter-correspondent' which
the Marines have set up but it seems that you have to be a practicing
newspaperman." He even tried to become a war correspondent with
the *New Yorker*, but because that position had already been filled, they
offered him a "job on their staff" instead, which Basso declined because they paid "nothing like the salary I am getting on *Time*." *Time*
could not send him abroad either, and notwithstanding his attempts to
pass the army's physical, in a letter of May 28, 1943, Basso tells Toto
that his weight was still 8 pounds shy of the mandatory 132 pounds
and that his bad right eye made him an unsuitable candidate for mili-

13. "Hamilton Basso, Dead: Novelist Wrote of Southern Life," *New York Times,* May
14, 1964, p. 35; Ikerd, "Hamilton Basso," 106.
14. Basso to Cowley, November 8, 1941, in Cowley Papers, NL.

tary service, anyway. To serve his country nonetheless, Basso then joined the Office of the Secret Service, the forerunner of the CIA, to "consult and advise . . . on problems and projects, perhaps best categorized as propagandistic."[15]

Basso's commuting between South Hadley, New York City, and Washington, D.C., Toto's complaints of boredom, and their financial situation put both the marriage and Basso under significant pressure. The couple spent their weekends arguing, and when Basso was close to a nervous breakdown, Toto sent him to Florida to unwind. Before he took the train to St. Augustine from New York City, he seemed to persuade his wife that nothing was the matter: "I am so cheered. Another publication in England, the Roosevelt book to write [this was never written], Scribners hot about the novel [*Sun in Capricorn*], Curtice crazy about John Applegate [i.e., *Mainstream*]—I can do it, can't I old darling. . . . It's fine really, to have this feeling of confidence again." This, however, was a false sense of security. When he began roaming the Florida beach and reading Toto's letters, the tension returned: "My sense of order, and a certain need I have for it, is as great—as yours—perhaps greater. I always hope to find . . . a way to restore that sense and feeling of order. So far I have been able to do it. The only order left in my life is the order that comes from home—therefore, when every weekend is devoted to nothing else but palaver about the 'situation,' I am almost completely disoriented from every thing when I get back to town." Reproaching his wife for picking out locales that turned out to be lonely or boring, Basso argued that he was trying his utmost, sustaining his wife and infant son and standing on his own feet rather than "asking . . . favors of the Reynals and Scribners of this world." Besides his worries about seeing his family through the war, he had sleepless nights over his growing loss of confidence in his work: "I cannot deny that I feel a keen sense of failure in my work and that, because of this, there has been a diminution of self-esteem which, if it continues, will eventually resolve itself into a lack of self-respect. It is this that has always kept me going and which I would not want to lose."[16]

From the Florida correspondence, of which we have only Basso's

15. Basso to Perkins, October 22, August 16, 1942, June 5, 1943, in SA; Basso to Etolia S. Basso, May 28, 1943, in Basso Papers, BL; Ikerd, "Hamilton Basso," 107.

16. Basso to Etolia S. Basso, February 24, 1942, and [*ca.* 1942], in Basso Papers, BL.

side, it is clear that whereas Toto was ready for a separation and perhaps even a divorce, her husband pleaded for another chance. Plucking oranges in the garden of fellow novelist Marjorie Rawlings, Basso contemplated his marriage. The daily letters to his wife vary in tone: some are argumentative, others meditative, and a few downright desperate.[17] The most revealing letter of this particular correspondence dates back to February 26, 1942:

> Truth is, honey, old-maid-dom withers me at my very roots. Nor can I say I'm sorry that it does. If you know me at all you should know that what I cannot live with, or by, is ordinary-ness. A villa or a garret. One or the other. Something dies in me when I have to live in between. (We're talking symbolically so don't do a Cowley on me). Perhaps it's a grievous fault in me. . . . Maybe you're right: maybe the boy ought to grow up ordinarily. But damn it all, I distrust that "ought" . . . is it better for him to grow up ordinarily with a more-or-less constantly depressed old man, or a little unordinarily with a more-or-less infrequently depressed old man? And how about you? How about it old sweetheart. Is it *really* what you want? Ordinaryness? . . . Is that the end-aim of your personal aspirations—as distinguished from what you want for me and Keith? If so, I've been wrong—wrong when I saw you in the bookshop, wrong during all those bad years you left me pretty much alone, wrong now.[18]

When Basso's mother jumped to the conclusion that her son had run off and subsequently apologized for his behavior to Toto, he was annoyed and told his mother that he had met a seventy-two-year-old heiress ("Imogine Van Dipple—you know, of the Pittsburgh Van Dipples—the steel people") whom he considered marrying.[19] He added that he had also fallen in love with a movie star ("her first name is Greta and her last name starts with a G"), and "there is a cute lady ex-

17. Etolia Basso denies the marital difficulties of 1942; Basso's correspondence of this time indicates otherwise.

18. Basso to Etolia S. Basso, February 26, 1942, in Basso Papers, BL. The bookstore Basso refers to is the Pelican Bookshop on Royal Street, New Orleans; the *Double Dealer* group gathered here, and it is where Ham and Toto first met.

19. Basso to Louise Basso, carbon copy enclosure in letter to Etolia S. Basso, March 16, 1942, in Basso Papers, BL.

plorer who wants me to share an igloo with her at the South Pole, and
I've had to avoid the whole chorus of a musical show that's here—ho
hum! . . . And if you ever dare to apologize for anything I do I will dis-
own you as Keith's grandmother and never speak to you again." This
is about the only light note in the Florida letters, together with Basso's
drawings and a corny poem for two-year-old Keith:

TO KEITH, BEING CURIOUS
Men each have a penis
Women have not.
It's not because
Nature forgot.

It's part of the great
Bright mystery
From whose depths
Come boys like thee.
The tiger's smile, the lamb's meek face

Were each begotten in its place
The fern, the flower, the bird, the tree
The fish that swim the caverned sea,
Are strands in the web that hold us all:
The poor, the proud, the great, the small.

How came the joining
Of this complex lot?
Because man has a penis
And woman has not.[20]

As time went by, the mood of Basso's letters grew more conciliatory
and with it the realization that separation was out of the question:
"Two people who get along so beautifully as we do *apart* ought to do
better *together*. That puzzles me greatly. And it's sheer moronic folly
for us to exhaust the other way we do with so much useless
talk. . . . Separation, which you have brought up so often wouldn't
work: I don't really think so."[21] After three weeks of Florida sunshine,
Basso was ready to go home again, and although we do not have Toto's
letters, it is clear that they had signed the peace to save their marriage.

20. Basso to Etolia S. Basso, March 6, 1942, in Basso Papers, BL.
21. Basso to Etolia S. Basso, March 2, 1942, in Basso Papers, BL.

While Basso was in St. Augustine, he met the Norwegian and Nobel Prize–winning novelist Sigrid Undset, who lived in the United States during the war. Basso was quite taken with her personality, especially after he found out that she had read both *Beauregard* and *Festival*, the English edition of *Days Before Lent*. Describing her as "magnificent," Basso told his wife: "You see this little monolith of a lady, formidable seeming, severe, holding some sort of mental ruler to rap the knuckles of bad American boys, and then with indescribable charm, she isn't any of these things—warm and wise and gentle and all of it played upon by a lovely sense of humor. We talked and talked and talked. Only now I am beginning to realize that I sort of forgot about Marjorie Rawlings. But she wasn't there—not in the presence of this other woman's compelling personal authority." Rather self-consciously he added: "Mme Undset is what a writer should be like—there would be a greater dignity to my craft if they were." Staying away from the writer's colony at St. Augustine, Basso kept mostly to himself, exhibiting once more his reluctance to mix with a clique of other writers. Besides that, he was hard at work with his new novel, establishing a routine of "up at 8, to work at 9, lunch at 1:30, loaf until 3:30, work until 6, dinner at 7:15, work until 10." On March 15, Basso reports that he is halfway through the book and has written the "crucial chapter"; although he had hoped he would have finished more, thinking he could "change the working habits" of "his modest lifetime and just 'write it roughly,'" he admitted that "it's still the same laborious process of getting page 1 in order before going on to page 2." In the same letter, he announced that *Sun in Capricorn* was going to be different stylistically: "It's certainly the most restrained writing I have ever done. Gosh the way I've slaved to get a paragraph into a line; to picture a scene in a paragraph. But it's good: that I know. And I have just made up my mind, sans any emotion or rhetoric—not to let it go until I have satisfied myself that it is as good as I can make it. I believe in everything I do—you know that. But this belief in this book is, or so I like to think, more sober and critical."[22]

Basso's concern for style may have been his only worry for *Sun in Capricorn*. The novel's subject, Huey Long, was colorful enough for the in-

22. Basso to Etolia S. Basso, February 28, 1942, March 2, 15, 1941, in Basso Papers, BL.

triguing political novel he intended to write. Basso's first impression of Huey Long occurred when he, as a young reporter, met Long during the Louisiana governor's race. Like many Louisianians, Basso was taken in by Long's hillbilly rhetoric: "I liked his similes and metaphors derived from the barnyard and the cornfield. . . . They understood him and liked him. I liked him too." Long's ability to sway an audience and his promises of new highways, bridges, lower gas and electricity rates, and free schoolbooks had widespread appeal in the poverty-stricken state. In 1928 Long was elected governor and Basso approved: "I thought that here was a young and forceful radical it would be well to support." After the corruption and abuse of Louisiana's oil barons, Long promised change, and he kept to his campaign promises: he improved infrastructure, dropped utility rates, abolished poll taxes, and taxed large corporations. In Basso's words, Long was the "first politician to win an enormous following by virtue of his attacks upon the evils and inequalities of our present social order."[23]

Although Basso was initially impressed by Long's social reforms, he grew disenchanted when the governor built a formidable political machine in order to gain complete control over the state legislature. Soon after the 1928 elections, the progressive reformer transformed into an absolutist megalomaniac. Basso was quick to pick up on the danger of Long, who had already begun planning his entrée to the U.S. Senate and the White House. Worrying about Long's eye on the presidency, Basso eventually compared him to Hitler and Mussolini: "Once Mr. Long reaches the White House we shall be living under a dictatorship. . . . If this sounds like an alarmist statement, I ask only that you remember the way democratic processes have been flouted in Louisiana. . . . Mr. Long has power equal to that of Hitler's."[24]

As Long climbed the political ladder, Basso's criticism became more inflammatory and emotional. After being kicked out of Long's hotel room by the National Guard, an incident he proudly referred to in both *Harper's* and the *New Republic*, Basso became increasingly resentful, and his epithets for Long changed from "young and forceful radical" to "clown," "paranoiac," "superman," "demagogue," "fascist," "dic-

23. Hamilton Basso, "Huey Long and His Background," *Harper's*, CLXX (May 1935), 663–73; Basso, "The 'Y' in Huey Long," *New Republic*, May 29, 1935, p. 177.

24. Hamilton Basso, "Der Führer and the Kingfish," *New Republic*, August 4, 1941, p. 163; Basso, "Huey Long and His Background," 673.

tator," and "Lucifer." In Basso's last article on Long, which appeared nine years after the senator's death, his harsh opinion had not mellowed: "I saw him . . . as a stripped-down example of the dictatorial idea whose only equipment was a brutal energy and the ability to sway thousands of people by the sound that rhetoric makes."[25]

Long after the senator's assassination, Basso would alert his readership whenever a new Long figure emerged. One such figure was Eugene Talmadge. Governor of Georgia from 1926 to 1946, Talmadge, or "Farmer Gene" as he was nicknamed, thrived on Long's political platform of agrarianism, populism, and religious fundamentalism. When he became a leading figure in southern politics and began to challenge Roosevelt, Basso warned against his divisionary tactics: "Talmadge is the first man in our history to declare for the presidency on a platform of hate—hatred of radicals, hatred of reform and, lowest and most despicable of all, hatred of the Negro."[26]

Long's heritage had left its mark on Louisiana, too. Pointing out that Long's henchmen had become the state's officers, Basso wrote that a "dictator [had] gone but the dictatorship" remained. In another *New Republic* article, Basso called for punishment of the corrupt mayor of New Orleans, Robert Maestri, and his two accomplices and Long heirs, Seymour Weiss and Richard Leche. Always favoring a mediating role of the federal government, he appealed to Washington for help: "A great deal of what is rotten in Louisiana will have to be cleaned up locally; but the federal government, if it finally means business, can help a lot."[27]

Basso's Long commentary covers more than a decade (1934–46). Whenever there appeared a new Huey Long book, Basso was the *New Republic* authority to review it. His importance as a Long critic has not gone unnoticed. Robert E. Snyder remarks that in the late twenties and early thirties, "Hamilton Basso stood, along with Hodding Carter,

25. As for the hotel room incident, described in the *New Republic*, of February 20, 1935, p. 41, Basso wrote, "I call Mr. Long my friend only because of our long acquaintance with each other. He once had me ushered out of his hotel room and once I was arrested by his National Guard" (Hamilton Basso, "The Huey Long Legend," *Life*, December 9, 1946, p. 109).

26. Hamilton Basso, "Our Gene," *New Republic*, February 19, 1936, p. 36.

27. Hamilton Basso, "The Death and Legacy of Huey Long," *New Republic*, January 1, 1936, p. 218; Basso, "Huey Long's Heritage," *New Republic*, August 30, 1939, p. 100.

Hilda Phelps Hammond, W. D. Robinson, and a host of others, at the forefront of those Louisianans who honestly and wholeheartedly believed that Huey Long's burgeoning power represented an abominable challenge to democratic concepts and institutions." In addition, Snyder notes that of these four, Basso was "the only one to openly and consistently grind his ideological axe against Longism." Based on Basso's extended coverage of (and initial respect for) Long, the critic Ladell Payne even went so far as to suggest that Basso might have been the model for Jack Burden in Robert Penn Warren's *All the King's Men*. And Russell B. Long, Huey's son, was so weary of Basso's swipes at his father, and in particular his profile of Long in *Life* magazine, that he wrote "In Defense of My Father," which was read in the U.S. Senate by Senator John Overton of Louisiana: "No man of our time has been more abused, vilified and misrepresented by the American press . . . than my father . . . he has been accused of being a ruthless dictator who would have destroyed our system of democratic government as well as with the charge as a noisy low-grade rabble rouser."[28]

But Huey Long did not only mesmerize the media. He is probably the most written-about governor in the American political novel: the forties saw the publication of four Huey Long novels, Basso's *Sun in Capricorn* (1942), John Dos Passos' *Number One* (1943), Adria Locke Langley's *A Lion Is in the Streets* (1945), and Warren's *All the King's Men*. While Louis D. Rubin, Jr., has written an extensive comparative analysis of these novels, here I will interpret *Sun in Capricorn* against the background of Basso's other works and his lifelong crusade against Longism.[29]

The story of *Sun in Capricorn* is similar to that of *Cinnamon Seed*. Like Dekker, the novel's protagonist, Hazzard, is orphaned at an early age and adopted by his Uncle Thomas and Aunt Caroline. Like Dekker, too, Hazzard is a shiftless character who has no ambitions and finally quits his uncle's law firm to become a full-time farmer. Hazzard's an-

---

28. Robert E. Snyder, "The Concept of Demagoguery: Huey Long and his Literary Critics," *Louisiana Studies*, XV (1976), 81; Ladell Payne, "Willie Stark and Huey Long: Atmosphere, Myth or Suggestion," in *Twentieth-Century Interpretations of "All the King's Men*," ed. Robert H. Chambers (Englewood Cliffs, N.J., 1977), 112; *Congressional Record*, Senate, 80th Cong., 1st Sess., 1947, XCIII, Pt. I, 438.

29. Louis D. Rubin, Jr., "All the King's Meanings," in Rubin, *The Curious Death of the Novel: Essays in American Literature* (Baton Rouge, 1967), 224–26.

tagonist is Gilgo Slade, an exaggerated version of *Cinnamon Seed*'s Harry Brand. As in Basso's 1934 novel, in which the Blackheaths' fate is inversely proportional to Brand's rise, in *Sun in Capricorn* the downfall of Hazzard's family is intertwined with Slade's rise. As Hazzard jokes: "Gilgo Slade was the central planet in our modest solar system. We told time by him as it were" (*S*, 40). Ironically, the day that Slade announces his candidacy for the U.S. Senate, Hazzard breaks the news that he wants to leave the law profession to raise mules.

While the novel has an undertone of mockery, which is primarily due to Hazzard's ridicule of Slade and his overall cynical view, the book is committed to a suspenseful plot. When Hazzard falls in love with a married woman, Erin, he gives Slade the opportunity to do some mudslinging against his uncle, who also happens to be Slade's political opponent in the race for the Senate. Though Hazzard and Erin try to escape the public's notice, the damage has already been done, the loudmouthed Slade yelling over the radio that his opponent's nephew is running around with a whore. The novel's climax, which because of its carnivalesque atmosphere is somewhat reminiscent of the Mardi Gras parade in *Days Before Lent*, occurs when Hazzard and Erin get stuck in the traffic accompanying Slade's roadshow. Cornered by a policeman who wants to arrest Erin for violating the moral code, Hazzard tries to find a way out by conceiving the madcap idea of murdering Slade. Before he can actually do so, Slade is assassinated by Quentin, Hazzard's cousin and Thomas' son. Like Long's assassin, Quentin is murdered by Slade's bodyguards, and just as there were speculations as to why Carl Weiss committed his crime, so are there all sorts of rumors as to what Quentin's motive might have been, until finally the papers decide that he "had been temporarily insane and killed Gilgo in the unfortunate belief that he was avenging the family honor" (*S*, 264). The book ends with a conversation between two men who wonder whether Slade was "the greatest man since Jesus Christ" or simply "a smart bastard" (*S*, 266). According to Snyder, this conversation fixes "in broad outline, the dichotomous conceptual framework from which all evaluations of Longism, literary as well as historical, have traditionally been constructed."[30]

While basing Slade on Huey Long's character and behavior, Basso

---

30. Snyder, "The Concept of Demagoguery," 81.

tends toward exaggeration, preferring grotesque caricature to realistic depiction. Slade's physical deformity—his mouth "must have been a foot wide" and his left foot has only three toes (S, 66)—is a manifestation of his mental deformation. Slade, like Long, is a conspicuous public figure who draws attention to himself by violating conventional standards of dress and acting outrageously. As the Long historian Alan Brinkley notes: "Long remembered the value of buffoonery in winning national press attention during his term as governor. Once again, he played the clown: receiving the press in his hotel room wearing lavender silk pajamas; insisting that potlikker be added to the menu in the Senate dining room; wearing flamboyant pink shirts, purple ties and white suits to the Capitol."[31] Long's pajamas episode is recounted in both *Sun in Capricorn* and *Cinnamon Seed*. In *Sun in Capricorn*, the hotel room reception assumes a fantastic, kermis-like air. The room is filled with eccentric cocktail-drinking people who all wait for Slade to appear. When he finally does, the crowd is hushed, for Slade is wearing "a green silk dressing-gown and matching bedroom slippers that flapped against his naked heels" (S, 79). Underlining the vulgarity of the scene, Hazzard takes note of Slade's indifference to the fact that "certain intimate parts of his body were almost completely exposed" (S, 88). Harry Brand, Basso's earlier representation of Long, is marked by a similar lack of sophistication and manners. Not only does he wear "flashy neckties" and receive a French battleship crew in his nightshirt, but also like Long, he champions "corn-pone and pot-liquor as man's highest gastronomical achievement."

The ingenious psychology of Long's campaign speeches, carnivalesque parades, and the ballyhoo of his circuslike shows have been vividly recreated in the book. While Snyder praised this aspect of the novel, writing that *Sun in Capricorn* "tells us a great deal about the concept of demagoguery and the minds of the people who use it," Gordon Milne thought Basso's power lay in his portrayal of Long's "superb evangelism and common touch as well as his unbridled ambition and underhanded strategy." One of the novel's reviewers, Gwen Bristow, was equally impressed, noting that Slade's campaigning sent shivers down her spine: "[Basso] writes so vividly that anybody who

31. Alan Brinkley, *Voices of Protest: Huey Long, Father Coughlin, and the Great Depression* (New York, 1982), 42.

remembers those wild campaigns cannot read these descriptions without a reminiscent shiver." In a letter to Cowley, Basso wrote that *Sun in Capricorn* meant to unveil the dynamics of dictatorship: "The leader, the group-insignia, the sinister associates, the hollow hanger-ons, the worshipful dispossessed lower-middle class mass—they are all there. . . . I sure in hell was not interested in writing a novel just about Huey Long."[32]

A political nightmare come true, *Sun in Capricorn*'s neurotic vision may have been fed by Basso's distress while writing parts of the book in Florida: the world seemed to be coming apart with Hitler's successful occupation of Europe and the Japanese bombing of Pearl Harbor, and Basso's private world was coming undone, too. The state of mind induced by fatigue and haunting marital problems may have fueled Hazzard's cynicism and the novel's paranoid vision of a democracy turned police state.

Though Basso conveys Long's reign of terror masterfully, Slade's character is flat and empty. He is no more than a looming background presence, and his physical disfigurement—his toes having been accidentally chopped off and then snatched away by a hungry cat—endows him with the kind of grotesque absurdity characterizing the maimed characters of O'Connor and McCullers. If one is to read *Sun in Capricorn* as an ambitious literary work, Slade's one-dimensionality and physical absurdity cripple the novel. In the same way, Hazzard never develops into a round, convincing character. Despite his strong point of view, he is overly passive and weak. Caught up in the simple plot of "man falls in love with woman and becomes the victim of a calumnious political campaign," Hazzard's colorless character turns the novel into a straightforward action novel, a novel of suspense, or, to use Louis Rubin's phrase, "a cheap thriller."[33]

32. Both Basso and Warren borrowed from Long's campaign speeches; Long's "The people . . . and not Huey Long, rule the State" is remarkably similar to Stark's "You are the state. You know what you need" (*All the King's Men*, 110). Compare also Willie's "Look at your pants. Have they got holes in the knees?" (110) to Slade's "How many of you good people have ONE suit of clothes?" (*S*, 254–55). Snyder, "The Concept of Demagoguery," 83; Gordon Milne, *The American Political Novel* (Norman, Okla., 1966), 133; Gwen Bristow, "Gilgo Slade of Louisiana," *Saturday Review of Literature*, September 18, 1942, p. 16; Basso to Cowley, June 12, 1942, in Cowley Papers, NL.

33. Rubin, "All the King's Meanings," in Rubin, *The Curious Death of the Novel*, 225.

In view of the novel's weaknesses, and especially when compared with *All the King's Men*, there remains little to be said for what one may well call Basso's worst novel. However, as an attempt to lampoon an important episode in Louisiana's political history, *Sun in Capricorn* has some documentary value. The extremity of the novel can best be ascribed to Basso getting carried away by the Long phenomenon after he had warned against the dangers of Long in article after article. Thus one should not judge the work as an ambitious piece of fiction but acknowledge, with Snyder, that the novel's political significance outweighs the book's gravest flaws.

Finally, *Sun in Capricorn* should be seen as a clear departure from *Wine of the Country*. Where the latter was supposed to blend the novel of ideas with intense psychological drama, *Sun in Capricorn* was not going to have the "emotion or rhetoric" but would be "sober and critical." Basso wrote Perkins that he was trying to "tell this story simply, simply: no introversions, no long passages of philosophical comment: let that be there, unwritten, between the lines."[34] Accordingly, there are no flashbacks, there is no editorializing, and there is no commentary about the South. Instead, we have a rapidly paced story and dialogue marked by a remarkable prosaic sobriety. Regardless of the view of Louis Rubin, who spurned the novel from a purely aesthetic point of view and discarded the work as a "slight affair" and "indifferent art," *Sun in Capricorn* does not pretend to be a great work of art but is a caustic caricature of southern populism and demagoguery.

Because Basso's work required him to be in New York more often and because he wanted to keep his job but "his family too," he asked Perkins, who lived in New Canaan, Connecticut, whether he should consider moving to New Canaan or nearby Westport. The family finally settled in Weston, Connecticut, and moved into "an old two-story frame house with a barn and eight acres of land." Because the house was far from the railroad station, whence many Westonians commuted to their jobs in New York City, it was relatively cheap. Van Wyck Brooks and his wife, Elinor, who already resided in Weston, had helped them find the place. Brooks first met Basso in 1942. At the time,

---

34. Basso to Etolia S. Basso, March 15, 1942, in Basso Papers, BL; Basso to Perkins, February 15, 1942, in SA.

he was so charmed by Basso that he told Ellen Glasgow about the Louisiana novelist. In reply, she remarked that Basso was "one of the very few younger Southern novelists whose prose had distinction."[35]

Soon after the Bassos moved to Connecticut, Elinor Brooks fell ill and died. The Bassos tried to console Brooks and invited him over for dinner frequently. This was greatly appreciated by Brooks, who, whenever the Bassos went traveling, would keep them up to date in postcard after postcard. Basso reciprocated the correspondence when Brooks traveled. These letters convey various impressions of life in Connecticut and Keith's upbringing. Looking back on his childhood, Keith remembered his father as a genuine friend. Although Basso was very disciplined about his writing schedule, withdrawing mornings and afternoons, he took time to teach his son how to fish, play baseball, and do chores around the house and garden. He also encouraged Keith to read, was interested in what he had read, and stimulated his reading of the newspaper. Keith rebelled against the reading schedule set up for him, and, years later, when he excelled at Harvard, Basso recalled his son's recalcitrance in a letter to his wife: "Do you remember those days when he wouldn't 'read' and I used to say that if we were very lucky he might someday catch fire?"[36]

Keith recalled only one incident of discipline. After a visit to the hardware store, the ten-year-old boy proudly showed his dad a faucet that he had snatched off the shelves. Basso grew silent, took his son into the woods, broke off a stick, and spanked the boy—according to Keith, "the only time he ever hit me." While Toto corrected the small errors in her son's life, Basso waited for the big mistakes to occur, such as Keith's decision to study journalism. Having seen too much of journalism himself, Basso dissuaded his son, who became an anthropology professor instead.

Though Keith was fully aware of his father's writing career, Basso never talked about his work or invited his son to read and comment on his novels. Yet Keith did notice the spells of depression and quiet when the writing was not going well. In addition, there was his father's self-effacement and refusal to take himself and his writing seriously. In an

35. Basso to Perkins, June 5, 1943, in SA; Ikerd, "Hamilton Basso," 109; Van Wyck Brooks to Basso, July 28, 1943, in Basso Papers, BL.

36. Keith H. Basso, interview with the author; Basso to Etolia S. Basso, June 15, 1960, in Basso Papers, BL.

interview with the *Herald Tribune*, Basso underscored that sentiment with the following comment: "It has always puzzled me how the notion got started that authors are interesting people. Think what happens—a man germinates an idea, he sits on it for months, rarely moving from the incubator, and in creation's own time, if luck and persistence are with him, he hatches out a book. A subwayman's life is livelier by far." Being extremely modest, Basso disliked displays of pride in others, and a diligent worker himself who would rewrite a whole page "if a single word seemed wrong," he did not want to be around people who showed off. Convinced that "nothing worthwhile in life comes easy," he also distrusted people who did not talk about the difficulty with which they had accomplished something.[37]

For this reason also Basso continued to be annoyed with intellectuals, critics, and literary people. Brooks, who was ill at ease with the neighborhood's literary gatherings, was delighted to have found a kindred spirit: "I am glad to hear that you have escaped the fashionable circles of the Lyons Plains Road . . . we made rather a policy of keeping out of things, when we first went to Westport, and I cannot quite regret it but it gives one a feeling, in the end, that one doesn't belong anywhere." The correspondence between the two men can be described as warm and mutually ingratiating. Compared to his tough-minded correspondence of the thirties, Basso's letters to Brooks are pleasant and soft-spoken. They reveal a smooth and natural style, which Brooks characterized rather appropriately as Basso's "charming air of casualness"—the hallmark, too, of his writing for *Life* and *Holiday*.[38]

Besides get-togethers with Brooks, who on one of his birthdays crawled underneath a table when his guests started loudly singing "Happy Birthday," the Bassos saw much of Malcolm and Muriel Cowley, the painter Peter Blume and his wife, Ebie, and the writer Peter de Vries and his wife, Katinka. Keith remembered the Connecticut crowd vividly, mostly because he was dragged along and was bored while the adults talked. Recalling Peter Blume's studio as one of the more exciting places to visit because of all the paintings, Keith was most im-

37. Hamilton Basso, "Some Important Fall Authors Speak for Themselves: Hamilton Basso, Up from New Orleans," *New York Herald Tribune Book Review*, October 24, 1954, p. 4; Malcolm Cowley, typescript notes for Basso's eulogy, in Cowley Papers, NL; Keith H. Basso, interview with the author.

38. Brooks to Basso, February 19, 1945, August 31, 1960, in Basso Papers, BL.

pressed with Malcolm Cowley's joviality. Like his father, Cowley was interested in what Keith was reading, and when Keith expressed his enthusiasm for Hemingway's fisherman stories, Cowley disappointed the boy by remarking that Hemingway was perhaps not such a great fisherman at all.

The Bassos also kept up with friends from the past, like the critic Edmund Wilson and the playwright Lillian Hellman. Basso knew Hellman from New Orleans. Like the Bassos, she had moved to Connecticut, and together with her partner Dashiell Hammett, she entertained the Bassos on a number of occasions. While Toto remembered meeting an inebriated and wickedly witty Dorothy Parker there, Keith recalled the brand-new crossbow that Hammett allowed him to play with. Upon leaving, the Bassos found the crossbow in their car trunk, and when they protested that Keith could not accept such a gift, Hammett reassured them, saying that some things should belong to the people who really want them.

While Basso kept his network of literary friends going, he was not drawn to the literary scene per se and found more satisfaction in serving on the local school board. At the same time, life was perhaps a little too dull; compared to the rural and mountain discomforts of the thirties, life in Connecticut was convenient but also suburbanly subdued. Missing the stimulation of his peers, Basso confided in Brooks: "The number of people worth talking to seem[s] to get fewer and fewer year by year." In the same letter Basso complained about the severe winter, which besides slowing down the building of his outdoor study, delayed his writing: "Just wrote a couple of short stories, the first pieces of fiction since 1941." Because of his breakdown in 1942 and an illness that was finally diagnosed as an adrenalin deficiency in 1945, Basso felt like "the wind" had been taken "out of his sails." In a letter to Van Wyck Brooks of December 22, 1945, Basso mentions this condition for the first time: "And so along with 3/4 of the other people who inhabit the American Dream, I'm taking pills [and get] little work done." The medication worked, however, for Toto reported in a letter to Brooks that his pills made Basso "like he was years ago, chirpy and whistley, bright eyed etc."[39]

39. Basso to Brooks, January 29, December 22, 1945, in Brooks Papers, PP; Etolia S. Basso to Brooks, January 8, 1946, in Brooks Papers, PP.

According to Malcolm Cowley, there was a remarkable slackening in Basso's production after 1943; always having been a cautious writer, he became "excessively careful," feeling "a continual need to challenge himself, to prove himself, to surpass himself." Cowley probably based this comment on a letter of 1947 in which Basso told his friend that his new novel, *The Greenroom* (1949), was "crawling" along: "It's bad when the creative and critical lobes are working at the same time. And then too, there is my increasing reluctance to publish—my indifference really. . . . I can't see the point of publishing another novel. The bilge we get these days! So it has to be good enough, in itself, to be a protest against the bilge." His opening of a *New Yorker* book review with "Nobody is going to be so foolish as to argue that the novel is flourishing particularly these days, because it just isn't," may well have been a reflection of his own writer's block. Basso's perfectionism often hampered his writing. As Cowley remembered; "He worked with difficulty, and usually produced five or six drafts of a work before bringing it to his publisher." He set the same high writing standards for his son. One day, when Keith presented his father with an essay for which he had received an A, Basso, upset with the essay's sloppy prose, crumpled it up and placed Keith in a private school. "Language was important in our family and to be used with care," Keith recalled in an interview of 1992. Basso's precision, fondness for language, and intense devotion to proper usage was also mentioned at his funeral, when one of his friends observed that he "died without writing a slipshod sentence."[40]

In the winter of 1947 Basso revisited New Orleans. Showered with attention from old friends, Basso felt like a "debutante." Although moving back to New Orleans seemed a constant temptation to the Bassos, they decided against it every time they returned to the city. Besides their belief that one simply cannot go home again, they thought the place unsuitable for Keith. Perhaps it was his father's death a year earlier that made Basso's 1947 visit take on a sentimental hue: climbing the tower of the cathedral that was such a landmark in his first novel, Basso looked out over the city and walked by the "house where I was born, black and empty and deserted, all my childhood at the bottom of a well." As always, the trip inspired his writing, or as he wrote his wife: "I am getting bigger on the inside with my novel; if I don't start giving birth soon, I may pop."[41]

The Greenroom was finally finished in 1949, six years after the nonfiction work *Mainstream* and seven years after *Sun in Capricorn*. The time lag between *The Greenroom* and Basso's earlier work is significant, for with this novel Basso abandoned his often-used formula of the intelligent young southerner coming to terms with himself and life in the small town. The protagonist, Rufus Jackson, is not even a southerner but a young man from Arizona, a state the Bassos had explored on a number of trips in the forties. The novel is not set in the South, either, but takes place in Europe. In Basso's only "international" novel, the reader finds himself in a village in Provence that bears a strong resemblance to St. Paul de Vence, where the Bassos had lived for a few months in the late thirties. The novel is also set in the late thirties; like the Bassos who left Europe as soon as the war became imminent, Rufus leaves when the Germans invade Austria.

Unlike Basso's earlier heroes, whose family history is revealed as the story unfolds, Rufus remains a blank. All we know is that he is a young widower who has a daughter. A failed playwright, Rufus is an assistant editor at a large publishing house. Overworked, as was Basso in the early forties, Rufus vacations in France and is kindly requested by his editor Charlie Shannon, who greatly resembles Charles or "Charlie" Scribner, to find out if the famous American and Nobel Prize–winning novelist Mrs. Porter is still working on her memoirs. The protagonist's mission to probe the affairs of a famous and virtually inaccessible author would be recycled in *The View from Pompey's Head*. While the young man's encounter with the novelist may have been inspired by Basso's meeting of the Nobel laureate Sigrid Undset, the actual confrontation with Mrs. Porter could have been modeled on Basso's dealings with Mrs. Wolfe: after Thomas Wolfe's death, Perkins had asked Basso to find out if the Wolfe family held any of the writer's papers. At the same time, Mrs. Porter is unmistakably based on the grande dame of American letters, Edith Wharton.

41. Basso to Etolia S. Basso, February 2, 1947, in Basso Papers, BL.

Already upon Rufus' first visit it becomes clear that Mrs. Porter is a difficult woman. When Rufus inquires about her memoirs, she answers evasively that it is "a question of writing truly" (*G*, 37), a statement that leaves him bewildered. Fortunately, he learns from Nora Marsh, the English girl staying with Mrs. Porter, that her work is in progress. Nora is unhappily married to Mrs. Porter's nephew, an alcoholic and would-be artist, Charles. Overly protective of Charles, Mrs. Porter has decided to save his marriage.

Rufus falls in love with Nora and consequently faces Mrs. Porter's antagonism and foul temper. On the night that Rufus and Nora decide to marry as soon as she settles the divorce, Charles shoots himself in the shoulder, an accident that Mrs. Porter uses to accuse Rufus and Nora of driving her nephew to suicide. Although Rufus finds out that it was really a drunken accident and realizes that Mrs. Porter is a pathetic old woman who conjures one lie after another, he cannot persuade Nora to come with him to America. Her feelings of guilt, the call of wifely duty, and her decision to stay with Charles after he promises to better his life preclude a happy ending. The open ending saves the novel from falling to the level of the supermarket romance, yet at the same time Nora's self-sacrificial role, which is typical of the Basso female, is melodramatic.

The Greenroom proves once more that Basso was successful neither in handling romance nor in portraying females his own age. Older women, however, like Mrs. Porter and the Princess de Cloville, and, in the early novels, characters like Aunt Olivia and Celia, are sharply drawn and intriguing. Like Edith Wharton, Mrs. Porter spends her old age in a French mansion, and like the great novelist, she inhabits a past with which Rufus is unfamiliar. Having published her first novel around the turn of the century, she thinks that to people of Rufus' generation, she has come to "represent the same thing as gas lighting, Turkish corners, and silver pheasants with bonbons" (*G*, 32). Like Wharton, too, whose quarrels with her publisher have recently been brought to attention by Mark Aronson's article "Wharton and the House of Scribner: The Novelist as a Pain in the Neck," Mrs. Leslie Porter is blamed by her publisher for always "causing a commotion" (*G*, 68).[42]

42. Mark Aronson, "Wharton and the House of Scribner: The Novelist as a Pain in the Neck," *New York Times Book Review*, January 2, 1994, pp. 7–8.

Van Wyck Brooks was particularly impressed with the Porter character: "What a feat it was to paint and not paint Edith Wharton, to create an entirely different person who was yet teasingly like the woman with the 'small cold heart' . . . Your Mrs. Porter goes right on living long after one has read the book." The playwright S. N. Behrman thought Mrs. Porter was based on Somerset Maugham, who also had a house in the south of France. Interestingly, Basso did a *New Yorker* profile of Maugham and probably used the author's aloofness as an inspiration for Mrs. Porter: "[Maugham] lives behind walls—a wall of reserve, a wall of gentlemanliness, a wall of exquisite good manners. No one has ever been able to penetrate the barriers he has erected between himself and the world."[43]

Besides Mrs. Porter's coldness, her lack of charity, her evil machinations, her interference in other people's lives, and her desire for building walls around her mansion and herself, she exhibits a "fondness for drama" befitting an actress who prepares herself for the "big scene" (G, 147). Rufus notices Mrs. Porter's theatrical inclinations the moment he meets her; observing that "she likes to hold the centre of the stage," he perceives her apparent distress after Charles's pseudo-suicide as a pretense: " 'Act III, Scene II,' his mind said sarcastically. 'The big final scene' . . . He recalled the opening line of what was generally considered her finest book, The Chronicles of Catherine. It was perhaps the most famous line she had ever written: 'She began each day with a rehearsal, closeted in the greenroom of her soul' " (G, 63, 247).

The stage metaphor is a favorite of Basso's; he used it extensively in *In Their Own Image*. However, while the metaphor in that book was used as a means for the rich to shut themselves off from the realities of the poor, in *The Greenroom*, Mrs. Porter resorts to drama to conceal the essentially empty life she leads. She is a *"farceur,"* Rufus decides, "not a jester or buffoon . . . but in the sense of one who habitually indulges in mystifications . . . her life was more tragically empty than he would have ever believed" (G, 250–51). Though a great writer and a successful artist, Mrs. Porter has failed as a human being. Her personal life is marked by a "lack and want of love." She tries yet fails to make up for this lack by clinging to Charles. In the end, she alienates not only Rufus

---

43. Brooks to Basso, August 26, 1949, in Basso Papers, BL; Hamilton Basso, "A Very Old Party—I," *New Yorker*, December 30, 1944, p. 24.

and Nora, but also the people—Charles and Philip Lennox, her estranged lover, who comes to prefer his coin collection to her—with whom she hoped to spend the rest of her days. As in a Hollywood drama by Eric von Stroheim, Mrs. Porter is ultimately left brooding in her mansion surrounded by a staff of gray-haired servants.

The Princess de Cloville, with whom Rufus builds up a warm and enriching relationship, is the antitype of Mrs. Porter. Though she looks like an ugly "cleaning woman," a description that deflates Rufus' romanticized idea of the European aristocracy, she has authority and charm. Unlike Mrs. Porter, who accumulated fame and fortune through her art, the princess squandered her family fortune by gambling, a game of oblivion she indulges in to make herself forget she is no longer young and "fit for love" (*G*, 166). Notwithstanding the princess' promiscuous past and a life that knows neither achievements nor success, she is a loving human being who faithfully stays at the deathbed of her lover, the Marquis de Vernay, and who lends a sympathetic ear to Rufus' problems.

In his discussion of *The Greenroom*, Joseph Millichap paid some attention to the Jamesian framework of the novel. The premise of the innocent American who gains his maturity once he is exposed to the ways and whims of the Old World is germinally present in the book. The French peasant in the town square, who harps on the essential "immaturity" of Americans, underscores this idea, as does the misbehaving and "ugly American" Spike Carruthers. Millichap goes so far as to argue that the idea of *The Greenroom* may have actually been inspired by Henry James's *The American* (1877): Millichap believes that like Christopher Newman, Rufus Jackson is prevented by the family from marrying the woman of his dreams. But whereas Christopher is unable to decipher the codes of the French family, the de Bellegardes, Rufus must face not a family but a single woman who is not even European but American. Furthermore, although Rufus does play the innocent American when it comes to regarding "anything over a hundred years old as one of the relics of antiquity" (*G*, 121) and to having romanticized perceptions of European nobility, he is by no means the impressionable young man that Christopher Newman is.

On the contrary, having lost his wife and exhibiting a profound sense of responsibility as a parent, Rufus is a dependable character who has none of the immaturity for which his countrymen are blamed.

To bring out his good behavior and decency, the narrator sets him off against the boisterous Spike Carruthers. Compared to Carruthers, Rufus is decent to the point of dullness. Also, his passive behavior vis-à-vis the manipulative Mrs. Porter and his stoical resignation after he has given up Nora do not ring true. An explanation for his impassivity may be sought in the fact that we never really get to know him. Whereas Tony, Dekker, David, and Jason have all been rounded out by their family history, flashbacks, and the exposition of their ideas, Rufus' portrait lacks such illumination. Hence, he is slightly colorless and flat. Because Rufus is neither a strong character nor a convincing innocent abroad, the supposed clash of cultures does not truly materialize. Consequently, it is difficult to see the novel in terms of a "Jamesian lesson that the New World is fallen as well as the Old, [and] that the American Adam must experience this fall in order to discover his mature place in life"; in the end, Rufus simply gets on with life, and though looking back sentimentally, he does not—like Isabel Archer and Christopher Newman—appear to have undergone a profound change of character or to have learnt "his lesson."[44]

Where does this leave us in our final estimate of the novel? Both Ikerd's and Millichap's praise seems inflated. Although the novel is tightly plotted and the characterization of Mrs. Porter one of its strongest points, the book is shallow and commercial in its orientation. With *The Greenroom*, Basso's oeuvre clearly took a new turn. Moving away from the serious subject matter of his thirties novels, Basso headed for fixed-formula *Trivialliteratur*. He replaced the southern setting and southern hero with an altogether different milieu and protagonist, and omitted his customary editorializing and flashbacks to rely solely on straightforward narration. The social realism and consciousness-raising of the early novels made way for romance and mystery, and as such, *The Greenroom* is the crossroads at which Basso's southern *Bildungsroman* changed into a version of the popular mystery and detective novel.

To be sure, Basso's inclination toward popular literature was something he was not fully aware of himself, and one may suggest that both the death of Maxwell Perkins and the author's transfer to Doubleday, a more commercially minded publisher than Scribner's, pushed him in

44. Millichap, *Hamilton Basso*, 97.

the direction of the belletristic novel. In letters to Charles Scribner and his new editor at Doubleday, Basso would complain that he missed the sensitive supervision of Perkins and that all publishers were really only interested in sales. While in the early years Basso would aim his ammunition at the intellectuals of his day, in later years publishers became his target. Rufus maintained that "publishing was looking for *War and Peace* and hoping to come across another *Gone with the Wind*. Publishing was too much talk . . . too many cocktails, too many experts, too many people who wanted advances, and too many young women who thought they were celebrities because they once sat four tables away from James Thurber or Ernest Hemingway" (*G*, 31). These comments, as well as Mrs. Porter's condemnation of the commercial interests of publishers ("a book has become as much a commodity as a sack of potatoes" [*G*, 140]), truthfully reflect Basso's opinion of the publishing trade.

Because the novel sold relatively well and because the majority of the reviewers were taken by the book's charm, its picturesque setting, and the powerful character of Mrs. Porter, *The Greenroom* was considered for dramatization. Basso had initially asked the playwright Samuel Behrman, whom he must have known through the *New Yorker*, to dramatize the novel. Behrman, however, declined. Though he thought the novel "a natural" for a play, he was "too worn out from the theater" to take it on.[45] In the end, the book was converted into a CBS radio play and a television play by the Canadian Broadcasting Company.

For income in the forties, Basso had to resort to journalism for *Time*, the *New Yorker*, and later, *Life* and *Holiday*. Although he liked having contact with other writers on the magazines' staffs, he saw journalism as a necessary evil that gobbled up the time he wanted to spend on his novels. Besides writing three rather middling novels during this decade, Basso was wrapped up in the composition of *Mainstream*, his book of essays on American history. Like *Beauregard*, the lively essays reveal Basso's personal slant on such historical figures as Calhoun, Jefferson, Lincoln, Long, and Roosevelt.

In the forties especially, Basso's scattering of his talent over differ-

---

45. Samuel N. Behrman to Basso, November 3, 1949, in Basso Papers, BL.

ent genres of writing did not benefit his novelistic career. Add to that the death of the supportive Maxwell Perkins and we find a dejected Basso, who, in January 1949 had to leave for the Georgia Sea Islands to get away from the "terrible, terrible burden of work" and a "sense of failure" that would not go away. Indeed, his doubts were such that when he went to Los Angeles for *Holiday* in the spring of 1949, he told Toto that he was setting out a few traplines "in case we are ever in need of a beaver."[46] At the same time, he simply could not abandon fiction: in a postscript to the same letter, he told Toto: "I think I want to start another novel: do you mind?" While his novel writing in the forties suffered from a degree of stagnation, his short stories for the *New Yorker* make up for the lag in his longer fiction.

Basso joined the *New Yorker* in 1944. Starting at the bottom of the hierarchy, he contributed to the "Talk of the Town" column but was soon promoted to reviews, profiles, and short stories. Founded in 1925, the *New Yorker* was intended as "smart, sophisticated, irreverent, urbane, and not written for the old lady in Dubuque," or so its founding editor, Harold Ross, maintained. Ross's nitpicking, rude, flamboyant, yet brilliant editorship turned the *New Yorker* into a high-quality magazine of combined commentary, wit, literature, humor, profiles, travelogues, reviews, and the local news of New York City. Over the years, the magazine managed to attract a great number of talented writers, cartoonists, and critics, and by the time Basso joined the staff, the *New Yorker* "had become the Vatican City of American cultural life." As Bob Gottlieb (the third editor, who succeeded William Shawn in 1987) remarks, "It came to be that if the New Yorker said it, it was so."[47]

When Shawn took over from Ross in 1952, the magazine's slant changed slightly, to a more serious vein. Accordingly, the magazine came to defend "the environment [and] eloquently condemned bias and hatred." Also, attuned to the Cold War climate, Shawn's *New Yorker* "made clear to readers that the proliferation of atomic weapons was suicidal." Although William Shawn's shy, gentle personality differed immensely from Ross's, he was equally gifted and carried on what had become the *New Yorker* tradition. According to Etolia Basso,

46. Basso to Etolia S. Basso, January 24, March 25, 1949, in Basso Papers, BL.
47. Robert McCrum, "The New Corker!" *Guardian Weekly,* October 11, 1992, p. 19.

her husband was very impressed with Shawn's editorial skill, which Brendan Gill remembered by its "silences, hesitations, sidelong glances of [Shawn's] very blue eyes [and] tentative baton-like strokes in the air of his dark-green Venus drawing pencil." And Joseph Epstein writes that "writers who worked under [Shawn] felt a fealty toward him of a kind owed to a kindly, tolerant, and wise father. . . . He did everything possible to make writers feel stability in their working lives. Once he was committed to a writing project, he stayed committed."[48]

As for the ambience of the *New Yorker* offices, both Philip Hamburger and Joseph Mitchell recall that at the time that Basso was involved with the magazine, there was a "familial sense to the place." Mitchell reminisced in an interview how "At the old New Yorker . . . a lot of us would go out to lunch together: Liebling and Perelman and Thurber, who was idiosyncratic and funny. Now everybody goes in and out." Etolia Basso remembers that when her husband and Harold Ross went to lunch one day, they noticed a huddle of three jittery men crossing a busy New York street. The three were E. B. White, James Thurber, and Alexander Woollcott. Upon recognizing them, Ross said: "They are my three best men and they can't even cross a street." Although this anecdote seems to indicate otherwise, from Brendan Gill's complacent *Here at the New Yorker* (1975) one may draw the conclusion that Basso's regular contributions to the magazine did not make him a true insider.[49] This may have had to do with the fact that he did not live in the city but commuted to the office once or twice a week. Another reason may be that Basso was often uncomfortable in the company of other writers.

However, one fellow writer (and fellow townsman) that Basso felt relatively close to was the novelist and humorist Peter de Vries. De Vries, who died in 1993, wrote the following about his relationship with Basso and their work for the magazine:

48. Philip Hamburger, "Thoughts About the New Yorker," *New Leader,* July 13, 1992, p. 11; Brendan Gill, *Here at the New Yorker* (New York, 1975), 11; Joseph Epstein, "Talk of the Town," *Times Literary Supplement,* September 4, 1992, p. 6.

49. Verlyn Klinkenborg, "This Was New York. It Was," *New York Times Book Review,* August 16, 1992, p. 7; Etolia S. Basso, interview with the author, February 18, 1994; Gill, *Here at the New Yorker.*

We first became acquainted in those rabbit warrens at the New Yorker, where we had no editorial connection with the magazine at all. He took the veil as book critic, while also writing stories for "the book" on his own, which I did likewise functioning editorially in the art department: cartoons, captions etc. I can't think of Ham's even imagining such a post for himself. Neither the one nor the other had written a story till we found it published in "the book." I had no idea who his editor was, and don't even now. This miraculous magazine simply appeared, behind all that talent and toil. "Nobody can touch it," Ham once remarked as we roosted at a lunch counter.[50]

Basso's "Profiles"—of playwright Eugene O'Neill, of novelist Somerset Maugham, of artist Charles Prendergast, and of French philosopher Jean Wahl—are penetrating and detailed, but as they were written under the strict and meticulous guidance of Harold Ross, they are virtually interchangeable with those by other writers. The same applies to Basso's book reviews. Unlike his *New Republic* writings, which were much more colored by his own and the magazine's politics, Basso's *New Yorker* pieces had to adhere closely to the magazine's format. The short stories, on the other hand, are delightfully Bassoesque, and it is regrettable that he wrote so few of them.

The six *New Yorker* stories can be classified as hunting and fishing tales, a genre made famous by Hemingway's Nick Adams stories and Faulkner's "The Bear." Significantly, Basso's stories deviate from the conventions of the genre that emphasize the ritual of the hunt, the test of manhood, and the rites of initiation. Instead, the stories demythologize the hunt and criticize the violence involved. Possibly Basso, who was not a great hunter himself and despised any sort of violence, wanted to show that the hunt does not live up to its mythical reputation.

The stories can be divided into groups of two. The first two, "The Age of Fable" and "The Edge of the Wilderness," are autobiographical fishing stories.[51] In the first piece, Peter Maxwell and his six-year-old son Patrick walk through the mountains of North Carolina. Nostalgic

---

50. Peter de Vries, letter to the author, April 2, 1992.

51. Hamilton Basso, "The Age of Fable," *New Yorker*, June 30, 1945, pp. 17–20; Basso, "The Edge of the Wilderness," *New Yorker*, September 20, 1947, pp. 71–75.

for the past, Peter sees himself in the small, climbing figure of his son; the child's avid curiosity about the trout and the old Cherokee Indian they will be meeting on their way reminds him of his own childhood enthusiasm. Patrick obviously pictures the Indian as some figure out of his storybooks at home, and Peter realizes that the boy's expectations may be too high.

When they reach the Indian's hut, the Indian, who is no more than an old man in dirty overalls, warns them that the river does not harbor fish anymore. They travel on to the river, but Patrick wants to go home: disappointed with the appearance of the Indian, who to the boy's mind is "not an Indian" but a "dirty old man," Patrick assumes his father has also lied about the trout. Although Peter tries to rouse his son's interest for the fishing, when he sees that Patrick has stubbornly made up his mind, he decides to leave. At that very moment a huge trout explodes from the water, and although Peter hooks it momentarily, the fish gets away. This event triggers a change of heart in the child. On their way home, he babbles on about the fish they nearly caught and about the real Cherokee Indian they will be passing again. His son's happiness brightens Peter's fortieth birthday, the day on which "the age of fable was past." This story was based on an actual event, for on June 22, 1947, Basso wrote to Malcolm Cowley: "I caught a 12 inch trout the other day. Keith, not to be outdone, went out all by himself the next morning and brought home a [*sic*] 11 inch one. You've never seen a happier boy. One of the reasons for the generations, I am sure, is for all the old emotions to be renewed and discovered again, the bright ones and the dark."

Joseph Millichap explains the story's title, "The Age of Fable," as something that the child ultimately recreates for his father. With Indians no longer looking like Indians and a river that is empty, the age of fable is not past but gains a new dimension thanks to the child's imagination. Although the fishing trip is a failure from the fisherman's point of view, it nonetheless manages to bring father and son closer together. This is also the objective of the hunt in southern culture, the bonding experience between father and son being essentially more important than the actual outcome of the hunt.[52] Most of Basso's hunts are unsuccessful, the hunt being subservient to the lesson the hunter is supposed

52. Wyatt-Brown, *Southern Honor*, 195–96.

to learn. As Hazzard explains to Erin, who objects to deer hunting: "It's not just going out and shooting a deer. It's part of the way you live" (*S*, 126).

In "The Edge of the Wilderness" Patrick Maxwell uses foul language, and in a bedside chat his father explains to him that the difference between corral and ordinary language is that the former should be used only rarely. The story was inspired by the nine-year-old Keith Basso; having spent the summer on an Arizona ranch, the boy told his neighbor in Weston that her cookies were "damn good." Like Patrick's father, Basso reprimanded his son at bedtime. As for Patrick, when he goes out fishing the next day, he catches sunnies only; because he once caught a twelve-inch trout, he is not pleased by small fish anymore. As he gazes into the water, a man approaches him, wading noisily through the river. The two start a conversation, and Patrick asks the man if he has not got any rubber boots. Proudly, the man explains that he does not need any because he is wearing special pants. He asks the boy if he has ever seen such pants, and Patrick says he has not. This pleases the man: "I'm glad you said that . . . Real glad. Because if you'd said you had, then I'd have known you were telling a whopper. And I don't take kindly to boys who tell whoppers. You know why? . . . Because I'm a minister of the Gospel, that's why." The minister then goes on to tell Patrick that he works for the Baptist Church in Piney Knoll, Mississippi, and that his pants can also be used for baptism: "Do you know what I do when I baptize a person? I take him and dunk him under the water and hold him there. He gasps and chokes, he kicks and he thrashes, but I keep him down. Yes sir."

Patrick, who does not like the man's talk, decides to ignore the minister in his baptismal pants and concentrate on his fishing. But the man does not leave, and asks Patrick if there are any fish in the river. Patrick confirms this and tells the man offhandedly that he caught a twelve-inch trout the other day. To the boy's angry frustration, the man does not believe this, but before he can insist he did catch such a big fish, a car stops by the roadside to pick up the minister. As the man climbs ashore, Patrick curses him, using the worst language he can think of: "The old grown-up stinker . . . Calling that pair of pants *baptizing* trousers! As if I'd believe that! . . . And he tried to make out that I was telling a lie, the old goddamn stinking grown-up bastard!" Although Patrick is aware of the promise he made to his father, he also knows "that this was one of the times when ordinary language just wouldn't do."

As with "The Age of Fable," the fishing experience is not about the rites of fishing but teaches us that the adult world is flawed and insincere. The contrast between the disarming spontaneity of the honest child and the hypocrisy of the minister, who preaches to the child that he should not tell any whoppers and then goes on to tell a lie himself, is beautifully ironic. The story's autobiographical overtones—Patrick is based on Keith and the unsympathetic minister may have come forth out of Basso's anticlerical sentiments—add to its authenticity and effect.

The next two stories, "A Kind of Special Gift" and "The Broken Horn," are southern tall tales.[53] The first is the story of the narrator's uncle, Zebulon. Although Uncle Zebulon is not a great hunter, he takes great pride in the dogs he breeds. His favorite dog is Bess. In the barber shop, which harks back to the beauty (and gossip) parlor of Eudora Welty's "Petrified Man," Zebulon likes to brag about Bess's hunting qualities. To Zebulon's horror, Bess falls ill and, together with all his other dogs, dies of rabies. Bess's death breaks Zebulon's heart. He goes out on long walks by himself, and one day, when the narrator meets his uncle in the fields, Zebulon tells him that he has developed a strong sense of smell that is similar to Bess's. Elaborating on how rabbits, quail, and bucks smell, Zebulon tells his nephew that it is a "kind of special gift," which, because it brings him closer to Bess, makes him grieve no longer.

The narrator, who has the naïveté of a child, believes his uncle and tries to improve his own smell, "sniffing his way across pea fields" and encouraging his friend, Booker-T, to do the same. While doing so, they come upon a crowd, led by Uncle Zebulon and his hunting buddy, Major Bedford. Apparently, Zebulon had boasted about his acquired sense of smell in the barber shop, and challenged by one of the shop's patrons, he had decided to prove it and hunt something down. The whole town gathers to watch this spectacle, but before Zebulon can demonstrate his gift, two of his brothers take him home. The next day

53. Hamilton Basso, "A Kind of Special Gift," *New Yorker*, February 4, 1945, pp. 24–27; Basso, "The Broken Horn," *New Yorker*, October 6, 1945, pp. 28–33.

he is sent to Alabama to rest for three months. Returning home, Zebulon resumes his former routine, breeding dogs and going on hunting escapades with the Major. Occasionally, though, the narrator meets his uncle on his country walks and observes that "he would always be standing very still, rapt and absorbed and he seemed to be smelling very hard."

The story has a strong comic element that borders on the grotesque, that popular portraiture device in southern literature.[54] One may further note that once more, Basso's hunt is not the central event of the story. Instead, the hunt and its rituals are mocked. There is no glorification of male courage, no conquest of the wilderness, and no test of masculinity. Rather, we see a somewhat pathetic older man who, mourning his dead dog, imagines he has inherited his pet's keen smell. Although Zebulon's "gift" is fantastic and farcical, the story is not extreme in its grotesqueness but actually rather subtle in its quiet understatement.

The same applies to "The Broken Horn," which has the same setting and characters as "A Kind of Special Gift." However, this time Major Bedford is the protagonist. Bedford, who drives an old Buick, is finally persuaded by his wife to buy a new car. To break it in, the Major, Zebulon, and his nephew go on a hunting expedition. As they are driving along, a deer jumps in front of the car and causes the vehicle to veer into a ditch. Furious over what has been done to his brand-new car, Bedford crawls out and tries to shoot the escaping deer. He misses yet finds a piece of the buck's horn that was broken off in the crash. Holding it in his hand, the Major vows he will kill the buck before the hunting season is over. Thus the Major becomes obsessed with the deer, which for some mysterious reason he does not manage to shoot. Like the bear in Faulkner's story, and like the deer, Old Red, in Basso's *Wine of the Country*, the buck survives onslaught after onslaught, becoming "more a creature of fable than a living thing; no animal, it seemed, had ever possessed so dark and cunning a wisdom before."

Ironically, as the hunting season draws to an end and the Major frantically hunts, the buck is finally killed by a single bullet fired by a

54. Skaggs, *The Folk of Southern Fiction*, 256.

small, thin man who found him nibbling at a plum tree in his back yard. Again, the hunt is demystified, and although the story resembles the conventional hunting story in which an animal becomes almost invincible, the anticipated climax gives way to both the anticlimax of the buck's easy killing and the story's moral that monomaniacal obsessions merely lead to disappointment.

The last two stories are more serious than the others. Both relate the violence of the hunt to the violence of war, and both deal with the hunter's reluctance to kill. "King Rail," a less successful story than "The Wild Turkey," introduces the reader to "railbirding," which is a special kind of bird hunt from boats, practiced mostly in the South.[55] The story is told by one of the guides, who takes people out on the water and positions the boat in places where rails fly up. One day he takes a young man on board. It is the first rail hunt for the young man, who has been in the war in China. As the birds are few, the guide works himself into a sweat to find the best spots for shooting. After two or three shots, the young man comments—much to the irritation of the guide—that it feels like shooting "sparrows from a rickshaw." In what the guide interprets as contempt, the young war veteran empties his gun, and as he does so, an enormous king rail flies up. The guide is boiling inside, knowing that only few men in their lifetime get the chance to shoot a king as big as a rooster. Weeks later, the guide hears from another guide that the young man, who missed his once-in-a-lifetime chance, had not enjoyed the hunt; the guide's hard labor had reminded him too much of the hardworking Chinese. Hence the guide is nicknamed "Gung Ho." The story's linking of the hunt to the war is interesting but perhaps not as effective as the war associations of "The Wild Turkey."

This last story deals with two brothers, Robert and Paul. They are sitting in a blind, waiting for turkeys. As they wait and whisper, it becomes clear that Robert wants his younger brother to shoot a turkey before he goes off to war. At this point, the story appears to move in the direction of the traditional initiation story. Paul, however, is anxious about using his gun because on a previous duck hunt with Robert, he had forgotten to put on his safety catch when climbing over a fence.

55. Hamilton Basso, "King Rail," *New Yorker*, October 18, 1947, pp. 97–103; Basso, "The Wild Turkey," *New Yorker*, March 18, 1944, pp. 25–27.

The gun went off and hit Robert in the leg, which then had to be ampu-tated. While they are waiting for the turkeys, Paul cannot dispel this incident from his thoughts, and when a group of turkeys finally ap-pears, he cannot bring himself to fire: "The explosion would be just like the explosion that tore off Robert's leg, and the turkey would die in its own blood, and for an instant, as Paul squinted down the barrels of his gun, he stared into a future which he wished he could escape."

Paul lowers his gun and confesses he will not shoot; while the turkeys fly away, alarmed by the sound of his voice, Robert jumps up, firing angrily after the birds, but loses his balance because of his stump. Robert then cries, upset with Paul's apparent cowardice and his own inability to join the army. Paul tries to console him, and although he knows that he has failed as a hunter, he feels relief and release: "There was a sudden lightness in all the places where fear had been, almost a giddiness, and for an instant, as a wild re-joicing mounted in him, he was afraid that he was going to shout aloud."

One may want to remember here that Basso's hunting stories were written at a time that the world was being torn by war. In this light, the stories, and "The Wild Turkey" especially, seem to underpin a pacifist message. All of Basso's hunts are failures, signifying the futility of man's instinct to kill. Human values, particularly the distinction be-tween right and wrong, are more important in these stories than the event of the hunt itself. Accordingly, in the first two tales, we learn that the strengthening of human bonds can take place without a successful hunt and that a child's honesty is preferable to adult hypocrisy. In the second set of stories, we learn that obsessions can lead to madness and alienation, while in the last two pieces, we are taught that killing is not as glamorous as it has been made out to be. In all these stories, the hunt is demythologized. Basso's own dislike of hunting can be seen as a rebellion against his southern identity. Whereas in southern culture the hunt is a revered realm of experience through which fathers teach their sons manliness, Basso implies that virility can be acquired through less violent means.

Clarence Ikerd was mistaken in discarding these stories, saying that Basso "was still grappling with the problems of defining character with innuendo or a few swift strokes, and these emerged as too broad and simple and yet puzzling because not sufficiently explained." Reading these remarkable stories, one cannot help but regret, like Joseph Millichap, that Basso wrote so few. Their autobiographical candor, humor, use of the southern grotesque, and local color, as well as their subtle southern "otherness" in their debunking of the hunt, turn them into jewels on the crown of Basso's oeuvre.[56]

56. Ikerd, "Hamilton Basso," 114; Millichap, *Hamilton Basso*, 140.

6

The Final Years

In the fifties Basso's work achieved widespread popular appeal. The sociocritical articles of the *New Republic* and the *New Yorker* had given way to travel writing and general interest articles for *Holiday* and *Life*, and Basso's 1954 novel, *The View from Pompey's Head*, was an instant best-seller. Citing his son, who had asked Basso why he wrote for popular magazines if all people did was throw magazines away, Basso expressed awareness of the commercial direction that his work had taken. When Malcolm Cowley accused him of "milking the big magazines," Basso admitted that he "would like to be able to do some of the things that all the intervening years have been a kind of preparation for. But there is always that living to earn!" He also said that if he had to earn his living "by writing the stuff that goes between the advertisements—pure commercialism," he wanted to get paid for it: "And the bigger the pay the better, provided I don't have to write what I don't feel or believe." Gearing so much of his writing to the big magazines and a mass audience caused feelings of isolation. Claiming that he was indifferent to Cowley's criticism that both his literary and political pursuits were marked by "simple-mindedness," he nonetheless resented "sitting on an island, isolated from the intellectual fashions and currents of the time, especially the currents that swirl around the rocks of literature and politics."[1]

Most of Basso's trips for *Holiday* came as a welcome break after the completion of another book. On the road or at sea, Basso sometimes complained that he missed his family, but though he may have insisted that "the only 'fun' left to me, and the most 'fun' I have ever known, or ever care to know, is you [Toto], the boy, my house in the backyard [i.e., Basso's outdoor study] and a real job of work to sink my teeth in," he knew that his trips were an excellent remedy for the "failure of nerve" he suffered whenever his writing had drained him.[2]

Clarence Ikerd has observed that in the *Holiday* pieces, which were later compiled in Basso's book of travel stories, *A Quota of Seaweed* (1960), "Basso always tried to focus on the people . . . rather than on either the scenery or the economic, social or political conditions of the countries." Evidence of Basso's remarkable talent for making contact and moving the people he met can be found in a letter of condolence that R. W. Bailey, a sailor, wrote upon learning about Basso's death in 1964. Having encountered Basso on a freighter in 1957, the sailor reminisced in his letter to Toto how he and Basso had enjoyed each other's conversations and had visited an old Spanish fortress in Omoa, Honduras: "We hired a car and after an hour of bad roads arrived at our destination. We found it being utilized as a prison for political prisoners much to our surprise. After one turn around the parapets followed by jeers and outstretched hands we disappointedly returned."[3] The two men then walked down the beach and witnessed a beautiful sunset that made Bailey conclude: "I shall never forget Omoa and will remember Mr. Basso as a gentle man who was able to fully observe and enjoy even the most commonplace events in life." Bailey got it right, for Basso's travel writings, consisting of articles and letters home, are anecdotal and witty narratives revealing the writer's eye for detail, his incisiveness, and his great storytelling talent.

The trip that prompted *The View from Pompey's Head* was made in January 1951. Largely meant as a recuperative journey—Basso had fallen

---

1. Basso to Cowley, June 22, 1949, January 9, 1951, in Cowley papers, NL.

2. Basso to Etolia S. Basso, March 23, 1949, April 15, 1950, in Basso Papers, BL.

3. Ikerd, "Hamilton Basso," 133–34; R. W. Bailey to Etolia S. Basso, June 1964, in files of Etolia S. Basso.

off his son's horse and needed "thirty stitches" to put his face "back together again"—the trip included stops at Savannah, Charleston, and
the islands off Georgia and the South Carolina coast. His return to the
South was highly inspirational: not only did he come up with the idea
of southern Shintoism after a southern belle told him at a Charleston
dinner party, "We're like the Japanese; we eat rice and worship our ancestors," but he also realized that the Charleston-Beaufort-Savannah
triangle would be an excellent setting for his fictional town, Pompey's
Head.[4]

Interestingly, whereas Basso polished up the image of the plantation South in an article for *Holiday*, writing that Savannah and its sur-
roundings were the South "of the great mansions, of beautiful women
and gallant men, of blooded horses, of purebred hounds, of Negroes
working in the fields and of all the other elements that went into the
creation of that rather Technicolor dream," in his notebook he mocked
the region, observing that one "can't turn anywhere in the South without smelling that stale smell of gentility." One should note here that
Carson McCullers had first been asked to write the Savannah and
Golden Isles article. According to McCullers' biographer, Virginia
Spencer Carr, the piece never came off successfully; the *Holiday* editor
"objected that she put too much of Lillian Smith and Miss Smith's social consciousness into [the] article. . . . Most of the blame lay, however,
thought Carson, on a prejudiced Southern editor who refused to see
the South as it was." Apparently Basso was better at keeping his opinions to himself, for while glorifying Savannah's extraordinary architecture in the *Holiday* piece, in his notebook he made fun of the fact that
Savannah prided itself on having never seen a lynching. Likewise, Basso's criticism of what he called Shintoism was much less concealed in
his notebook. Ridiculing Charlestonians' obsession with tracing back
their ancestors to the founding fathers of the city, he observed that the
Savannahians' ancestors came out of "the debtor's prisons of
England," while "in New Orleans one never hears of an ancestress
who was numbered among those famous juvenile delinquents of the
early 1700s who were known as the 'casket girls' and sent over from
France to provide . . . for the woman hungry colonists of Louisiana."

    4. Hamilton Basso, "Why I Wrote the View," *Literary Guild Review* (November 1954),
3; Basso, "Savannah and the Golden Isles," *Holiday*, X (December 1951), 56.

Having exiled himself in the North, the author became more censori-
ous of the South, though sometimes more so in his private than in his
public writings.[5]

Although it appears that in later years Basso was no longer as preoccupied with the South as he had been in the thirties, southern matters were still on his mind. After the landmark Supreme Court desegregation decision of 1954, Basso sent letters to several newspapers to
plead for careful implementation of desegregation. In a letter to the editor of the New York *Times*, which he had written after long conversations with Luther Hodges, governor-to-be of North Carolina, he condemned segregation but also asked for a moderate approach in
desegregation so as to avert race riots. Congressman Stewart Udall of
Arizona, who on June 14, 1955, introduced a bill to promote school in-
tegration through a federal aid program, quoted extensively from the
letter and stated that Basso's comments had had "considerable influence" on his remarks and "the tenor" of his bill.[6] The racial question in
the South was never far from Basso's mind, and although he was not a
conspicuous spokesman for black civil rights, the issue of race surfaced
as a significant motif in most of his southern novels.

In September 1951 Basso went on a cross-country drive for *Holiday*.
Having failed to persuade Cowley to come along, he went alone and
jotted down his observations in an amusing travel diary. Leaving Weston on September 24, Basso headed west, and while crossing the Hud-
son River, he reflected that compared to the roaring Mississippi and
Missouri rivers, it was no more than a "literary creation" and a
"stream" at best. In a similar fashion, he debunked Route 1: "A quite
talented poet has written a long poem about it but it has no poetry for
me (That poem wasn't so hot either)."[7]

Driving through New Jersey—where, he mentioned, the industrial
smells might have delighted Walt Whitman but did not please him—

5. Virginia Spencer Carr, *The Lonely Hunter: A Biography of Carson McCullers* (New
York, 1976), 422; Hamilton Basso, "Savannah, Georgia; 3 February 1951" [travel diary]
(Typescript in Hamilton Basso Papers, HT).

6. Ikerd, "Hamilton Basso," 124; Stewart L. Udall to Hamilton Basso, February 17,
1956, in Basso Papers, BL.

7. Hamilton Basso, "An American Notebook 1950–1951" (Typescript in Hamilton
Basso Papers, HT), n.p.

Basso arrived in Pennsylvania Dutch country ("big, bosomy, capable of endless bearing . . . a Rubens Venus done in terms of crops and earth") and made the following note on the "Persistence of National Types": "I had lunch in the town of Hamburg, founded in 1779 on the east bank of the Schuylkill . . . Everybody in the lunchroom had the same kind of face you see in Dürer etchings; I passed the salt to St. Jerome."

After staying at the Hershey Hotel in Hershey, Pennsylvania ("new addition to the list of dumps"), Basso headed for U.S. 40 and Gettysburg. He was taken around the battlefield at Gettysburg by a guide who thought that Basso was a northerner because of his Connecticut license plates, and he was amused when the guide sneered at Confederate-minded southerners: "I had a lady from Texas the other day and she talked worse about Lincoln than some people talk about Truman." When, in his turn, Basso confided that he had written a book on Beauregard, he was even more amused when the guide replied, "Ah yes . . . where was he at the time of Gettysburg?"

As Basso later roamed the battlefield by himself, he ruminated somewhat sentimentally (and rather characteristically): "Here was written . . . the final surge of the feudal jousting, plantation South. It crashed against something quite opposite—the burgeoning force of the Industrial Revolution—and when it fell back it was done. The slaves were freed, the insult to man's condition was erased and the way was paved for the coca cola barons to take over." Though Basso did not subscribe to the Agrarian creed, as he grew older he became suspicious of big business and believed that industry had wiped out too many scenic parts of the southern countryside. As for Abraham Lincoln, whom he called a "patron saint" in *Mainstream* and praised as a man who equaled Mark Twain by doing what "Dante . . . did for Italian—making [English], that is, a medium of major expression" (*M*, 69), he could not conceal his admiration and bowed his head at the place where Lincoln delivered his Gettysburg Address: "I don't know though, if I was bowing to Lincoln or the magic and wonder of those magnificent words."

Moving inland, Basso noted regional and other differences: "All hill women are uglier than cows; attractiveness seems to stop around 500 feet." Later in his diary he even mused that since crossing the George Washington Bridge he had not seen a pretty face, to which he added a note to the grandchildren he would never have: "I have always been a careful observer of landscape and I trust that you, too, will see beyond the trees." While being a great charmer who, according to Keith, "always had a twinkle in his eye," Basso was never a flirt but treated women with respect and southern regard.[8]

On September 26, Basso was driving through Columbus ("the hickest of all hick towns") on his way through Ohio, and though he was an experienced and confident traveler, he made a self-conscious comment about his hat: "I came on this trip wearing a corduroy hat that I bought from an Army surplus store in Portsmouth, Maine—it drew almost as much attention as if it had wings." The next day he reached Theodore Dreiser's Terre Haute ("Now I know why Theodore Dreiser turned into Theodore Dreiser. This place in itself comes close to being an American tragedy"). Having visited the Midwest the summer before with Keith and Toto, Basso still felt like a complete stranger in America's cornbelt: "The whole South is home, I feel a certain sympathy with the East, and the West is where my heart is—but this region! I might as well be among the Arabs. And yet, in its self-containedness, its lack of outside influences, it is probably the most 'American' part of the country . . . but the people, no! And I always feel the crushing weight of conformity; I'm beginning to resent the stares at my innocent corduroy hat."

Reaching Vandalia, Illinois, on September 28, Basso paid tribute to Lincoln by having ham and eggs across from the old statehouse where Lincoln had been a legislator. Trying to find out who of the Midwestern writers portrayed the region and its people most truthfully, Basso came to the conclusion that Edgar Lee Masters really captured Illinois: "There was something phony about Sherwood Anderson, as there is about Carl Sandburg, and Dreiser was just hitting back at Terre Haute . . . But Spoon River is right; it's the kind of poetry this Illinois country could produce. 'But Douglas! / People out yonder in Proctor's Grove / A mile from its courthouse steps / Could hear him roar.' That does it somehow; it's the right rhythm and the right tack; it's Illinois." Revealingly, Basso added that he had met Masters once when he was "too young to appreciate" him: "I am sorry I never had the chance to tell him how much understanding of the prairie country he has given me."

On October 3, crossing a "muddy" Missouri River, Basso arrived

8. Keith H. Basso, interview with the author.

"west." Wiring Toto that he had made it to Kansas, he told her of the soaring temperatures and how he had a wicked sunburn because he had been driving with his roof down: "My nose . . . would go good with Tartar sauce." Pleasantly surprised at the large black population in Topeka (the "descendants of the Negro 'Exodusters' who came here in 1879–80. The oldest and most concentrated Negro community is called 'Tennessee Town'—nobody seems to know why"), Basso still found the women he met en route unattractive and boasted chauvinistically that he liked "what we have in New Orleans better."

From Topeka he drove to Denver via Oakley. Approaching the Rockies on October 5, Basso reflected on the "mixed blessings" of the moving frontier: "And the frontier wasn't all peaches and cream either; as a country we got lynch-law, vigilantiism [*sic*], 'to hell with book-learning,' etc., from it along with possibly, T. Jefferson's idea of 'frontier democracy.' " Four days later he crossed the Great Divide, and marveling at the beauties of the desert, he reached Salt Lake City on October 10: "I don't believe in this city; it doesn't want to be there. It's an affront to logic—but here, giving off rather the same feeling as Kansas City, it most definitely is." From Salt Lake City he drove to Elko, Nevada, where he joined a group of locals for a beer. Again a "note to my grandchildren" followed: "What I mean, young uns, is that I sometimes find more companieros in men with rednecks than I do with those with white skins."

Arriving in Reno on October 12, Basso went for a walk in the hills and hit upon a frontier theory, which he called "Basso's Law": "What makes the West the West is this—the Puritan influence never got beyond Kansas; it broke against the Rockies and then fell back. . . . And it is with the 'Rocky Mountain' frontier—Colorado and Nevada especially—that we get more of violence, vigilantiism [*sic*] etc. that the frontier persists." Basso's interest in frontier history prompted a desire to write a book on the fur trade. "Sick of the reexaminations of the reexaminations of the reexaminations of Melville, Henry James, Hawthorne, and even more sick of the notion that the U.S. and the whole of its history is no larger than the eastern seaboard," he hoped to write a biography of Sir William Drummond Stewart, "whose trail" he had first picked up in New Orleans. Basso surrendered the idea when he read Bernard DeVoto's *Across the Wide Missouri* (1947). But because he could not let go of Stewart's story, he asked DeVoto about Mae Reed

Porter, who had already announced she would write a Stewart biography. DeVoto responded promptly that Basso should go ahead, for Porter was, in his opinion, "a rich, grasping, stupid woman, with a monstrous ego and a tireless faculty for self-advertising. She cannot write at all and she is entirely incapable of doing even the most elementary research."[9] (Despite DeVoto's caustic dismissal, Mae Reed Porter did write the biography, entitled *Scotsman in Buckskin: Sir William Drummond Stewart and the Rocky Mountain Fur Trade* [1963].)

Because of DeVoto's advice that Stewart's life would not be the proper start for a book on the fur trade, Basso decided against the biography but could not help but notice the uncanny resemblance of Mae Reed Porter, as described by DeVoto, to Mrs. Porter of his *Greenroom*: "A most curious thing. My last novel, an entertainment called The Greenroom, was built around an oldish woman, a writer that a good many critics decided was Mrs. Wharton, as she wasn't, who in her own way was a kind of tiger and who played a considerable amount of hell. I called her Mrs. Porter, reaching into the blue for a name and drawing her character from nothing but my own imagination. She has more than a little in common with your Mrs. Porter, however, and I wouldn't be fool enough, having invited the jinx, to step directly in its path. No thank you."[10] Though Basso was still keen on writing about the fur trade and collected many books on the subject, the project never made it into a book. However, as he drove west and contemplated America's pioneer past, fur trade history often entered his mind.

Basso finally made it to San Francisco after three weeks, 3,708 miles, and seventy-one pages of his journal. Before abandoning his travel impressions, he expressed his love for the City by the Bay: "The circumstance of my having been born in the French Quarter makes it hard for me to see New Orleans as objectively as I might but I have to agree with the old statement . . . that there are only three truly distinctive cities in the United States—New York, New Orleans and San Francisco." Writing home, he further confided in Toto that San Francisco was, like New Orleans, "a Tom town": "For a time I was fairly convinced that the Tabby in me had finally triumphed over the Tom, but sister, the Tom

9. Basso to Bernard DeVoto, August 11, 1951, DeVoto to Basso, August 21, 1951, in Basso Papers, BL.

10. Basso to DeVoto, August 26, 1951, in Basso Papers, BL.

sure broke loose that night in Elko!"[11] As always, when Basso went on long trips by himself, he would start to miss Toto in more ways than one: "I don't let myself think how beautiful you are; not too much—it has now got to the point when all I want to do is make love to you all night long—sweetly, gently, roughly—all kinds of ways—yep, we've moved out of the sign of the Tabby into the constellation of the Tom."

The year 1952 was a quiet one; while Basso was steadily working on *The View from Pompey's Head*, he published little with the exception of an introduction to William Herndon's *Exploration of the Valley of the Amazon* and a review of Phillip Graham's *Showboats: The History of an American Institution* in the *American Historical Review*. As he was finishing *The View from Pompey's Head* in the spring of 1953, Basso contracted meningitis and had to be hospitalized. According to Malcolm Cowley, this was typical: "At some point toward the end of every novel, Ham would begin to suffer from physical complaints, often serious." Returning from the hospital, Basso got up immediately and went to work for the Weston school board. This put him back in bed with "more pains in this battered thing I call my head and a few more pounds of terramycin."[12]

In search of better health and with the proofs of *The View from Pompey's Head* under his arm, Basso boarded a Norwegian freighter for Brazil to pen a travel piece on Rio de Janeiro and write an in-depth article on the southern plantation squires who left for South America after their defeat in the Civil War. As always, Basso ran into a number of interesting characters aboard the ship; while he suspected the Belgian Mrs. Hardy of being the "Ancient Mariner in a new guise" ("Her eye is as glittering, she talks just as endlessly and maybe somewhere on her person, she is carrying the same albatross"), he became friends with a couple he met on board, the Limas, after helping them out. When the ship arrived in Rio, Mrs. Lima fell ill with a serious fever. Fearing that they would not be able to disembark, they called on Basso, who played doctor by stuffing the poor woman with aspirin and liquids; later on, Basso admitted that he went out of his way for the couple because he identified with Paul Lima: "I saw in Paul Lima, that rushing warmth of

---

11. Basso to Etolia S. Basso, October 14, 1951, in Basso Papers, BL.
12. Malcolm Cowley, Typescript notes for Basso's eulogy, in Cowley Papers, NL; Basso to Cowley, May 15, 1953, in Cowley Papers, NL.

his, the impulsive and indiscriminate going out to people, something of myself: a raw, naked manifestation of that same feeling, which, in myself, has become . . . both more civilized and more repressed . . . I had identified myself with Paul Lima; every time he got hurt, I was hurt; every time he was rebuffed, I was rebuffed."[13]

Returning from South America, Basso finally finished *The View from Pompey's Head*. The book had taken so long because Basso had been particularly picky, or as he would tell Robert Cantwell of the *Saturday Review of Literature*: "It seems the older one gets, the more demands one makes. I think that in this book I started out making the severest demands on myself, and I have lived up to the demands better than in any other book."[14]

Comfortably placed on the New York *Times* best-seller list for forty weeks, selling more than 75,000 copies, and sold to the movies for $100,000, *The View from Pompey's Head* was the breakthrough that Basso had long been waiting for. However, just as one cannot argue that Melville's *Typee* (1846) was a better book because it sold more copies than *Moby-Dick* (1851), so is it equally impossible to claim that *The View from Pompey's Head* was a masterpiece because it was so popular. Indeed, after a thorough reading of the work, one may be inclined to agree with James E. Rocks that this "well-known novel should not . . . be the only work for which Basso is primarily known or by which he is fundamentally judged." One should not see *The View from Pompey's Head* as the zenith of his literary career but as a book whose prime value lies in the writer's renewed preoccupation with the South and a resuscitation of Basso's old theme—the return of the native. Interestingly, the publication of *Pompey's Head* coincided with that of a number of articles in which Basso revisited the scenes of his New Orleans childhood.[15]

13. Hamilton Basso, "Letter from Rio de Janeiro," *New Yorker*, October 17, 1953, pp. 64–76; Basso, "A Reporter at Large: The Last Confederate," *New Yorker*, November 21, 1953, pp. 124–43; Basso, "Brazil 1953" [travel diary], August 2, 7, 1953 (Typescript in Hamilton Basso Papers, HT).

14. Cantwell, "A Southerner Returns," 15.

15. Rocks, "Hamilton Basso and the World View from Pompey's Head," 338–39. These articles are "A New Orleans Childhood," *New Yorker*, October 9, 1954; "The Talkative Windfall," *New Yorker*, December 4, 1954; and "Thanks to Saint Jude," *New Yorker*, May 7, 1955.

When critics suggested that Basso might have stolen his theme and use of the flashback from writers like J. P. Marquand and Thomas Wolfe, he defended himself vigorously, pointing out that he had employed the flashback as early as 1934, long before Marquand used the device. As for the return-of-the-native motif, Basso had used that in three of his earlier novels, too, and insisted that his renewed preoccupation with the theme in *Pompey's Head* came out of his personal experience "won over many years and occasionally at the cost of some pain." He further explained that the composition of *Pompey's Head* triggered "a few deeply felt observations about that part of the country to which I am united by the bonds of birth and affection. It was done in my own person and my own voice, to the very best of my ability." With *Pompey's Head*, Basso aimed to fuse his version of the novel of character (*Relics and Angels* and *Courthouse Square*) with his novel of ideas (*Days Before Lent* and *Wine of the Country*). Foremost, *Pompey's Head* should be seen as a kind of sequel to *Courthouse Square*, for while Basso referred to *Courthouse Square* as a "boy's book," he saw *Pompey's Head* as a "man's book."[16]

The novel's opening finds Anson Page in midlife and midcareer. Happily married to Meg and the father of two children, Anson is a promising lawyer and future partner of the law firm Roberts, Guthrie, Barlowe & Paul. But he is not content. Moping about in his New York apartment, he yearns for a southern spring. His desire is satisfied when Mr. Barlowe sends him home to Pompey's Head, a South Carolina town that derives its curious name from the classical Pompey, whose profile was said to resemble the jutting headland of the bluff as seen from the river where it had first been sighted by the town's founders. Anson is sent home on a mission. Lucy Wales, wife of the famous novelist Garvin Wales, has pressed charges against her husband's publisher, Duncan & Company, for embezzlement. She suspects Wales's editor, the deceased Phillip Greene, of embezzling twenty thousand dollars of her husband's royalties, and Anson has to find out whether Greene wrote checks to a certain Anna Jones in Wales's name or in his own. Anson is told to meet with the retired Wales, who is virtually kept prisoner by his wife on an island off the South Carolina coast. Because

16. Hamilton Basso to Mr. Highet, March 29, 1955, in Basso Papers, BL; Ikerd, "Hamilton Basso," 125.

the plot revolves around the supposed innocence of Greene and the mysterious relationship between Greene, Wales, and Anna Jones, the story includes a detective element, which may well have contributed to the book's popularity with the public.

More so than in Basso's preceding novels, the protagonist's homecoming involves an intense confrontation with his past. Once Anson gets off the train in Old Pompey, flashback follows flashback, a pattern that Louis Auchincloss parodied in "The Adventures of Johnny Flashback" in the *Saturday Review*.[17] Through Anson's recollections, we meet his family, who, like the Barondesses, "lost a certain amount of caste" because they demanded justice for one of their black townsmen (*PH*, 3). Anson remembers how Clifford Small, an old Negro who works in his father's hardware store, is sweeping the sidewalk one day when Mr. Henry Pettibone passes by. When Cliff happens to sweep some dust onto him, Pettibone proves true to his name, shouting at Cliff and pushing him through the shop window. Cliff's hand is so severely slashed that it has to be amputated, a tragedy that, though a little contrived, adds poignancy to the white man's ongoing mutilation of the black man. Page senior, who feels protective of Cliff because of the Smalls' loyal service to his family, encourages Cliff to sue Pettibone for compensation, and a kind of mini-Scottsboro case ensues.

At the trial, Anson recalls, Pettibone's defense is preposterous, his insistence on the importance of his caste revealing the town's engrained prejudice: "One of the tacit assumptions of Pompey's Head was that a person of consequence like Mr. Pettibone, in relation to a Negro like Clifford Small—in relation, indeed to almost any Negro—could do no wrong . . . a hot temper always being understood to be one of the proper possessions of a Southern gentleman" (*PH*, 179). Cliff is falsely accused of drunkenness but vindicated when, at the very last moment in the trial, Midge Higgins takes the stand and testifies that on the morning of the incident she had walked by and spilled the contents of her purse, and a sober Cliff had helped her pick them up. According to Anson, Midge's testimony, the word of a white woman against the

17. Louis Auchincloss, "The Adventures of Johnny Flashback (With Full Apologies to Hamilton Basso, John Brooks, and John P. Marquand, Jr.)," *Saturday Review of Literature*, October 22, 1955, pp. 11–14. In the piece, Auchincloss mocks the main character's susceptibility to lose himself in the past as well as the absurd Shintoism of the residents of the small town Pryde's Rock.

word of a white man, makes the jury change its mind and award Cliff fifteen hundred dollars in damages. But while Anson's wife, Meg, who is not a southerner, would like to see the outcome of the trial as a triumph of righteousness, Anson believes that the jury is swayed by what W. J. Cash called the cult of southern womanhood: "If in Pompey's Head there was an unspoken agreement that a person of consequence like Mr Henry Pettibone could do no wrong in relation to a Negro like Clifford Small, so was it understood that a lady always told the truth . . . even though Mr Pettibone was assessed the token payment of fifteen hundred dollars, and everybody understood it was a token payment, the jury, by upholding the principle that a lady never failed to tell the truth, was upholding him as well. . . . And so it was incorrect to look upon the jury's verdict as a victory for the forces of enlightenment" (*PH*, 247).[18]

Grateful for Midge's performance, Anson realizes that though she might be a Channel girl (a working-class girl), she is a true heroine. Though nearly engaged to Kit Robbins, Anson has a fling with Midge. His attraction to her is ambivalent: Although he cannot resist her sensuality, he is disappointed that she gives in so easily to his advances and seems so experienced in love making. Similarly, though he feels great sympathy for her, his Shintoist leanings prevent him from "getting mixed up with a Channel girl."

In another flashback, Anson remembers that Kit, the girl he was supposed to marry, turned out to be the worst Shintoist of them all when she told him cockily that his father supported Cliff merely because he hated Pettibone for "having the ancestors" that the Pages did not (*PH*, 185). Upon his discovery that Kit, too, was "wrapped in bandages as confining as the strips of silk with which the Chinese used to bind the feet of their female infants [and had] turned into a kind of

---

18. W. J. Cash, *The Mind of the South* (1941; rpr. New York, 1969). In his customary florid style, Cash writes on the cult of southern womanhood: "The upshot in this land of spreading notions of chivalry, was downright gyneolatry. She was the South's Palladium, this Southern woman—the shield-bearing Athena gleaming whitely in the clouds, the standard for its rallying, the mystic symbol of its nationality in face of the foe. She was the lily-pure maid of Astolat and the hunting goddess of the Boeotian hill. And— she was the pitiful Mother of God. Merely to mention her was to send strong men into tears—or shouts. . . . At the last, I verily believe, the ranks of the Confederacy went rolling into battle in the misty conviction that it was wholly for her that they fought" (89).

cripple," Anson quit his law firm, took out all his savings, and left for New York City.

Upon his return to Pompey's Head, Anson is sorely reminded of the mixed feelings he had for both Midge and Kit. To add to his emotional confusion, he becomes romantically involved with the girl next door, Dinah Blackford. Dinah, who had always been more of a little sister than a peer of Anson's, has grown into a pretty woman. Though she is a very sympathetic character, a consciousness of caste has not left her unaffected, either: after her family lost its fortune, Dinah was "tired of living like trash and . . . wanted to be back where [she] belonged," and so she married a member of the nouveaux riches, the former Channel boy Mico Higgins (*PH*, 326).

Given Dinah's loveless marriage and Anson's midlife crisis, it is not surprising that the two end up making love. Whereas Pompey's Head no longer fulfills Anson's sense of home and belonging, Dinah embodies home and an otherwise irretrievable past: "She somehow represented the lost security of the house on Alwyn Street, together with all else that was lost, the whole lost world of Sonny Page, and she promised comfort and release" (*PH*, 321). Anson's orgasm is both a sexual climax and a climax of personal fulfillment and release, in which past and present intermingle: "And when at last he possessed her, in a wholeness of possession he had never known or dreamed, past and present came thundering together and he was master and owner of it all. He seemed to have been released of a burden under which he had unknowingly labored all his life" (*PH*, 327).

But of course Anson did not return home to seek closure by means of midlife-crisis sex. His affair livens up the story, yet the reader is well aware that he has some business to attend to. Fortunately, Dinah is well connected and introduces her lover to Lucy Wales. On his first visit to the Waleses' Tamburlaine Island, Anson does not see Garvin Wales but has to deal with Lucy, who, variously described as a "mean, poisonous, trouble-making bitch," "evil in its most absolute form," and a "first class neurotic," is an amplified version of the devious Mrs. Porter in *The Greenroom* (*PH*, 46, 119, 318). When Anson tells Lucy about Anna Jones and asks who authorized the checks, she immediately assumes that Jones was Phillip Greene's mistress and that her husband had nothing to do with it. She tells Anson that he must come back another day to interview Wales.

When Anson returns to the island, he finds Wales a difficult and reticent old man. Wales initially denies knowing anything about the checks but eventually confesses that Anna Jones is his mulatto mother. Having escaped his cropper childhood by becoming a famous writer, Wales did not want the world to know that his mother had turned up with her marriage certificate to prove that he was her son: "I'd got out, I'd managed to climb from that white-trash mud, and now I was back in it again! But worse! Now I was a nigger into the bargain, trash and nigger as well!" (*PH*, 340). Wales's angry confession underscores the main theme of the book, or as Anson realizes: "Nobody . . . ever completely escaped. His father had called it Shintoism, which was as good a word as any, and what it offered was a kind of ready-made identity, something that could be slipped into a coat. Did it not explain them all?" (*PH*, 341). It certainly does explain the behavior of Lucy: having eavesdropped on the conversation, she calls Anson back to the island and makes up a story about her husband borrowing the money from Greene for a trip around the world. Her denial of the truth is rooted in Shintoism once more: "It was not deviousness and it was not madness. It was simply that she was Lucy Devereaux, and that, as Lucy Devereaux, she could not have been married all these years to the man whose mother was Anna Jones" (*PH*, 348). It is the Waleses' Shintoist keeping up of appearances that Anson finally comes to associate with the mindset in his hometown, or the "view" from Pompey's Head.

When Dinah asks Anson about his encounter with the Waleses, he sticks with Lucy's story. In fact, it saves him from telling the truth to his employer as well. This is a significant weakness of Anson's character, as is his remarkable lack of guilt over his one-night stand with Dinah. Equally difficult to comprehend is his indifferent farewell to Dinah; having declared his love to her and having called her "his girl," his subsequent "try to get to New York. I forgot to give you my address, but you can always find us in the phone book," is particularly shallow and contradictory (*PH*, 350). Likewise, the characterization of the Waleses is unpersuasive: they are almost too wicked to be convincing.

Another of the novel's prime weaknesses is its heavy reliance on the flashback. Anson's past may be interesting in light of the feelings he experiences upon coming home, yet the world of the past fails to connect with the world of the present. Rather than illuminating the actual story and plot, Anson's flashbacks seem merely symptomatic of his sentimental hunger for the past. Furthermore, although the subplot of the Pettibone case has clearly been inserted to illustrate the flawed southern justice system and Shintoism in practice, the trial is a trifle predictable.

The book becomes more rewarding when placed within the overall framework of Basso's life and work. Evidently, Anson's life resembles Basso's and those of his earlier protagonists in some respects. For instance, Anson's feelings for his father and grandfather are strikingly similar to Basso's own. Just as Basso extolled his grandfather over his father, Anson boasts about the business instinct of his New England grandfather and belittles his father for not having been the businessman his grandfather was. Like Basso, too, who told Edmund Wilson that he was trying to make up for the failures of his father, Anson's escape from Pompey's Head is said to have been partly triggered by his desire to atone for his father's mistakes (*PH*, 321). Additionally, Anson's sense of double exile must have been close to Basso's own feelings: when Meg refers to her husband as a "lapsed Southerner" who has left the South but is still "full of complications" because of it, we may readily assume that Anson shares these sentiments with his creator.

Most striking is Anson's resemblance to David Barondess. Like David (and Wolfe's Eugene Gant), Anson returns a man, and like David too, he experiences a sense of alienation and "homelessness." Besides feeling just as much a stranger in Pompey's Head as in New York City, Anson notes that "everything was the same and nothing was the same. It was like returning to a house you had rented to strangers and coming upon the changes they had made—it was the same house and the same rooms, and the clock in the hall had the same measured tick, but some of the furniture had been rearranged and the pictures were hung differently, and there was the lingering presence of alien shapes that made the house theirs, not yours" (*PH*, 76). Like David, Anson is struck by the "unreality" of the South, but where David had not made up his mind about whether to stay home or leave again, Anson has become a disenchanted southerner who describes his native region as "a kind of never-never land . . . the moss in the trees, the way the sun sets, the haze on the river and those fogs we get just before dawn, the magnolias in the moonlight and sometimes not only the magnolias but the mocking-birds as well—it's not real, only there it's real, and so the true reality is somehow lost and nothing seems improbable but the world as it actually is. We had too much of it . . . It led us astray . . . the moonlight-and-magnolia dream . . . It's over now, dead and gone for ever, but Mulberry betrays you into thinking that it isn't . . . Because of Mulberry, we're sort of anachronisms, you and I." (323–34). Because Anson is a mature version of David, we may disagree with Clarence Ikerd, who stated that *Pompey's Head* is just another novel in which a "young man" is "in conflict with society."[19] Whereas David is still caught in a tug-of-war with his hometown, Anson is through with such conflict; merely in conflict with himself, he returns to his hometown to see his rejection of the South confirmed and his homesickness cured.

Finally, what makes *Pompey's Head* especially intriguing is the inspiration it drew from the Perkins-Wolfe relationship as witnessed by Basso. Phillip Greene, who is described as a "man with more discoveries to his name than any editor in the business" and as a "truly private person" whose "solitariness . . . set him apart from other men," is unequivocally modeled on Maxwell Perkins (*PH*, 23, 103). Greene's relationship with Wales, which is not only seen as "one of the legends of American publishing" but also as something that "had become Duncan & Company's holiest possession," is obviously modeled on the Perkins-Wolfe friendship: "No two men could have possibly been closer" (*PH*, 29, 92). Like Wolfe, Wales is lost without Greene's supervision, and had it not been for Greene's steadfast resolve, Wales's first novel would have never seen the light of day. While Greene bears a close resemblance to Perkins—which comes out even more in the manuscript version of the novel—Wales is an amalgam of Thomas Wolfe, Eugene O'Neill, and Ernest Hemingway.[20] For example, Wales's

19. Ikerd, "Hamilton Basso," 125.

20. The following passage from the manuscript was omitted in the published novel, apparently because Greene came too close to Perkins: "The riddle of Phillip Greene, however, was not too difficult to come by. He was a man passionately devoted to the cause of literature. Moreover, he was a New Englander of the old breed. Born into a society which once held that the minister and the parson were of a higher worth than the merchant and the banker, and reared in a family which persisted in that view long after it had gone down in New England's general decline, he had a certain austerity of outlook which caused him to regard cocktail parties, official luncheons, and P.E.N. dinners as a rather frivolous waste of time. He didn't like them and he didn't particularly like the people who habitually went to them. He wanted neither to see nor be seen. His whole

"latent brutality, not vicious [but] more on the order of a willingness to slug it out in a bar-room brawl," as well as southerners' conviction that Wales's books gave the South a bad name, clearly remind one of Wolfe. But Wales's adventures as a "gold hunter, seaman and soldier" and his marriage to a domineering wife turn him into a possible alter ego of Eugene O'Neill. At the same time, Anson's and his colleagues' opinion that Wales's novels consistently deal with his adolescent fantasies is reminiscent of Basso's critique that Hemingway was too old to be having wet dreams.

The View from Pompey's Head received enthusiastic reviews. The critics praised the novel as Basso's "best," and Arthur Mizener wrote that he had come away from the book "feeling, not that we have seen something like a vision as with Faulkner, but that we have been listening to an amused and compassionate man who knows more about America than all the sociologists and advertising men put together." However, the novel has dated considerably. In spite of its successful preoccupation with southern Shintoism and its fictionalization of the novelist's experiences with Maxwell Perkins and Thomas Wolfe, the southern allure and atmosphere of works like *Cinnamon Seed* and *Courthouse Square* are traded in for a bland detective narrative, which, albeit deftly delivered, lacks the power and the passion of the early novels. Nevertheless, when the novel was brought out again in 1985, Jonathan Yardley of the *Washington Post Book Review* hailed the book as "a novel of Southern manners to rank with, if not above, the work of Ellen Glasgow, and a consideration of Southern social stratification worthy of Howard Odom [*sic*] or W. J. Cash." Yardley must not have been familiar with Basso's thirties novels, for as a southern novel, *Pompey's Head* adds

---

ambition was to help authors do their best work. . . . There was more to it than that, however. Phillip Greene was counsellor, confessor, banker, friend. All authors are troubled creatures and in Phillip Greene they found someone in whom they could endlessly confide. It sometimes seemed to Anson, after he came to know Greene, that most of his time was given to concerns that in most cases were only incidental to the job at hand—somebody had fallen in love with somebody's wife; somebody else was depressed because she had received such a brief letter in regard to the first half of her new novel; somebody . . . 'What Phil had,' Bliss said, 'and what most people don't have, was the ability to give' " ("The View from Pompey's Head" [Typescript in Basso Papers, BL], 169–70).

very little to what Basso had already accomplished in his earlier work.[21]

Although Basso must have been extremely pleased with the book's sales, he was modest about its success. While announcing to Van Wyck Brooks that the novel was going to be translated into seven languages, he confessed that writing was still "a trying trade. . . . Nothing is ever done. One climb leads inevitably to another. . . . In art there is no Everest. We make our own mountains and we are never done." Keith, who remembers reading about the rocketing book sales while away at school, was astonished to find that on his return home, his parents neither talked about it nor had spent a cent of the money: "Neither the climate nor the tempo of the household changed." Malcolm Cowley congratulated his friend generously, predicting that the book would not only sell well but be translated and made into a movie. Cowley's prediction came true, and Ikerd wrote that after *The View from Pompey's Head*, Basso "was more than ever in demand to attend conferences, judge contests and contribute articles. For the first time he was enjoying fame." The recognition by his peers came a year later, when Basso was elected to the National Institute of Arts and Letters, where, together with Cowley, he worked on Ezra Pound's release from the mental hospital where he was living.[22]

With the success of *The View from Pompey's Head*, Basso now had the luxury and financial security to decline articles and take his time to write the kind of book he wanted to write. Also, having become a much more visible figure in the literary world, he was deluged with fan mail from around the world and was also sent manuscripts by aspiring young writers. Remembering his own struggle for success, Basso was not only accessible but patient and encouraging. Also, as a senior writer he was consulted by the biographers of writers he had known. Thus Andrew Turnbull, F. Scott Fitzgerald's biographer, approached him in September 1957 and asked him to "throw a little light

21. Arthur Mizener, "Fiction Chronicle," *Sewanee Review*, LXIII (1955), 491; Jonathan Yardley, "Rediscovering a Novel of Manners," *Washington Post Book Review*, June 30, 1985, p. 3.

22. Basso to Van Wyck Brooks, February 14, 1954, in Basso Papers, BL; Keith Basso, interview with the author; Ikerd, "Hamilton Basso," 125.

on the relationships between Fitzgerald and Wolfe." In preparation for the biographer's visit, Basso made notes on Fitzgerald, which Turnbull thought "very just and perceptive."[23]

Having become somewhat of a local celebrity, Basso was invited to give a speech before the Friends of the Westport Library in June 1957. In his typical self-effacing manner, he was reluctant to speak at the library, or as he told the crowd that had gathered to listen to him: "If it was thought well that children should be seen and not heard, it strikes me as being no less desirable that writers should be heard and not seen."[24]

The speech composed for this occasion is the only full pronouncement of Basso's artistic creed. Obviously written to amuse the audience, the text can nonetheless be read as a convincing exposition of Basso's aesthetic persuasion. Opening with a rather clumsy definition of the novel ("a novel is an extended piece of fiction that is primarily concerned with people in motion"), Basso soon warmed to his subject, using such classics as *War and Peace*, *The Red and the Black*, and *Moby-Dick* as examples, and pointing out that one of the novel's purposes is entertainment. Admitting that "we live in a kind of rubbishy time" when entertainment is associated with "cheapness and vulgarity," Basso insisted that Shakespeare, Austen, Flaubert, Dostoyevsky, and other literary greats all wrote with entertainment in mind. Next to entertainment, the novel serves a moral purpose without becoming a "religious tract." Mentioning that all good art has a moral framework, Basso reminded his audience that this is why parents are concerned about what their children read.

Basso further stated that a good novel is a social document in that it should "at least suggest the containment of the whole particular condition of a whole unique society." At the same time, rejecting the mimetic theory of art, he argued that the novel, and art in general, does not imitate life or mirror the world but is a world in itself. Building on Ortega y Gasset's belief that a work of art is a departure from rather than a reflection of reality, Basso mentioned his old friend Thomas Wolfe as a novelist who was able to "erase our vision of reality and put in its place a much more intense vision of his own."

23. Andrew Turnbull to Basso, September 21, December 2, 1957, in Basso Papers, BL.

24. Hamilton Basso, "Readers and Writers," July 13, 1957 (Typescript in Basso Papers, HT).

Finally, Basso observed that because facts are "deceptive" and "total vision" is humanly impossible, fiction is in some ways closer to truth than reality: "Impious though it may sound, the novelist can play God. Nothing is hidden from him, nothing is concealed. He can approach as close to the truth as his genius permits. Take Natasha in *War and Peace*. We know more about her than we can possibly know about any human being, even those who are closest to us. She is far more than a truthful portrait. She *is* truth. That is the highest value of the novel. It leads us into the presence of truth." He closed his speech by reiterating his renewed faith in the novel and what he believed the genre stood for, namely "entertainment on the highest level . . . moral commentary . . . a social document and . . . a means of leading us into the presence of truth."

Toto had a hard time sitting through the speech as that afternoon she had been bitten by a copperhead snake. Though her husband had sucked out the venom and she had been treated with a serum, her foot was hurting. There can be no doubt about Basso's fame at this point: the headline "Wife of Novelist Suffers Snakebite" made both the local and national press. Toto was told to walk on soft surfaces, and thinking that a soft beach might quicken the healing, the Bassos decided to spend the winter of 1957–58 in the Bahamas. Expecting warm weather, they experienced a particularly cold spell all winter, and since their beach cabin had no central heating, Basso worked on his next novel sitting close to the kitchen stove.

Finishing *The Light Infantry Ball* in the fall of 1958, Basso took on another *Holiday* assignment to unwind from the arduous strain of delivering another bulky manuscript. From New Orleans, where he gave a talk in a journalism class at his alma mater, Tulane University, Basso boarded a freighter and sailed via the Panama Canal and the Galapagos Islands to Tahiti. He was sorely disappointed with his fellow passengers, the ship's crew, and the ship itself. He discussed the Bible with two Jehovah's witnesses and complained about the Danish captain, who was addicted to rum. He told Toto that the ship was dirty, hot, and unsteady: "This old woman wallows, day in, day out. Things bang and clatter all the time. I am bruised in three places." On November 25, he was relieved to set foot in Papeete: After the dismal journey on the dirty ship, where his only escape was Melville's *Redburn*, he welcomed the Edenic beauty of the island: "I ached to share it. I understood why, in the legends of the whalers and clipper-ships, it stood as Paradise."[25]

Basso was the guest of Bengt Danielson of the Kon-tiki expedition. Danielson lived in a tin-roofed house, which Basso thought the coziest of places during a rainstorm. While lounging at one of Papeete's side-walk cafés he met Paul Gauguin's son, whom he described as a drunkard and a jailbird. He found out that Gauguin himself ended up rather ordinarily, as he "took to keeping a store": "I have documentary evidence, published by the local historical society and I will present it when I get home." As in his other travel diaries and letters, Basso made room for his observations concerning the beauty of women. Writing that Tahitian women do not age well, he concluded that their beauty was based on myth: "It would be interesting to know how the legend of the Polynesian woman's beauty got started. Going back to the whalers and clipper ships, my guess is that after six or eight months at sea, most any woman would look pretty good, and that the relaxed sexuality of the islands must have stood in sharp contrast to New Bedford and Salem." After having driven the island's circumference, his image of Tahitian women was still the same: "I pity the man who by the standards of our western society falls in love with a Tahitian girl, or with any notions concerning the simple-hearted maiden who wants only to lie under the mango tree and make love." On December 2, Basso returned home, ready to correct the proofs of *The Light Infantry Ball*, which was to come out the following year.[26]

The Light Infantry Ball, the second part of a trilogy that Basso never finished, is a sequel to *The View from Pompey's Head* in its attempt to trace the vices, Shintoism, and racism of Pompey's Head to the town's antebellum origins. Lee Barker, Basso's editor at Doubleday, summarized the theme of the novel as "the way in which slavery destroyed the South from a moral and emotional point of view long before Sherman's armies did it from a physical one." Basso elucidated the theme in an elaborate synopsis for the novel.[27]

Drawing from Mary Chesnut and W. J. Cash, Basso argued that the

25. Basso to Etolia S. Basso, November 19, 25, 1958, in Basso Papers, BL.
26. Basso to Etolia S. Basso, November 26, December 1, 1958, in Basso Papers, BL.
27. Lee Barker to Basso, March 16, 1955, in Basso Papers, BL.

plantation legend was an incomplete and unfair representation of ante-bellum society, its prime misconception lying in its intentional slight-ing of the tensions that slavery and secession evoked. By upholding what John Calhoun called the "positive" blessing of that "peculiar in-stitution," the South isolated itself by becoming an anachronism in a world that had come to see slavery as an unacceptable social institu-tion:

> The South lay behind slavery as behind a chain of mountains. For all practical purposes, every contemporary current was shut out. Deliberately. Not to shut them out would have involved a questioning of slavery in the light of the world's opinion at the time. And slavery could not be questioned any longer. To do so, would be to realize its conflict with the modern world, which, lest it be stripped naked of its whole mythos, was what the South must deliberately refuse to realize. Its choice made, it must perforce deny the present and retreat further and further into the past. On its feudal base, it erected a feudal society. It adopted Sir Walter Scott as its spokesman and attempted to re-enact, because of the necessities of its own myth, the myth of the golden age of chivalry. And in large part succeeded. The planta-tion South was the last great fief, and its men and women the last sons and daughters of Launcelot and Elaine. Unless we under-stand this, we understand nothing.[28]

In *The Light Infantry Ball*, Basso tried to bring out the impact that slav-ery and secession had had on the individual in particular and southern society at large. Thus the novel's protagonist and scion of a prominent planter's family has to reconcile his abolitionist sentiments, preached to him by his northern college professors, with the proslavery argu-ments of his community and family, and is finally faced with the choice of either speaking his mind and running the risk of "being re-garded as an enemy of society, and perhaps challenged to a duel," or, "more temperately," keeping his mouth shut. By 1860, Basso writes, "Most mouths were kept shut," and the main character, John Bottom-ley, loyal to the ideas of his family and community, sides with the

---

28. Hamilton Basso, "Indigo Hundred, The Social Atmosphere of Pompey's Head" (Typescript notes for *The Light Infantry Ball*, in Basso Papers, BL), n.p.

South, joins the Confederate administration, and fights in the Rebel army.[29]

The Light Infantry Ball itself is less attractive than Basso's prospectus for the book. The novel opens with a duel, when John is challenged by the villain of the book—the social climber and megalomaniac Ules Monckton—at the light infantry ball. Like the Blackheaths and the Barondesses, the Bottomleys embody the planter family in decline. Thus, John, the heir, is soft with his slaves and is portrayed as a much weaker personality than his domineering father. His dipsomaniacal brother, Cameron, is not a great asset to the family either: he flees town after a brief romance with a Channel girl and his murder of her interfering brother. John's mother suffers from bad nerves. Her screams in the middle of the night reveal her fear of the retribution of black slaves, and her belief that the house is on fire also adumbrates the fate of the plantation South. Like her husband, she dies at the end of the war, their deaths symbolizing the end of the antebellum era. John's only sister, Missie, does not safeguard the Bottomleys' plantation dynasty, either, when she marries a middle-class doctor instead of a planter.

Unlike the disintegrating Bottomley family, the Moncktons are, like the Brands and the Slades, the new rulers of the South. While Gup Monckton, as editor of the town's only newspaper, *The News*, molds and manipulates public opinion in Pompey's Head, Ules tries to sway the sentiments of the city's administrators by preaching his fanatical secessionist views to members of the Agricultural Society. But his success as a public speaker remains limited, and once the war breaks out, he becomes a kind of evil Beauregard who wants to conquer the North and the rest of the Americas to convert these lands into slaveholding territories.[30] When the war draws to its close and defeat seems inevitable, Monckton fights on with the zeal of a madman and tries to set up guerrilla forces to strike back at the Union army. With the Bottomleys' decline and the Moncktons' rise to power, it is of some symbolic significance that at the duel, Ules shoots John in the shoulder and sets the Bottomleys' plantation, Indigo Hundred, on fire. Monckton himself dies a dramatic death in the flames.

29. *Ibid.*

30. Ules Monckton is the epitome of the southern "fire-eaters": they were the most fanatical supporters of slavery. Before he started *The Light Infantry Ball,* Basso had planned but never finished a book on the fire-eaters.

The story of the Bottomleys and the Moncktons, played out against the backdrop of secession fever, the war, and the South's capitulation, is interspersed with insights into John's unhappy love life. Like Tony and Anson, he first falls in love with the wrong woman. Utterly infatuated with Missie's teacher, Lydia Chadwick, John is devastated when she marries the much older Senator Stanhope, whose daughter Arabella chides John for being in love with her stepmother. Lydia is a female version of Ules Monckton, her marriage to Stanhope being the mere means to an end: like Ules, she is a social climber with political ambitions. John is blinded by his love for her but, like a hero in a Tolstoy novel, seeks solace in the agricultural life of his plantation, Deerskin, and is consequently referred to as a "hermit" and a "recluse."

While John frets at Deerskin and is tempted by what Basso would call the "availability" of the black woman, Cameron visits him to borrow money. Cameron is to announce his engagement on the eve of the light infantry ball, but he disappears and leaves his family no clue as to his whereabouts. Functioning as another one of Basso's "private eyes" John unravels the mystery of his brother's disappearance when he sees Cameron's saddle in Allbright's barber shop. Like Alcide Fauget, Allbright is a successful free mulatto, who assists Cameron in his flight from town. John, however, resents Allbright: having found out that the slick barber is really his father's half-brother, he does not want to be reminded of his family's miscegenation and treats the overly ingratiating barber with contempt. When Allbright refuses to identify the saddle as Cameron's, John leaves the shop angrily. In the end, John has to change his tune: as in a case of mistaken identities, Allbright, like Epstein in the manuscript version of *Relics and Angels*, Sam in *Cinnamon Seed*, and Alcide in *Courthouse Square*, turns out to be a noble character whose generosity is not acknowledged until the end.

At the outbreak of the war, John is called back to Indigo Hundred. Like Basso in the forties, John would have liked to be on the battlefield but ends up behind a desk, functioning as Stanhope's secretary. Unlike Basso's other protagonists, who, despite their family's demands, manage to hold onto their hearts' desires, John obediently complies with his father's and the community's wishes. Wanting to become an author or architect after college, John becomes a planter instead because his father tells him to. Similarly, when his father and the senator urge him to become Stanhope's assistant, John becomes a clerk even though he wants to be a soldier. John is not only passive and wooden—he was described as a "stick" by a *Times Literary Supplement* reviewer—he is also weak. His passive resistance, his disinclination to hold slaves combined with his unwillingness to change the status quo, his lusting after women slaves, and his pathetic dive into Lydia's shirtwaist when she stumbles over some geraniums, turn him into a wavering and unsympathetic character. Most reviewers commented on John's weaknesses, and when Basso's friend and southern critic Broadus Mitchell criticized his many inconsistencies, Basso claimed that John was never intended as an "especially heroic hero." His "low-boiling point in relation to that slave girl . . . and Lydia Stanhope's bosom" were simply illustrations of the "way he was": "He had to be a rather sex-starved man. And surely we can agree that the South, more than any part of the country, takes a kind of dank, humid view about sex—always, at least in John Bottomley's day, the easy availability of the Negro woman, and at the same time, the sulphurous Calvanistic [*sic*] image of hell, fire and brimstone."[31]

Apart from his lack of sexual control, John's psychic ability to see through things and solve mysteries immediately is highly unconvincing. One look at the Channel girl is apparently enough for John to know that Cameron killed her brother. And when John's clerk rouses the suspicion that Stanhope might be smuggling cotton, one glance at Lydia reveals to him that Stanhope is indeed smuggling and that Lydia is his accomplice. Besides these contrived epiphanies, John is extremely changeable in his emotions. Although continually depressed over his failure to have an amorous relationship with Lydia, once he finds out that she has a hand in the smuggling conspiracy, he bans her from his thoughts, apparently with ease. Fleeing into the arms of the pretty Arabella, with whom he has always had a teasing brother-sister relationship (like Anson and Dinah), he asks her to marry him after a single kiss. The novel's romance, perhaps heightened by the exaggerated chivalry of antebellum times, is of a dimestore romance quality and, as such, a letdown for the serious reader.

The novel's finale, which echoes the ending of *Gone with the Wind* (1936), is equally disappointing because of its overcharged dramatiza-

31. "Agincourt and After," *Times Literary Supplement*, December 4, 1959, p. 705; Basso to Broadus Mitchell, September 22, 1959, in Basso Papers, BL.

tion. When the haggard-looking John returns to Indigo Hundred, Ules is about to set the house on fire after an impassioned speech from the porch. Allbright tries to stop him but Ules shoots him in the chest, and while Missie holds the fatally wounded mulatto in her arms and the house bursts into flames, Arabella seeks comfort in John's arms, telling him, "There'll be another light infantry ball" (*LIB*, 476). This ending was misinterpreted as indicating Basso's allegiance to the preservation of antebellum society. Basso, however, meant the opposite with Arabella's statement: "As I wrote that line, and then puzzled it, into wanting to come as close as possible to the right note, the exact pitch, I thought it had an ironic tinge. As I still do. Standing where Arabella stood, I could see the South as trying to have another light infantry ball, vainly and foolishly attempting to pretend that it had not walked into oblivion."[32]

Another misconception on the part of the critics was the assumption that *The Light Infantry Ball* was a historical novel. While Riley Hughes described the novel as a "book of deft historical perceptions," and Earl W. Foell suggested, less complimentarily, that it is a "historical reconstruction" with operetta characters, Granville Hicks claimed that the book is not the "kind of superior historical novel it was obviously intended to be." However, already in 1954, when Basso was drawing up the first plans for the novel, he was telling Van Wyck Brooks that he wanted to take the families of *Pompey's Head* and "go back to Pompey's Head during the Civil War, writing a modern novel in that setting." Similarly, in his letter to Broadus Mitchell, he wrote that he detested the historical novel and tried to "overcome" the genre by avoiding "a single historical character on the stage." In conversation with Lee Barker, Basso further stressed that though the novel was set in the nineteenth century, *The Light Infantry Ball* was in "no sense a historical novel." The question of course remains whether one can define a novel as "modern" when it draws so elaborately and accurately from plantation and Civil War history. Clearly, Basso had done a great deal of historical research, and the southern newspapers of the 1860s among his notes for *The Light Infantry Ball* indicate that the novel was not drawn from the imagination alone.[33]

32. Basso to Mitchell, September 22, 1959, in Basso Papers, BL.

33. Riley Hughes, "The Light Infantry Ball," *Catholic World*, CLXXXIX (August 1959), 400; Earl W. Foell, "Basso's Civil War South," *Christian Science Monitor*, June 4, 1959;

Malcolm Cowley was one of the few reviewers who understood what Basso really wanted to do with his Civil War novel. Possibly he and Basso had spoken about the book before it came out. Never calling it a historical novel, Cowley argued that the author's aim was "not to evoke the pastness of the past, not to celebrate the pageantry and valor that have gone with the wind, but rather to seek in the past for the seeds of the present." Also, Cowley was the only critic who understood that Ules Monckton, representing the group of fanatic secessionists and fire-eaters who were responsible for the tragedy of the South, was in fact a more important character than John.[34]

In spite of Cowley's perceptive critique and Basso's appreciation of his friend's review, Cowley did not lavish praise on the novel. On the contrary, the review has a negative undertone that Cowley may have tempered on account of his friendship with Basso. Thus while pointing out the writer's serious intentions, Cowley did not relish the novel's "costume romance," "detective story," and "theatrical" ending. Curiously, although Basso thanked Cowley in a first letter written from the Holland-America Line, in a later letter he referred to the review again and asked Cowley why he had cleaned out the "sewer."[35] It is possible that Basso had first read the review in haste because of his trip to Scandinavia and then, on rereading it, had become disgruntled with his friend's tone.

Basso was upset with most of the critics. Some of them commended his knowledgeable analysis of antebellum society and secessionist politics, yet most deplored the figure of John Bottomley and the novel's cheap romance. Few understood, as did his friend Newton Arvin, that Basso had tried to treat "the war years from the Southern point of view without special pleading, melodramatic sentimentality, and a nagging defensiveness; and . . . to generate . . . a kind of imaginative sympathy with the South of that intensely tragic moment that all the Confederate romanticizing literature from now on till Doomsday could never evoke." Basso's attempt to view the southern plantation legend from a

---

Granville Hicks, "Pompey's Head, 1861–1865," *Saturday Review of Literature,* June 6, 1959, p. 16; Basso to Brooks, October 23, 1954, in Brooks Papers, PP; Basso to Mitchell, September 22, 1959, BL; Barker to Basso, March 16, 1955, in Basso Papers, BL.

34. Malcolm Cowley, "The Life and Death of a Fire Eater," *New York Times Book Review,* June 7, 1959, pp. 1, 33.

35. Basso to Cowley, June 5, 1959, March 28, 1960, in Cowley Papers, NL.

different angle was perhaps not as successful as he had hoped, but the novel was nonetheless applauded by Caroline Tunstall of the *Herald Tribune Book Review*, who spoke of Basso's courageous "new approach to the subject" of southern myth.[36]

Although critics like Cowley, Arvin, and Tunstall recognized and honored Basso's objective in that *The Light Infantry Ball* was to serve as a "corrective," countering the "customary, conventional picture of the ante-bellum South," the majority of critics placed the novel in the *Gone with the Wind* tradition, which ironically was precisely the school that Basso had always been writing against.[37] In spite of his desire to tell the truth about the South, Basso's southern realism of the thirties settled into a sort of blend of pessimism and mythologization. Where in his thirties work southern virtues and vices are usually seen in perspective, in his later work the South turns into a locale of nightmares and madness (*Wine of the Country*), political paranoia and despotic populism (*Sun in Capricorn*), and finally Shintoism (*The View from Pompey's Head*). At the same time, the South is presented as a place of moonlight, magnolias, romantic love, and Civil War intrigues (*The Light Infantry Ball*). Tossed between homesickness and the realization that he could not go home again, Basso became less objective. In his fiction of the forties and fifties, the South is a land of extremes, and whereas some exiled writers manage to understand their country of origin better once they have the distance and detachment of living elsewhere, in Basso's case, exile was detrimental to his fictionalization of the South. Rather than continue his rebellion against the plantation legend, he (albeit unintentionally) reinvented the old myths, a phenomenon that surfaces most painfully in *The Light Infantry Ball*. Owing to its many ambiguities and flaws, the book is not at all representative of either Basso's actual views of the South or his distinction as a novelist.

In the summer of 1960, Basso went to Europe to pen a travelogue on Scandinavia. His letters home disclose that he was no longer the avid traveler he had been even a few years earlier. Bored as always by landscapes, he did not care for the fjords. Furthermore, he was shocked and

36. Newton Arvin to Basso, June 8, 1959, in Basso Papers, BL; Caroline Tunstall, "Story of Secession Days in Old Pompey," *New York Herald Tribune Book Review*, June 7, 1959, p. 3.

37. Basso to Mitchell, September 22, 1959, in Basso Papers, BL.

surprised by the anti-American sentiments of the Scandinavians: "Maybe our techniques of mass production are responsible: certainly the rock and roll influence seems to have penetrated everywhere; certainly you can drink Coca Cola in 72 different languages . . . and why are the shop windows full of such junky, tasteless stuff? Why such awful 'modern' domestic architecture? Blame the U.S. if you like—and they do like: we are the international whipping boy . . . but let's not forget the corroding influences of the two world wars which, unless I have misread my own experience, we didn't start."[38]

He further observed that he no longer got on with the natives, and with the Swedes in particular, who, according to him, did not smile enough: "I'm a great smiler when I am in foreign parts, as you know, and I can always tell myself, truthfully, that in Tahiti and Samoa I did get along with the natives—Here though—Oh rats!" Cooped up for long periods on board ship, Basso was always greatly interested in his fellow passengers. On his Scandinavian trip, he compared them to the Dutch he and Toto had met on their trips aboard the *Rotterdam* and the *Maasdam*: "I remember the Dutch as being more gay—'the jolly Dutchman; the dumb Swede; the bone-head Norwegian'—perjorative [*sic*] symbols, each one . . . and yet they sometimes ring true."[39]

The letters from Scandinavia are tinged by a kind of travel fatigue; Basso confessed that he did not "care to come abroad again. I can't deny my own country (which is for one thing the only country I'll ever have) and yet I cringe from an identification with these American tourists who are now beginning to arrive—the noisy, loudmouthed ones; the first batch of unclean beatniks." His tour of northern Europe had few crescendos, with the exception of his first midsummer night witnessed "aboard the Oslo Fjord when on toward three o'clock in the morning the sky still was luminous and the sea was inky black—that was the one and only bang . . . that first light night . . . was the only time I've been away: when the accustomed and the familiar fell behind, and for an instant . . . I was different than before." Conditioned by the exotic environment of Louisiana bayous and the city of New Orleans, Basso had more of a rapport with Tahitians, Cubans, and Latin Americans than with the more reserved and sometimes cold Swedes, Norwe-

38. Basso to Etolia S. Basso, May 31, 1960, in Basso Papers, BL.
39. Basso to Etolia S. Basso, May 23, June 19, 1960, in Basso Papers, BL.

gians, and Finns. The Danes, on the other hand, were, according to Basso, a "pleasure-loving people, relaxed and inherently gay . . . so with my own temperament being what it is, how can I not like these people?"[40]

His Scandinavian travelogue completed *A Quota of Seaweed* (1960), a book of travel pieces of which the majority had already come out in the *New Yorker*. Looking back on his oeuvre, Basso would come to think favorably of this book and his other work of nonfiction, *Mainstream*. He may even have preferred these books to what he considered his weaker novels—*Relics and Angels, In Their Own Image*, and *Sun in Capricorn*. Contemporary readers might agree, placing Basso's nonfiction work, journalism, and short stories on a higher plane than some of his novels. As comes out very clearly in the letters and the travel diaries, Basso's talent was sometimes better suited for "the shorter distance than the longer distance," an expression Basso himself used to contrast Henry James's shorter fiction to his novels.[41]

In 1961 Basso made his last extended trip abroad and realized that he had grown tired of travel; his trip to Trinidad was the worst of all his foreign travel. In his letters home, he complained of the oppressive heat, the dirt, and the crowded streets. The letters are depressing, and the darkness and fatigue that Basso found so hard to "explain" may have been an early foreboding of the lung cancer that would be diagnosed one and a half years later. Besides his mental and physical exhaustion, he was disturbed by the colonial and racist mentality of Trinidad's white elite: "What has got me down, after but one day of socializing, is the worms-in-the-milk-bottle quality of the lighter skinned society . . . when whites try to live in these climatically and ethnically non-white societies, they sort of get 'rendered' and boiled down, spiritually, by the heat: and then all these globules of this and that come to the surface . . . in some way or other, despite high tea and dressing for dinner and so forth, people simply go 'bush.' " Always sensitive to the insensitivities of whites vis-à-vis blacks, he was not pretending or striking a pose when he told his wife that he preferred a chat with the black locals to sherry with the white patriciate.[42]

40. Basso to Etolia S. Basso, June 6, 17, 19, 1960, in Basso Papers, BL.

41. Tape recording of a conversation among the Bassos, the Blumes, and the Brookses, June 9, 1955, taped at the Bassos' home in Connecticut, in Basso Papers, HT.

42. Basso to Etolia S. Basso, October 27, 1961, in Basso Papers, BL.

It irked Basso that after the success of *Pompey's Head*, he was recognized as a famous writer: "They have discovered that a 'writer' (damn the word!) can like Shakespeare's jew [*sic*] laugh, weep, rejoice and so on, which has finally alleviated their original unease [but] I can be a dangerous man. Just as dangerous as if I presented the classic conventional image of the 'writer,' unwashed and superior and flagrantly immoral, instead of this ultra-protective coloring it has pleased me to adopt." On his trip to Trinidad he was followed around by an inquisitive couple whom he named "Mr and Mrs Joe from Toledo." After they had found out Basso was a writer, Mrs. Joe kept asking him what he thought of the new design of the *Saturday Evening Post*, "which she and Joe emphatically didn't like. . . . Such decent, decent people," Basso sighed, "and such a woeful handicap, whenever they set foot abroad; and also, I am afraid when they stay at home."[43]

To steer clear of both American tourists and Trinidad's upper crust, Basso avoided cocktail parties and kept mostly to himself. Trying to relax to get rid of the weariness in his bones, he was already planning his next novel, which was to take place in Tahiti. He gave the first draft the tentative title "The Swing of the Compass," and on his way home he wrote Toto: "I was able to 'see' one vitally important episode close to the end of the book. . . . I 'saw' the whole first part that is already written and the question is this—whence came it out? The four S-s? The heat heavy enough to touch? Les negres comme le Congo? . . . My sullen privacy for nearly a week? . . . Or Mrs Joe from Toledo?"[44]

The unfinished manuscript of "The Swing of the Compass" shows that Basso was still interested in the detective element but was also being innovative by using a polyphonic narrative for the first time. The story begins in the faculty room of a college campus where Professor Guildford has sherry with the young historian Andrew Tenniel. Guildford tells Tenniel that a rich widow will donate one million dollars to the college if one of the professors writes a biography of her cousin, the forgotten botanist Wallace Pembroke Graves. Graves died in the Pacific, where he attempted to lay out a kind of South Seas Kew Gardens. Guildford encourages Tenniel to do the job.

43. Basso to Etolia S. Basso, November 4, 6, 1961, in Basso Papers, BL.
44. Basso to Etolia S. Basso, November 18, 1961, in Basso Papers, BL.

Although Meredith Beers, a fellow scholar whom Guildford calls a "constipated ape," is one of the likely candidates for the book, the widow favors Tenniel because she admires his article about the colonial gardens of America. The tension and petty arguments between Tenniel and Beers—who, like the closet scholar Casaubon in George Eliot's *Middlemarch* (1871), has written a "key to all mythologies" and who, like the New Critics, claims that "a novel should exist as a poem exists, in itself, independent of any external references, even psychology"— evince Basso's satirical view of universities and stuffy intellectuals.

Tenniel's scholarly insecurities and mockery of academe remind one of Kingsley Amis' *Lucky Jim* (1954), a novel Basso may well have read. Like Basso, who was sometimes embarrassed to admit he was a writer, Tenniel does not boast of his own profession, and like Tait Ravenwill in *Wine of the Country*, he fears the ivory tower life that Guildford leads: "Here it was, [Tenniel] thought, the classic example—the insulated, impractical academic; the 'professor' in quotation marks; the foolish fellow who spent his own time and other people's money ferreting out knowledge as wearisome as it was useless."[45]

While Tenniel starts his research, we meet Michele Sarlat, a Frenchwoman who, after an unhappy childhood and disastrous marriage to a wartime traitor, is tired of fending for herself and marries the childless widower Lindvall. The couple live on Akivani (Basso's fictional version of Tahiti). The link with Tenniel's story is laid when we learn that Lindvall owns the Graves gardens. Michele has typical Basso traits: her mother having died in childbirth and her father having been killed at sea, she is an orphaned heroine; and like Dekker and Hazzard, she is raised by an aunt and uncle in Paris. Also, like the typical Basso grandfather, Michele's grandfather Joseph Quinet takes on mythical proportions. Michele remembers him as someone who mingled with the Impressionists in Paris and who, like another Gauguin, left for Tahiti to paint and plant. The tie with her grandfather is strong: "Because of the several paintings from brush of her grandfather, which were as much part of the atmosphere of her childhood in the Rue Labineau as her lofty balcony and the bells of St. Sulpice, she felt closer to him, more

---

45. Hamilton Basso, "The Swing of the Compass" (Typescript in Basso Papers, BL), 211, 242. The unfinished manuscript of the novel was not given to the library until 1971, after Etolia Basso had tried to sell it to Viking.

identified and lineal, than she did to her mother. It was not difficult to summon up the image of her grandfather (generally he was seated at one of the sidewalk tables of the Nouvelles Athenes in the company of those great ones, agreeing, dissenting, signalling to a waiter for another drink), whereas her mother, no matter how hard she tried to visualize her, remained a shadowy, wraithlike figure lost in the forlorn ghostliness of that deserted house no more than a mile down the road."[46]

Like her literary brother David Barondess, Michele dwells on the past. And she, too, is melancholic, lonely, and homesick. Beyond that, we know very little of her; the manuscript was never finished. What we do get to see, however, is Tenniel's quest for biographical facts. Aided by his various interviews with people who knew Graves, we gradually conceive a portrait of the botanist. Tenniel's interviews are undoubtedly inspired by the interviews Basso had done for his *New Yorker* profiles. Interestingly, rather than submit his characters to the conventional question-and-answer game, he allows them long dramatic monologues that give the narrative its polyphonic nature. Though not as arcane as the monologues in some of Faulkner's novels, the effect is the same: from the different speakers' conflicting impressions of and experiences with Graves, we have to distill the identity of the real Graves, who, all in all, appears to have been an eccentric and self-indulgent *doppelgänger* of Garvin Wales. The use of the multiple viewpoint suits Basso well: having a keen ear for dialogue, he makes the interviewees sound so natural that the monologues appear to be transcripts of taped interviews.

Unfortunately, we do not know how the novel would have ended. Knowing that Michele married out of convenience and that Tenniel is divorced and unhappy in love, it is likely that with Tenniel's research leading him to Lindvall, the two are bound to meet and fall in love. But many questions are left unanswered: What will the confrontation between Lindvall and Tenniel be like? What will Tenniel find out about Graves, and why does Ralph Maitland, a relative of Graves, insist on the family's right to privacy and threaten to sue Tenniel if he publishes?

Like *Pompey's Head*, "The Swing of the Compass" has a mystery plot, the amateur detective here being a historian. As in *Pompey's Head*, too, Basso relies heavily on the flashback, which explains but mostly slows down the action. Such criticism aside, "The Swing of the Compass"

---

46. *Ibid.,* 199.

shows promise and potential. Its hero and heroine, Andrew and Michele, are neither the wooden characters of *The Light Infantry Ball* nor the hollow society figures of *A Touch of the Dragon*, the novel Basso worked on after he put aside "The Swing of the Compass." Instead, Andrew and Michele are much rounder characters. Michele seems sensitive and intelligent, and Andrew is a much more stimulating character than the stiff John Bottomley and the shallow Sebastian Venables in *A Touch of the Dragon*. This may be explained by Basso's easier identification with a shy historian than with a plantation squire or a society beau.

In this manuscript, albeit incomplete, Basso had clearly regained the old vigor and verve of his thirties novels, in which character, atmosphere, and feeling took precedence over plot and story. "The Swing of the Compass" feels genuine where *The View from Pompey's Head*, *The Light Infantry Ball*, and *A Touch of the Dragon* feel forced and artificial. In part, the authentic flavor derives from Basso's successful and natural handling of the polyphonic narrative; in part, also, the story's strength seems to come from his recapturing of the poetic voice he had last used in his thirties novels. Thus the natural beauty of Akivani is akin to the local color enchantment of the Louisiana landscapes of his early work: "For all practical purposes, her eyes opened on the island of Akivani. The ceaseless murmur of the reef, the crash of a coconut falling to the earth, the slatting of palm trees in the wind, the waiting silence before a rain, the voice of a native girl singing far away."[47] We must be careful not to overestimate an unfinished work, yet the 378 pages of the manuscript give us more than an inkling of how the novel might have turned out. In retrospect, one can only regret that Basso did not finish a novel that combined the virtues of both his early and his later talent.

When Basso was diagnosed with cancer in 1963, he abandoned the Tahitian novel and turned a long short story, "Edwina," into a short novel that was to bear the title *A Touch of the Dragon* (1964). When Malcolm Cowley gave the eulogy at Basso's funeral, he noted that the novel was written under sentence of death, a feat representing Basso's willingness to sacrifice "his life to his literary integrity and his passion for honest craftsmanship. Like his friend Thomas Wolfe, he was a hero and martyr of the act of writing." The smooth and light narrative cer-

47. *Ibid.*, 200.

tainly seems unaffected by Basso's impending death, yet this deathbed work is not, as Clarence Ikerd believes, "one of the finest novels" Basso wrote. Its forced social comedy and satiric delineation of a dull upper-crust milieu make this polished novel of manners a tedious prolongation of *In Their Own Image*.[48]

The narrator, Sebastian Venables, is not a hero of momentous action but a Jamesian observer. His failures as a writer and a husband serve as a kind of sideline to the story of Edwina Deydier's ruthless rise to power. Set against the background of midwestern high society, which seems as interested in ancestor worship as southern society is, Edwina's ascent to the top is witnessed by Sebastian. She achieves her preeminence by writing a dog column for a society magazine and by marrying the pretentious literary critic Covington Leeds. Leeds's rediscovery of the ignored writer Gervase Peale becomes one of the pillars to Edwina's glory, but when Peale turns out to be an impostor, something which Leeds failed to uncover, Edwina gets rid of her husband, just as she disposes of her elkhounds when they no longer serve the furthering of her "career." As Edwina is a compounded caricature of Lydia Stanhope, Ules Monckton, Lucy Wales, and Mrs. Porter, she is evil personified. The novel ends with a tennis match held on a Caribbean island where Edwina's social set vacations. As fanatical on the tennis court as she is in real life, Edwina beats her opponent, the wife of the English governor, whose heart condition causes her sudden death after the match. Edwina marries the governor and thus finally satisfies her voracious ambition for power and status.

Like *In Their Own Image*, *A Touch of the Dragon* is greatly weakened by its cardboard characters. Even Edwina, who receives most of the attention, is a shallow creation. Though she is positively wicked, she is more often irritating. Behaving like a spoiled child and using her money as a prop to achieve her goals, she hovers like some evil spirit over Sebastian, who knows neither money nor goals in his life. Sebastian's sense of failure and his wife's difficulty to conceive may be related to Edwina's curse—the "touch of the dragon" of the title. Sebastian actually wonders if Edwina "might not be akin to one of the

48. Cowley, typescript notes for Basso's eulogy in Cowley Papers, NL; Ikerd, "Hamilton Basso," 135. Apparently, "Edwina" was a short story that Basso had submitted to *Harper's* in 1960: "They liked the story, but they said it was too long for one issue and did not lend itself to being split up" (133).

unfortunate chilling persons we read about in the books of demonol-
ogy that belong to the same period as the old rectangular maps, a creature who casts no shadow and has no soul" (*TD*, 204). Whatever the
case, once Edwina has reached her goal, Susan, Sebastian's second
wife, announces she is pregnant, and the couple are set to live happily
ever after.

Despite the malevolent shadow Edwina casts over other people's
lives, her diabolical nature is attenuated by her extreme silliness: for instance, she pours a carton of milk and cracks an egg over her head
when she is angry with someone else. Her malice is further weakened
by her essential phoniness; like Mrs. Porter and the pretenders of *In
Their Own Image*, she hides behind a façade: "Just as she lived beyond
her cultural means, so did Edwina overextend her emotional capital.
There were these feelings she believed she ought to have—feelings
about politics, feelings about books. . . . She was like an actor who, after
a shattering display of violent emotion—Othello, for example—wipes
away his agony with his greasepaint" (*TD*, 36–37). Because of
Edwina's capricious character, it is difficult to take her seriously.

The reviews were mixed. Those who recommended the novel admired the figure of Edwina and labeled the book as "entertaining."
Those who thought the book was slick rather than entertaining criticized Edwina's superficiality. One of the reviewers wondered: "I cannot for the life of me see what the late Hamilton Basso was about in de-
ploying all that taste and skill for the production of such a poisoned-
chocolate-box villainness as his Edwina Deydier, whose upper-
suburban bitchiness could only be properly handled . . . in the old-
fashioned kind of woman's magazine."[49] However much Edwina was
applauded or sneered at, none of the reviewers took note of the implied sexism of Edwina's creation, for Sebastian seems to argue that female ambition is improper and blemishes feminine beauty. According
to him, Edwina has the potential to be beautiful, but her zeal and hard
work turn her into a freak. Covington Leeds, on the other hand, who is
equally ambitious and despicable, is nonetheless a more dignified
character than the overbearing Edwina, who, not surprisingly, is said
to be taller than most men. Regrettably, Edwina's portrayal, together

---

49. Norman Shrapnel, "Manner over Matter," Manchester *Guardian Weekly*, February 18, 1965, p. 11.

with the marginal delineation of the majority of his female characters, confirms that Basso, though a firm supporter of black emancipation, was blind to the plight of women.

As for Covington Leeds, he is a kind of Harold Stearns gone astray. Like Stearns, who reiterated the theme of the artistic aridity of American soil, Leeds harps on his "disenchantment with the contemporary culture of the United States" (*TD*, 123). Like Stearns, too, whose promise soured, Leeds is "awarded . . . a top-most place among the writers of the war generation who had failed to live up to their promise" (*TD*, 124). Leeds represents the kind of literary critic and poet that Basso detested so much, and as can be expected, Sebastian voices his creator's opinions when he deplores the academic seriousness of literary criticism and describes Leeds's claptrap writings as "snake oil" and as obsessed with the theme of the "barren wasteland of contemporary culture and the sad lot of the artist" (*TD*, 24, 162). Sebastian also scoffs at Leeds's division of novelists into "two all-inclusive categories, 'wet flies' and 'dry flies'—'dry fly' novelists being those who sought to attract the reader by the 'superficial lure of surface appeal' (Dickens and Trollope being cited as examples), while the 'wet fly' novelists (Proust, Joyce, and D. H. Lawrence) were described as seeking a more valid engagement in the darker, murkier, more meaningful depths of human experience" (*TD*, 240). Leeds's sympathy lies with the "wet flies," and he and Edwina, who champion Joyce as the Picasso of the novel, "stand as representatives of the new age, the modern man and woman." In contrast to Leeds and Edwina, who embrace the avant garde, Sebastian feels as Basso may have felt in the company of Malcolm Cowley and Matthew Josephson, that is, "old-fashioned almost to the point of being [a] pathetically backward primitive, who, by some freakish piece of luck, had managed to survive" (*TD*, 62–63, 114).

Notwithstanding his Bassoesque discussions of literature and art, Sebastian is not a commendable character at all. Just as we cannot truly hate Edwina because she fails to be an antagonist in the full sense of the word, we do not feel much sympathy for Sebastian because of his insubstantiality. Sebastian is simply too weak, or as Elizabeth Janeway argued: "Edwina needs a fullfledged, involved character to oppose her and bring the book to a climax, just as the dragon needs a dragon killer. But this dragon simply stubs her toe while St. George stands by and reports the details."[50] Part of Sebastian's sketchiness lies in his being a sideline commentator rather than an active protagonist.

Incidentally, *Sun in Capricorn* and *A Touch of the Dragon* are Basso's only novels that have first-person narrators. Basso may have wanted to avoid the intimacy of a first-person narration by turning Hazzard and Sebastian into characters who do not take themselves seriously. In this way, he directs our attention to their absurd and monomaniacal opponents, Slade and Edwina. Like Hazzard, Sebastian is unambitious and passive. Whether it is their embitterment or simply their outlook on life, with both characters there is an undertone of mockery in everything they say. One may even consider them unreliable narrators, and in this respect, Sebastian certainly resembles Fitzgerald's Nick Carraway, who is also an outsider-observer of the cushioned lives of the idle rich, in *The Great Gatsby* (1925).

Also poorly conceived is Sebastian's lack of distinction or purpose. Although he shares a few traits with Anson Page and Rufus Jackson, who also have to deal with malevolent women, where Anson and Rufus have a clear assignment and reason to meet with their antagonists, Sebastian has no such sense of mission. He does not get entangled with Edwina at any point, but being of marginal importance to her set, he "could only watch her progress from a distance, like a dweller in an Alpine valley who gazes at a solitary climber high upon the peaks" (*TD*, 62). It is this distance and the certainty that Sebastian will never confront the dragon lady that rob the novel of its suspense. Sebastian's prolonged fascination and obsession with Edwina even become a little wearisome, his observations being no more than an extended study into the perversity of the ambitious female.

Neither a continuation of what Basso had written nor the promise of a new departure, *A Touch of the Dragon* should not be seen as a summation of the novelist's career. Because the publication of the novel coincided with Basso's death, some reviewers took the opportunity to acclaim his entire oeuvre but unfortunately based his importance as a writer on his later and more popular books. Thus most critics discussed Basso's entertaining ability; as the *Spectator* critic noted, *A Touch*

---

50. Elizabeth Janeway, "Nobody Loves Edwina," *New York Times Book Review*, March 22, 1964, p. 33.

of the Dragon offers "easy reading for a train journey." William B. Hill, more complimentarily, called Basso an "artistic novelist [who] does not splash words on paper, does not try to be esoteric, uses none of the common devices for getting attention; he does plot a novel carefully and he writes beautiful prose." Hill further referred to Basso's "careful craftsmanship," a term that Cowley would also use in his eulogy. Though surely a flattering epithet, "craftsmanship" does not equal "genius" or "exceptional talent," nor does it purport any sort of lasting legacy.[51]

More praise came from William Barrett, who told his readers that Basso "never screams or roars at the reader; his is the quiet voice of a man of the world speaking calmly of the things and people he has observed dispassionately but sympathetically." Some critics associated this style with the pitch of the *New Yorker*, or as John Coleman put it: "In many ways [Basso] must have been an editor's delight: *his* tone so uncannily caught the ideal *New Yorker* tone of alert but well-bred and slightly withdrawn worldliness. It was 'civilised' without being too committed to civilisation." In his *Journals*, John Cheever also alluded to this "civilized" style, which he ascribed to the influence of the *New Yorker*'s first editor, Harold Ross: "[Ross] taught me that decorum can be a mode of language—born of our need to speak with one another—and a language that, having been learned, was in no way constraining."[52]

Basso's last novel was brought out not by Doubleday but by Viking. Although Basso's editor at Doubleday, Lee Barker, wanted to publish the book, Basso felt pressured, as Barker was hoping for the same kind of best-seller that *Pompey's Head* had been. Finding Barker's preoccupation with "book-clubs, motion pictures, and best-sellerdom too wholly at odds" with his own approach to writing, Basso explained in a letter: "The nub of the matter, however, is that I don't want to write another 'big' novel—not by any definition of bigness that hinges on weight or bulk or the number of printed pages. As a writer, I am interested in as many readers as I can get. I am wholly disinterested however, in 'aim-

---

51. Neville Braybrooke, "Innocence and Experience," *Spectator*, February 19, 1965, p. 6; William B. Hill, "A Touch of the Dragon," *America*, April 11, 1964, p. 515.

52. William Barrett, "Reader's Choice," *Atlantic Monthly*, CCXIII (April 1964), 143; John Coleman, "First Person Singular," *Observer*, February 14, 1965, p. 13; John Cheever, *The Journals*, ed. Benjamin Cheever (1991; rpr. London, 1993), 340.

ing' for a readership, or trying . . . to give the reader what he wants. In what I have written since I came to my belated maturity, leaving aside the question of merit, I have tried to express certain values—values completely at odds with those implied by the very term 'big novel.' In short, I have nothing in my mind or trunk that I feel, quite hard-headedly, that Doubleday would really care to publish."[53]

Nine months before Basso's death, his illness was declared terminal after an operation to remove one cancerous lung revealed that the cancer had already spread to his sternum. The doctor, who would admire the courage with which the Bassos took the bad news, advised them to escape the winter cold of Connecticut. They followed his advice and rented a ground-floor apartment in Scottsdale, Arizona. Keith, who was a promising graduate student in anthropology at Stanford, joined them for what was to be their last Christmas together.

From the moment Basso learned that he only had a few months to live, he kept up his spirits and dutifully worked on the last pages of his novel. Joking with the nurses, he told them that he was not sick at all. He informed his doctors that they should no longer worry as the medicine men on the Apache reservation where Keith worked as an anthropologist had held a "sing" for him to exorcise "Malakai," or the evil spirit.[54] In the same upbeat frame of mind, Keith wrote his father a little poem to congratulate him on the completion of *A Touch of the Dragon*:

> . . .
> And now he can roam
> Or even go home
> Til Viking comes through with the galley.
>
> He may sit and go about musin'
> On the tale of Sebastian and Susan
> Now that it's done
> He should have some fun
> Maybe he'll blow, and go crusin'.[55]

After Christmas, however, Basso took a turn for the worse. Because the Arizona hospitals lacked sophisticated x-ray equipment, the Bassos hurried back to New Haven Hospital. The radiation treatment that fol-

---

53. Basso to Barker, June 29, July 17, 1962, in Basso Papers, BL.
54. Etolia S. Basso to the author, May 28, 1992.
55. Keith Basso to Basso, October 9, 1963, in files of Etolia S. Basso.

lowed brought some relief and prompted Peter de Vries's comment that his friend's "apparently handsome reaction to radiation" was going to stand him in good stead. But Basso's overall health deteriorated quickly, and the publication of *A Touch of the Dragon* in March did little to alleviate the pain. In April, Basso returned to the hospital and de Vries mourned that the world was "unravelling like an old sock," as all his friends were falling ill. Nonetheless, Basso remained hopeful until the very end, confiding in Cowley that "if I get well . . . I want to drop everything I have done in the past—that's the effect of an illness like this—and strike in some new direction."[56]

Basso lost consciousness for several days and then died peacefully in the company of his wife and his mother on May 13, 1964, in New Haven Hospital. When Keith was asked about his father's death, he replied: "His final thoughts, I'm almost certain, were of my mother, and as death approached he gave no sign of fear. He had suffered enormously, and I like to think he was grateful when at last there was no pain." Upon his death, obituaries appeared in all the major magazines and newspapers. His funeral was attended by many, and the letters of condolence Toto received speak of Basso's sharp mind, charm, charisma, and warm interest in others. The New York *Times* editor R. L. Duffus summed it up best when he wrote Toto on May 15, 1964: "It is hard to judge what life meant to a man so calm, composed and philosophical, but I think all your friends will agree that he seemed to be happy in his work and his home life."[57]

Born and bred in the South but buried at the tree-lined cemetery of Emmanuel Church in Weston, Connecticut, Hamilton Basso, that "medium-size man with graying hair, a strong nose, a quick and easy smile and a courteous affability," rests in peace. After thirty-four years of virtual neglect of his most important work, his legacy may get lost in the many cracks of the American canon. But the books remain, and, with them, Basso's unique testimony of a southerner who repeatedly tried but eventually could not go home again.[58]

56. Peter de Vries to Basso, January 20 and April 1964, Basso to Cowley, [1964], in Basso Papers, BL.

57. Keith Basso, letter to the author, February 15, 1994; R. L. Duffus to Etolia Basso, May 15, 1964, in possession of Etolia Basso.

58. John K. Hutchens, "The Architect of Pompey's Head," *New York Herald Tribune Book Review*, October 31, 1954, p. 3.

Bibliography

NOTE ON SOURCES

The bulk of Hamilton Basso's papers can be found at the Beinecke Rare Book and Manuscript Library at Yale University. The collection contains the full typescripts and, in some cases, notes as well as galley proofs of five of his books: *The Greenroom* (typescript and dramatization of the novel for a radio play); *The Light Infantry Ball* (notes, typescript, and galley proofs); *A Quota of Seaweed* (typescript); *A Touch of the Dragon* (typescript); and *The View from Pompey's Head* (notes and typescript). The novel unfinished at Basso's death, entitled "The Swing of the Compass," is part of the same collection, as is Basso's early and unpublished work, consisting of short stories, poems, and a worthwhile novelette, "The Ladies of the Land." One can further find notes and typescripts of miscellaneous articles Basso wrote for the *New Yorker* and *Holiday*.

The author's correspondence at the Beinecke is dominated by letters to his wife, Etolia Simmons Basso. The ninety-two letters, spanning 1942–60, cover Basso's travel through California, Denmark, Finland, Florida, Jamaica, Norway, Sweden, Tahiti, and various other places. The letters are anecdotal and lively and often served as the preliminary pieces to the actual travelogues for *Holiday*. The remaining letters in the Beinecke collection (about five hundred in all) reveal that Basso corresponded with many fellow writers and other interesting contemporaries. Letters to Basso include those by Sherwood Anderson, Edward Aswell, Bruce Bliven, Peter Blume, Van Wyck Brooks, Erskine Caldwell, Robert Coates, Malcolm Cowley, e.e. cummings, Jonathan Daniels, Bernard De Voto, William Faulkner, Otis Ferguson, F. Scott Fitzgerald, Ellen Glasgow, Nadine Gordimer, Lillian Hellman, Eugene Jolas, Matthew Josephson, Somerset Maugham, Broadus Mitchell, Carlotta O'Neill, Maxwell Perkins, Katherine Ann Porter, Marjorie Rawlings, James Thurber, Stewart Udall, Sigrid Undset, Peter de Vries, Thornton Wilder, Edmund Wilson, and Thomas Wolfe. The Thomas Wolfe folder also holds a copy of Wolfe's famous 28-page farewell letter to Maxwell Perkins and a copy of his short story "The Child by Tiger." For a stimulating record of Basso's life and ideas in the thirties, one should consult the forty-four letters that Basso wrote to his friend Matthew Josephson, to be found in the Matthew Josephson Papers at the Beinecke Library.

Basso's good relationship with Maxwell Perkins has been documented in his letters to the editor, all available in the Scribner's Archives at the Harvey S. Firestone Library at Princeton University. For more personal insights into Basso's character, one should read his letters to Sherwood Anderson and Malcolm Cowley in the Sherwood Anderson Papers and Malcolm Cowley Papers at the Newberry Library in Chicago. Likewise, Basso liked to share his innermost thoughts with Thomas Wolfe: the total of twenty letters that he wrote to the Asheville novelist are divided between the Houghton Library at Harvard University (Thomas Wolfe Papers) and the Wilson Library at the University of North Carolina at Chapel Hill (North Carolina Collection). Basso's letters to Van Wyck Brooks are more reserved in tone but nevertheless interesting for a glimpse of the author's life in Weston, Connecticut; these letters (twenty in total) are kept among Van Wyck Brooks's papers at the Patterson-Van Pelt Library at the University of Pennsylvania in Philadelphia.

Finally, the Hamilton Basso Collection at the Howard-Tilton Memorial Library at Tulane University in New Orleans holds the typescripts of Basso's debut novel *Relics and Angels;* five typescripts of unpublished short stories; five travel diaries; a copy of a speech Basso delivered at the Westport, Connecticut, public library in 1957; and the typescript for the profile of William Faulkner that was to appear in the July 28, 1962, issue of the *Saturday Review.* The same collection contains a tape recording of June 9, 1955, in which Basso asked Van Wyck Brooks about Henry James. This sole record of Basso's distinct southern drawl also reveals very clearly the author's social graces and refined sense of humor. In the same library one can find four interesting letters from Basso to Lyle Saxon (in the Lyle Saxon Collection). Equally worthwhile for its rendering of literary New Orleans in Basso's days is Cathy Chance Harvey's Ph.D. dissertation, "Lyle Saxon: A Portrait in Letters, 1917–1945" (1980), also to be found at the Howard-Tilton Memorial Library.

Hamilton Basso is mentioned sparsely in surveys and books on southern literature, and few scholars have written articles, let alone book-length studies, on him. Clarence Frye Ikerd was the first to write a full critical biography in the form of a doctoral dissertation (University of North Carolina at Chapel Hill, 1974); Joseph R. Millichap put the novelist on the map more definitively with *Hamilton Basso* (1979) in the Twayne series. Millichap later contributed a perceptive entry on Basso in Robert Bain and Joseph Flora's biographical dictionary *Fifty Southern Writers After 1900* (1987). Since Ikerd had the opportunity to interview many of Basso's contemporaries while they were still alive, I relied on his dissertation for biographical information. Millichap's work, on the other hand, was especially helpful for its sound interpretations of Basso's works.

James E. Rocks declined doing a book on Basso but nonetheless wrote an excellent fifteen-page survey of the novels, entitled "Hamilton Basso and the World View from Pompey's Head," *South Atlantic Quarterly,* LXXI (1972). Finally, for more bibliographical information, I would like to refer the reader to the footnotes and the following listing, which includes a comprehensive review of Basso's works.

PUBLISHED WORKS OF HAMILTON BASSO

Novels

Relics and Angels. New York, 1929.
Cinnamon Seed. New York, 1934.
In Their Own Image. New York, 1935.
Courthouse Square. New York, 1936.
Days Before Lent. New York, 1939.
Wine of the Country. New York, 1941.
Sun in Capricorn. New York, 1942.
The Greenroom. New York, 1949.
The View from Pompey's Head. New York, 1954.
The Light Infantry Ball. New York, 1959.
A Touch of the Dragon. New York, 1964.

Short Stories

"I Can't Dance." *transition,* XVI (June 1929), 127–32.
"The Fabulous Man: A Story." *Scribner's Magazine,* XCVII (April 1935), 217–18.
"Me and the Babe: A Story." *New Republic,* April 24, 1935, pp. 308–10.
"The Wild Turkey." *New Yorker,* March 18, 1944, pp. 25–27.
"A Kind of Special Gift." *New Yorker,* February 24, 1945, pp., 24–27.
"The Age of Fable." *New Yorker,* June 30, 1945, pp. 17–20.
"The Broken Horn." *New Yorker,* October 6, 1945, pp. 28–33.
"A Glimpse of Heaven—I." *New Yorker,* July 27, 1946, pp. 24–28.
"A Glimpse of Heaven—II." *New Yorker,* August 3, 1946, pp. 28–32.
"The Edge of the Wilderness." *New Yorker,* September 20, 1947, pp. 71–75.
"King Rail." *New Yorker,* October 18, 1947, pp. 97–103.
"The World of Caspar Milquetoast." *New Yorker,* November 5, 1949, pp. 40–61.

Poetry

"Brain." *Double Dealer,* VII (April 1925), 139.
"Questioning." *Double Dealer,* VIII (May 1926), 339.
"Rain on Aspidistra." *transition,* XXII (February 1933), 11–15.

Nonfiction

"Flood Water." *New Republic,* June 22, 1927, pp. 123–24.

"New Orleans Letter." *transition,* XV (February 1929), 149–50.

"Black Beowulf." *New Republic,* September 30, 1931, pp. 186–87.

Beauregard: The Great Creole. New York, 1933.

"The Seasonings of 'Old Hickory.' " *New Republic,* April 19, 1933, pp. 286–87.

Review of E. Merton Coulter's *A Short History of Georgia. New Republic,* December 13, 1933, p. 149.

"Five Days in Decatur." *New Republic,* December 20, 1933, pp. 161–64.

Review of Edward Larocque Tinker's *Bibliography of the French Newspapers and Periodicals of Louisiana. Books Abroad* (October 1933), 427.

"Mr. Senator, Come Clean!" *New Republic,* February 21, 1934, p. 54.

"About the Berry Schools: An Open Letter to Miss Martha Berry." *New Republic,* April 4, 1934, pp. 206–208.

"A Spotlight on the South." *New Republic,* April 18, 1934, pp. 287–88.

"The Divided Southern Front." *New Republic,* May 9, 1934, pp. 360–62.

"The End of a Trilogy." *New Republic,* June 20, 1934, p. 161.

"Textile Trouble—2 Gastonia: Before the Battle." *New Republic,* September 19, 1934, pp. 148–49.

"Two Sides of the Barricades—II: Lockout." *New Republic,* October 10, 1934, pp. 238–39.

"Mr. Hearst Sees Red." *New Republic,* January 16, 1935, pp. 260–71.

"Let's Look at the Record." *New Republic,* February 20, 1935, pp. 41–42.

"The Riot in Harlem." *New Republic,* April 3, 1935, pp. 209–10.

"Huey Long and His Background." *Harper's,* CLXX (May 1935), 663–73.

"Anderson in America." *New Republic,* May 1, 1935, p. 348.

"Mr. Hearst's Apostolic Creed." *New Republic,* May 8, 1935, pp. 358–61.

"The 'Y' in Huey Long." *New Republic,* May 29, 1935, p. 177.

"Radio Priest—In Person." *New Republic,* June 5, 1935, pp. 96–98.

"Letters in the South." *New Republic,* June 19, 1935, pp. 162–63.

"Deep Dark River." *New Republic,* August 21, 1935, p. 54.

"The Pulse of the Nation." *New Republic,* August 21, 1935, pp. 41–43.

"Some Recent Novels." *New Republic,* August 21, 1935, p. 54.

"Nothing to Say." *New Republic,* September 18, 1935, pp. 166–67.

Review of the first issue of the *Southern Review. New Republic,* September 25, 1935, p. 195.

Review of *The Letters of Jonathan Swift to Charles Ford,* edited by David Nicholas Smith. *New Republic,* October 16, 1935, p. 279.

"Nemesis in the Cotton Belt." *New Republic,* November 13, 1935, pp. 24–25.

"King of the Finks." *New Republic,* December 4, 1935, p. 108.

"The Kingfish: In Memoriam." *New Republic,* December 18, 1935, p. 177.

"The Death and Legacy of Huey Long." *New Republic,* January 1, 1936, pp. 215–18.

"Mountain View." *New Republic,* January 1, 1936, p. 232.

"The Old and the New South." *New Republic,* February 12, 1936, pp. 26–27.

"Our Gene." *New Republic,* February 19, 1936, pp. 35–37.

"No Insinuation." *New Republic,* April 1, 1936, p. 224.

"Fog in Alabama." *New Republic,* May 27, 1936, p. 79.

"Thomas Wolfe: A Portrait." *New Republic,* June 24, 1936, pp. 199–202.

"The Liberty League Writes." *New Republic,* July 22, 1936, pp. 319–21.

"Why the Southern Novel?" *New Republic,* July 22, 1936, p. 331.

"The Little Hitlers at Asheville." *New Republic,* September 2, 1936, pp. 100–101.

"Orestes in Alabama." *New Republic,* September 30, 1936, p. 231.

"A Story-Teller's Novel." *New Republic,* October 7, 1936, pp. 259–60.

"Two Mid-American Novelists." *New Republic,* October 21, 1936, p. 318.

"Cardinal Pacelli and Father John." *New Republic,* October 28, 1936, pp. 343–45.

"No Decision." *New Republic,* November 11, 1936, pp. 54–55.

"Books in Brief." *New Republic,* December 2, 1936, pp. 153–54.

"Books in Brief." *New Republic,* December 30, 1936, p. 282.

"Thomas Wolfe." In *After the Genteel Tradition,* edited by Malcolm Cowley. New York, 1937.

"The Floundering Fathers." *New Republic,* February 17, 1937, p. 50.

"Herndon's Story." *New Republic,* March 31, 1937, p. 245.

"Maury Maverick: A Portrait." *New Republic,* April 21, 1937, pp. 315–17.

"At Home and Abroad." *New Republic,* May 12, 1937, pp. 24–25.

"Mr. Basso vs. Mr. Whipple." *New Republic,* June 30, 1937, p. 225.

"Unbranded Steer." *New Republic,* August 11, 1937, p. 11.

"Bayou People." *New Republic,* September 1, 1937, p. 108.

"Thomas Mann and a New Humanism." *New Republic,* March 9, 1938, pp. 120–23.

"South Wind." *New Republic,* June 1, 1938, pp. 97–98.

"Italian Notebook." *New Republic,* June 15, 1938, pp. 147–49.

"The Catholic Church in Politics." *New Republic,* December 21, 1938, pp. 202–203.

"God's Angry Newspapermen." *New Republic,* March 1, 1939, pp. 107–108.

"Huey Long's Heritage." *New Republic,* August 30, 1939, pp. 99–100.

"The Future of the South." *New Republic,* November 8, 1939, pp. 70–72.

"The Fate of H. G. Wells." *New Republic,* December 13, 1939, pp. 234–35.

"Artists' Artist." *New Republic,* January 15, 1940, pp. 91–92.

"Dixie: Then and Now." *New Republic,* February 5, 1940, pp. 185–86.

"Hats in the Ring: Young Mr. Dewey." *New Republic,* February 12, 1940, pp. 201–203.

"Hats in the Ring: Caucus Jack." *New Republic,* February 26, 1940, pp. 266–69.

"Can New Orleans Come Back?" *Forum,* CIII (March 1940), 124–28.

"Hats in the Ring: Monsignor Jim." *New Republic,* March 11, 1940, pp. 333–36.

"Hats in the Ring: Burton the Bronc." *New Republic,* April 22, 1940, pp. 527–30.

"See America First." *New Republic,* May 20, 1940, p. 677.

"Hats in the Ring: Jedge Hull." *New Republic,* May 27, 1940, pp. 720–23.

"New England Chatbook." *New Republic,* June 17, 1940, pp. 831–32.

"That Man in the White House." *New Republic,* July 22, 1940, pp. 106–108.

"The Great Profile." *New Republic,* July 29, 1940, pp. 146–47.

"Thomas Wolfe: A Summing Up." *New Republic,* September 23, 1940, pp. 422–23.

"Der Führer and the Kingfish." *New Republic,* August 4, 1941, pp. 162–63.

"The Long State." *New Republic,* October 27, 1941, pp. 563–64.

"Faulkneriana." *New Republic,* August 31, 1942, pp. 261–62.

Mainstream. New York, 1943.

"Ellen Glasgow's Literary Credo." *New York Times Book Review,* October 17, 1943, pp. 5, 53.

"Oh, Bury Me Not." *New Yorker,* July 15, 1944, pp. 66–69.

"Tonio Kröger in Egyptian Dress." *New Yorker,* July 22, 1944, pp. 53–56.

"A Very Old Party—I." *New Yorker,* December 30, 1944, pp. 24–34.

"A Very Old Party—II." *New Yorker,* January 6, 1945, pp. 28–38.

"Philosopher." *New Yorker,* May 12, 1945, pp. 27–32.

"Gift Books and Books for Gifts." *New Yorker,* December 15, 1945, pp. 118–20.

"The Huey Long Legend." *Life,* December 9, 1946, pp. 106–108.

Introduction to *The Red and The Black,* by Marie-Henri Beyle (Stendhal). New York, 1947.

"The Roosevelt Legend." *Life,* November 3, 1947, pp. 126–47.

Introduction to *The World from Jackson Square: A New Orleans Reader,* edited by Etolia Simmons Basso. New York, 1948.

"The Boys in the Upstairs Room." *The World from Jackson Square: A New Orleans Reader,* edited by Etolia Simmons Basso. New York, 1948.

"Boom Town, Dream Town." *Holiday,* III (February 1948), 26–41, 124–26.

"The Tragic Sense—I." *New Yorker,* February 28, 1948, pp. 34–38.

"The Tragic Sense—II." *New Yorker,* March 6, 1948, pp. 34–38.

"The Tragic Sense—III." *New Yorker,* March 13, 1948, pp. 37–40.

"Three Rivals." *Holiday,* IV (October 1948), 40–55, 97.

"Bayou Country." *Holiday,* VI (October 1949), 52–63.

"Los Angeles." *Holiday,* VII (January 1950), 26–47.

"The Wonderful Game of Baseball." *Holiday,* VII (May 1950), 42–45.

"St. Louis." *Holiday,* VIII (October 1950), 34–49.

"The Boswell Detective Story." *Life,* December 4, 1950, pp. 93–104.

"Jamaica Journal." *Holiday,* IX (March 1951), 98–102.

"Proud Pageant." *Life,* July 2, 1951, pp. 36–44.

"There's a Lot of Room in Wyoming." *Holiday,* IX (August 1951), 26–39.

"Savannah and the Golden Isles." *Holiday,* X (December 1951), 44–57.

Introduction to *Exploration of the Valley of the Amazon,* by William Lewis Herndon. New York, 1952.

Review of Philip Graham's *Showboats: The History of an American Institution. American Historical Review,* LVII (1952), 1053–54.

"Havana." *Holiday,* XII (December 1952), 64–70.

"San Francisco." *Holiday,* XIV (September 1953), 26–41.

"Letter from Rio de Janeiro." *New Yorker,* October 17, 1953, pp. 64–76.

"A Reporter at Large: The Last Confederate." *New Yorker,* November 21, 1953, pp. 124–43.

"New Orleans Childhood: The House on Decatur Street." *New Yorker,* October 9, 1954, pp. 89–101.

"Some Important Fall Authors Speak for Themselves." *New York Herald Tribune Book Review,* October 24, 1954, p. 4.

"Why I Wrote the View." *Literary Guild Review* (November 1954), 3–6.

"The Talkative Windfall." *New Yorker,* December 4, 1954, pp. 163–64.

"Thanks to St. Jude." *New Yorker,* May 7, 1955, pp. 86–93.

"If Tortugas Let You Pass." *American Heritage,* VII (1957), 46–49.

"Our Far-Flung Correspondents: There Is Indeed But One Ronda." *New Yorker,* September 8, 1956, pp. 116–32.

"Our Far-Flung Correspondents: Encounter in Puerto Cortes." *New Yorker,* October 12, 1957, pp. 98–117.

"A Reporter at Large: South Sea Diary." *New Yorker,* June 13, 1959, pp. 41–43.

"Our Far-Flung Correspondents: R.L.S." *New Yorker,* December 5, 1959, pp. 213–20.

A Quota of Seaweed. New York, 1960.

"Journey to Scandinavia." *Holiday,* XXIX (May 1961), 42–55, (June 1961), 90–96, 101–106, 170–75, XXX (September 1961), 70–71, 83–85.

"William Faulkner." *Saturday Review,* July 28, 1962, p. 12.

UNPUBLISHED WORKS OF HAMILTON BASSO

Beinecke Library, Yale University. Hamilton Basso Papers.

"Attitude." Typescript short story. [*ca.* 1926].

"Burden of Sin." Typescript short story. [*ca.* 1926].

"Burial." Typescript short story. [*ca.* 1925].

"Debutante." Typescript short story. [*ca.* 1925].

"Design." Typescript poem. [*ca.* 1926].

"Early Rhythm." Typescript poem. [*ca.* 1926].

"Epilogue." Typescript notebook. [*ca.* 1926].

"Epitaph." Typescript poem. [*ca.* 1926].

"Exam." Typescript short story. [*ca.* 1925].

"Finale." Typescript short story. [*ca.* 1925].

"Finesse." Typescript short story. [*ca.* 1925].

"Fire-side Portrait." Typescript poem. [*ca.* 1926].

"For a Pagan Love." Typescript poem. [*ca.* 1926].

"Gates Open." Typescript short story. [*ca.* 1925].

"The Greenroom." Typescript and radioscripts of novel. 1949.

"Greenwich Village." Typescript notes. 1926.

"Holiday." Typescript short story. [*ca.* 1925].

"Ladies of the Land." Typescript novelette. [*ca.* 1929].

"The Light Infantry Ball." Typescript novel. 1959.

"Litany." Typescript poem. [*ca.* 1926].

"Longfellow." Typescript short story. [*ca.* 1925].

"Miscellaneous." Typescript notes. [*ca.* 1926].

"Momentary Digression." Typescript notebook. [*ca.* 1926].

"Nocturne." Typescript prose poem. [*ca.* 1926].

"Pin Wheel." Typescript short story. [*ca.* 1925].

"Pole." Typescript short story. [*ca.* 1925].

"Prologue." Typescript notes. [*ca.* 1926].

"Questioning." Typescript poem. [*ca.* 1926].

"Song." Typescript poem. [*ca.* 1926].

"Spatial Arrangement." Typescript poem. December 1, 1926.

"The Swing of the Compass." Typescript unfinished novel. 1961.

"Tahiti Diary." Typescript travel impressions. 1958.

"10:30 A.M." Typescript poem. [*ca.* 1926].

"Touch of the Dragon." Typescript novel. 1964.

Untitled typescript of short story. [*ca.* 1925].

"The View from Pompey's Head." Typescript novel. 1954.

"Walls." Typescript short story. [*ca.* 1925].

"What Else." Typescript poem. [*ca.* 1926].

"Years Change Verdia Crane." Typescript short story. [*ca.* 1925].

Howard-Tilton Memorial Library, Tulane University, Hamilton Basso Papers.

"An American Notebook." Typescript travel impressions. 1950–51.

"The Blue Chip." Typescript notes. [*ca.* 1945].

"Brazil." Typescript notes. 1953.
"A Candle for the Marquis." Typescript short story. 1939.
"A Feeling for Boa-Constrictors." Typescript short story. [*ca.* 1945].
"Havana." Typescript notes. 1953.
"The Headhunters." Typescript short story. [*ca.* 1940].
"Huh." Typescript short story. [*ca.* 1945].
"Jamaica Notebook." Typescript notebook. 1950.
"Readers and Writers." Typescript speech. June 13, 1957.
"Relics and Angels." Typescript novel. 1928.
"Savannah, Georgia; 3 February 1951." Typescript travel diary.
"William Faulkner." Typescript notes. 1962.

LETTERS

Beinecke Library, Yale University, New Haven
    Basso, Hamilton. Papers. Correspondence.
    Josephson, Matthew. Papers. Correspondence.
Harvey S. Firestone Library, Princeton University, Princeton
    Fitzgerald, F. Scott. Correspondence.
    Perkins, Maxwell. Correspondence.
    Scribner's Archives.
Howard-Tilton Memorial Library, Tulane University, New Orleans
    Basso, Hamilton. Papers. Correspondence.
    Saxon, Lyle. Papers. Correspondence.
Houghton Library, Harvard University, Cambridge
    Wisdom, William B. Collection. Correspondence.
Newberry Library, Chicago
    Anderson, Sherwood. Papers. Correspondence.
    Cowley, Malcolm. Papers. Correspondence.
Patterson-Van Pelt Library, University of Pennsylvania, Philadelphia
    Brooks, Van Wyck. Papers. Correspondence.
Wilson Library, University of North Carolina, Chapel Hill
    North Carolina Collection.
    Wolfe, Thomas. Correspondence.

INTERVIEWS WITH THE AUTHOR

Basso, Etolia Simmons. January 3, 1991; January 8, 16, 1992; May 4, 1992; November 6, 1993; February 18, 1994.
Basso, Keith H. January 25, 1992.

Brooks, Cleanth. October 15, 1991.

McCrady, Mary Basso. February 1, 1992.

SELECTED OTHER SOURCES

Aaron, Daniel. *Writers on the Left: Episodes in American Literary Communism.* New York, 1961.

Abernathy, Thomas. "Partizan Leaders." *Virginia Quarterly Review,* IX (1933), 443–47.

Account of Basso's wedding. *New Orleans Times-Picayune,* June 1, 1930, p. 6.

"Agincourt and After." *Times Literary Supplement,* December 4, 1959, p. 705.

Allen, Walter. *The Modern Novel in Britain and the United States.* New York, 1964.

Anderson, Sherwood. *The Letters of Sherwood Anderson.* Edited by Howard M. Jones and Walter Rideout. Boston, 1953.

Aronson, Mark. "Wharton and the House of Scribner: The Novelist as a Pain in the Neck." *New York Times Book Review,* January 2, 1994, pp. 7–8.

Auchincloss, Louis. "The Adventures of Johnny Flashback." *Saturday Review of Literature,* October 22, 1955, pp. 11–14.

Bain, Robert, and Joseph M. Flora, eds. *Fifty Southern Writers After 1900.* New York, 1987.

Bain, Robert, Joseph M. Flora, and Louis D. Rubin, Jr., eds. *Southern Writers: A Biographical Dictionary.* Baton Rouge, 1979.

Barrett, William. "Reader's Choice." *Atlantic Monthly,* CCXIII (April 1964), 143.

Barthelemy-Roussève, Charles. *The Negro in Louisiana: Aspects of History and His Literature.* 1937; rpr. New Orleans, 1970.

Basso, Etolia Simmons, ed. *The World from Jackson Square: A New Orleans Reader.* 1948; rpr. New York, 1972.

"Basso Wins Southern Prize." *Publishers Weekly,* February 3, 1940, p. 625.

Benson, Brian, and Mabel Dillard, eds. *Jean Toomer.* Boston, 1980.

Berg, Scott. *Max Perkins: Editor of Genius.* New York, 1978.

Blotner, Joseph. *The Modern American Political Novel, 1900–1960.* Austin, 1966.

——. *Faulkner: A Biography.* New York, 1974.

Bohner, Charles H. *Robert Penn Warren.* New York, 1964.

Bradbury, John M. *The Fugitives: A Critical Account.* Chapel Hill, 1958.

——. *Renaissance in the South: A Critical History of the Literature, 1920–1960.* Chapel Hill, 1963.

Bradbury, Malcolm. *The Modern American Novel.* Oxford, 1983.

Bradbury, Malcolm, and David Palmer, eds. *The American Novel and the Nineteen Twenties.* London, 1971.

Bradbury, Malcolm, and James McFarlane, eds. *Modernism, 1890–1930.* 1976; rpr. Harmondsworth, Eng., 1987.

Bradbury, Malcolm, and Richard Ruland, eds. *From Puritanism to Postmodernism: A History of American Literature.* London, 1991.

Bradford, M. E. *Generations of the Faithful Heart: On the Literature of the South.* La Salle, Ill., 1983.

Braybrooke, Neville. "Innocence and Experience." *Spectator,* February 19, 1965, p. 6.

Brickell, Hirschel. "Beauregard and Davis." *North American Review,* CCXXXV (1933), 478.

Brinkley, Alan. *Voices of Protest: Huey Long, Father Coughlin, and the Great Depression.* New York, 1982.

Bristow, Gwen. "Gilgo Slade of Louisiana." *Saturday Review of Literature,* September 18, 1942, p. 16.

Brooks, Cleanth. "What Deep South Literature Needs." *Saturday Review of Literature,* September 19, 1942, p. 8.

Brooks, John. "You Can Go Home Again, Young Man." *New York Times Book Review,* October 24, 1954, p. 1.

Brooks, Van Wyck. *Wine of the Puritans: A Study of Present-Day America.* 1908; rpr. London, 1974.

Butcher, Fanny. "A Story to Cure Fiction Blues." *Chicago Sunday Tribune,* October 24, 1954, p. 2.

Butcher, Margaret Just. *The Negro in American Culture.* 1956; rpr. New York, 1971.

Calverton, V. F. "The Bankruptcy of Southern Culture." *Scribner's Magazine,* XCIX (1936), 294–98.

Cantwell, Robert. "A Southerner Returns." *Saturday Review of Literature,* October 23, 1954, pp. 15–16.

Carr, Virginia Spencer. *The Lonely Hunter: A Biography of Carson McCullers.* New York, 1976.

Cash, W. J. "Literature and the South." *Saturday Review of Literature,* December 28, 1940, p. 18.

———. *The Mind of the South.* New York, 1941.

Cashman, Sean Dennis. *America in the Twenties and Thirties: The Olympian Age of Franklin Delano Roosevelt.* New York, 1989.

Castronovo, David. *Edmund Wilson.* New York, 1984.

Catton, Bruce. *The Centennial History of the Civil War.* Garden City, 1961.

Chamberlain, John. "Faith Plus Works." *New Republic,* August 9, 1939, pp. 25–26.

Chambers, Robert H., ed. *Twentieth-Century Interpretations of "All the King's Men."* Englewood Cliffs, N.J., 1977.

Chase, Richard. *The American Novel and Its Tradition.* 1957; rpr. Baltimore, 1990.

Cheever, John. *The Journals,* edited by Benjamin Cheever. 1991; rpr. London, 1993.

Churchill, Allen. *The Improper Bohemians: A Re-creation of Greenwich Village in Its Heyday.* New York, 1959.

Clark, T. D. *The Rural Press and the New South.* Baton Rouge, 1948.

———. *The Emerging South.* Baton Rouge, 1968.

Coates, Robert. "Five New Novels." *New Republic,* March 28, 1934, pp. 190–91.

Codman, Florence. Review of Basso's *The Greenroom. Commonweal,* LI (December 1949), 252.

Coleman, John. "First Person Singular." *Observer,* February 14, 1965, p. 13.

Cowley, Malcolm. *Exile's Return: A Literary Odyssey of the 1920s.* New York, 1951.

———. "The Life and Death of a Fire Eater." *New York Times Book Review,* June 7, 1959, pp. 1, 33.

———. "The Writer as Craftsman: The Literary Heroism of Hamilton Basso." *Saturday Review,* June 27, 1964, pp. 17–18.

———. *The Dream of the Golden Mountains: Remembering the 1930s.* New York, 1980.

———. *The Portable Malcolm Cowley,* edited by Donald Faulkner. New York, 1990.

———, ed. *After the Genteel Tradition: American Writers, 1910–1930.* Carbondale, 1964.

Daniels, Jonathan. "The Upper Crust." *Saturday Review of Literature,* April 13, 1935, p. 621.

———. "Native's Return." *Saturday Review of Literature,* November 7, 1936, pp. 11–12.

———. *A Southerner Discovers the South.* New York, 1938.

DeVoto, Bernard. *The Literary Fallacy.* Boston, 1944.

Doll, Mary Aswell, and Clara Stites, eds. *In the Shadow of the Giant, Thomas Wolfe: Correspondence of Edward C. Aswell and Elizabeth Nowell, 1949–1958.* Athens, GA., 1988.

Donald, D. H. *Look Homeward, Angel: A Life of Thomas Wolfe.* Boston, 1987.

Doren, Mark Van. Review of *Courthouse Square. Southern Review,* III (1937), 170–71.

Dupree, Robert S. *Allen Tate and the Augustinian Imagination: A Study of the Poetry.* Baton Rouge, 1983.

Durrett, Frances Jean Bowen. "The New Orleans Double Dealer." In *Reality and Myth: Essays in American Literature,* edited by William E. Walker and Robert L. Welker. Nashville, 1964.

Eagleton, Terry. *Marxism and Literary Criticism.* London, 1976.

———. *Literary Theory.* Oxford, 1983.

Eaton, Clement. *A History of the Southern Confederacy.* London, 1954.

———. *The Mind of the Old South.* Nashville, 1964.

Eckenrode, H. J. "Tragic Americans." *Yale Review*, XXII (1933), 841–44.

Edel, Leon. *Writing Lives: Principia Biographica.* 1959; rpr. New York, 1984.

Eisinger, Chester E. *Fiction of the Forties.* Chicago, 1963.

———. "Nice Young Man Meets Dragon Lady." *Saturday Review*, March 28, 1964, p. 43.

Epstein, Joseph. "Talk of the Town." *Times Literary Supplement*, September 4, 1992, p. 6.

Faulkner, William, and William Spratling, eds. *Sherwood Anderson and Other Famous Creoles.* 1926; rpr. Austin, 1966.

Feibleman, James. *The Way of Man: An Autobiography.* 1952; rpr. New York, 1969.

———. "Literary New Orleans Between World Wars." *Southern Review*, n.s., I (1965), 702–19.

Fitzgerald, F. Scott. *The Letters of F. Scott Fitzgerald,* edited by Andrew Turnbull. New York, 1963.

Foell, E. W. "Basso's Civil War South." *Christian Science Monitor*, June 4, 1959, p. 7.

Geismar, Maxwell. *Writers in Crisis: The American Novel Between Two Wars.* Boston, 1942.

Gelb, Arthur. *O'Neill.* New York, 1962.

Gill, Brendan. *Here at the New Yorker.* New York, 1975.

Glasgow, Ellen. "Heroes and Monsters." *Saturday Review of Literature*, May 4, 1935, pp. 3–4.

Gold, Herbert. *The American Novel Since World War II.* Greenwich, Conn., 1969.

Goldhurst, William. *F. Scott Fitzgerald and His Contemporaries.* New York, 1963.

Goldstein, Albert. "Mr. Basso, Mr. Mencken and Uncle Tom." *Southwest Review*, XX (1935), 11–12.

Gray, Richard. *The Literature of Memory: Modern Writers of the American South.* London, 1977.

Green, Rose B. *The Italian-American Novel.* Rutherford, 1973.

Gross, Seymour L., and John E. Hardy, eds. *Images of the Negro in American Literature.* Chicago, 1966.

Hall, James. *Hall's Dictionary of Subjects and Symbols in Art.* 1974; rpr. London, 1986.

Hamburger, Philip. "Thoughts About the New Yorker." *New Leader*, July 13, 1992, p. 11.

"Hamilton Basso." *Wilson Library Bulletin*, XIV (1939), 186.

"Hamilton Basso, Dead: Novelist Wrote of Southern Life." New York *Times*, May 14, 1964, p. 35.

Harvey, Cathy Chance. "Lyle Saxon: A Portrait in Letters, 1917–1945." Ph.D. dissertation, Tulane University, 1980.

Hesseltine, W. B. "Beauregard, the Great Creole." *Mississippi Valley Historical Review*, XX (1933), 422–23.

Hicks, Granville. "Pompey's Head, 1861–1865." *Saturday Review of Literature*, June 6, 1959, p. 16.

Hill, William B. "A Touch of the Dragon." *America*, XI (April 1964), 515.

Hobson, Fred Colby, Jr. "H. L. Mencken and the Southern Literary Renascence." Ph.D. dissertation, University of North Carolina at Chapel Hill, 1972.

———. *Serpent in Eden: H. L. Mencken and the South.* Chapel Hill, 1974.

———. *Tell About the South: The Southern Rage to Explain.* Chapel Hill, 1983.

———. *The Southern Writer in the Postmodern World.* Athens, Ga., 1991.

Hoffman, Frederick. *The Art of Southern Fiction: A Study of Some Modern Novelists.* Carbondale, 1967.

———. *The Little Magazine: A History and Bibliography.* Princeton, 1947.

Holman, C. Hugh. "Literature and Culture: The Fugitive-Agrarians." *Social Forces*, XXXVII (1958), 15–19.

———. *Three Modes of Modern Southern Fiction: Ellen Glasgow, William Faulkner, Thomas Wolfe.* Athens, Ga., 1966.

———. *The Immoderate Past: The Southern Writer and History.* Athens, Ga., 1977.

———. *Windows on the World: Essays on American Social Fiction.* Knoxville, 1979.

Homberger, Eric. *American Writers and Radical Politics, 1900–1939.* London, 1986.

Hope, F. "Free Woman." *New Statesman*, February 19, 1965, pp. 285–86.

Hughes, Riley. "The Light Infantry Ball." *Catholic World*, CLXXXIX (August 1959), 400.

Hutchens, John K. "On Books and Authors: The Architect of Pompey's Head." *New York Herald Tribune Book Review*, October 31, 1954, p. 3.

Ickstadt, Heinz, Rob Kroes, and Brian Lee, eds. *The Thirties: Politics and Culture in a Time of Broken Dreams.* Amsterdam, 1987.

Idema, Henry. *Freud, Religion, and the Roaring Twenties: A Psychoanalytical Theory of Secularization in Three Novels: Anderson, Hemingway, and Fitzgerald.* Savage, Md., 1990.

Idol, John Lane, Jr. *A Thomas Wolfe Companion.* New York, 1987.

Ikerd, Clarence Frye. "Hamilton Basso: A Critical Biography." Ph.D. dissertation, University of North Carolina at Chapel Hill, 1974.

Janeway, Elizabeth. "Nobody Loves Edwina." *New York Times Book Review*, March 22, 1964, p. 33.

Jones, Howard Mumford. "Social Notes on the South." *Virginia Quarterly Review*, XI (1935), 452–57.

Josephson, Matthew. *The Robber Barons: The Great American Capitalists, 1861–1901.* New York, 1934.

———. *Infidel in the Temple: A Memoir of the Nineteen Thirties.* New York, 1967.

Kazin, Alfred. "Intelligent Southern Realism." *New York Times Book Review,* August 6, 1939, p. 5.

———. *Starting Out in the Thirties.* London, 1962.

Kennedy, Richard S. *The Window of Memory: The Literary Career of Thomas Wolfe.* Chapel Hill, 1962.

King, Richard. *A Southern Renaissance: The Cultural Awakening of the American South, 1930–1955.* Oxford, N.Y., 1980.

Klausler, Alfred P. "Cool Prophets." *Christian Century,* August 26, 1959, pp. 972–73.

Klinkenborg, Verlyn. "This Was New York. It Was." *New York Times Book Review,* August 16, 1992, p. 7.

Knickerbocker, Kenneth. "Beauregard." *Sewanee Review,* XLII (1934), 110–12.

Kronenberger, Louis. "Return of the Native." *New Republic,* November 25, 1936, p. 122.

Kuehl, John, and Bryer Jackson, eds. *Dear Scott-Dear Max: The Fitzgerald-Perkins Correspondence.* New York, 1971.

Lasch, Christopher. *The New Radicalism in America.* New York, 1965.

Lathrop, R. Gail. "Thomas Wolfe and Partridge Hill." *Thomas Wolfe Review,* IX (1985), 27–29.

Lawrence, D. H. *Studies in Classic American Literature.* 1923; rpr. Harmondsworth, Eng., 1985.

Lawson, R. Alan. *The Failure of Independent Liberalism, 1930–1941.* New York, 1971.

Leitch, Vincent B. *American Literary Criticism from the Thirties to the Eighties.* New York, 1988.

Leuchtenburg, William E. *Franklin D. Roosevelt and the New Deal, 1932–1940.* 1963; rpr. New York, 1990.

———. *The Perils of Prosperity.* Chicago, 1958.

Lovett, Robert M. "Wine of the Country." *New Republic,* December 15, 1941, p. 835.

Lytle, Andrew. "A Confederate General." *New Republic,* May 31, 1933, p. 80.

———. *Southerners and Europeans: Essays in a Time of Disorder.* Baton Rouge, 1988.

MacKethan, L. H. *The Dream of Arcady: Place and Time in Southern Literature.* Baton Rouge, 1980.

"Map Making." *Times Literary Supplement,* February 18, 1964, p. 121.

May, John R. "Louisiana Writers in Film." *Southern Quarterly,* XXIII (1984), 18–31.

Mayfield, John S. Review of *Beauregard. Southwest Review,* XIX (1934), 23–25.

Mays, Davis D. "Sivilizing Moustache Pete: Changing Attitudes Toward Italians in New Orleans, 1890–1918." In *Ethnic Minorities in Gulf Coast Society,* edited by Jerrell H. Shofner and Linda V. Ellsworth. Pensacola, Fla., 1979.

McCrum, Robert. "The New Corker!" *Guardian Weekly,* October 11, 1992, p. 19.

McMillan, Dougald. *transition: The History of a Literary Era, 1927–1938.* Amsterdam, 1975.

McPherson, James. *Battle Cry of Freedom: The Civil War Era.* Oxford, Eng., 1988.

Mencken, H. L. *The Impossible H. L. Mencken,* edited by Marion E. Rodgers. New York, 1991.

Millichap, Joseph R. *Hamilton Basso.* Boston, 1979.

Milne, Gordon. *The American Political Novel.* Norman, Okla., 1966.

Mizener, Arthur. *This Far Side of Paradise: A Biography of F. Scott Fitzgerald.* Boston, 1949.

──────. "Fiction Chronicle." *Sewanee Review,* LXIII (1955), 484–94.

Mott, Frank Luther. *A History of American Magazines.* Cambridge, Mass., 1968.

"Mr. Basso's Princess." *New York Times Book Review,* September 18, 1949, p. 8.

Naipaul, V. S. "Dark Places." *New Statesman,* August 18, 1961, pp. 221–22.

Nelson, Raymond. *Van Wyck Brooks: A Writer's Life.* New York, 1981.

Neville, Helen. "Five Decisions." *Nation,* September 9, 1939, pp. 273–74.

"New and Noteworthy." *New York Times Book Review,* May 19, 1985, p. 85.

Nichols, Lewis. "Talk with Hamilton Basso." *New York Times Book Review,* October 24, 1959, p. 22.

Obituary of Hamilton Basso. *Time,* May 22, 1964, p. 72.

──────. *Illustrated London News,* May 23, 1964, p. 829.

──────. *Newsweek,* May 25, 1964, p. 41.

──────. *Publishers Weekly,* May 25, 1964, p. 52.

O'Brien, Michael. *Rethinking the South: Essays in Intellectual History.* Baltimore, 1988.

"Old Spain and the New World." *Times Literary Supplement,* September 15, 1961, p. 617.

Parks, Winfield. "Six Southern Novels." *Virginia Quarterly Review,* XIII (1937), 154–60.

Pells, Richard H. *Radical Visions and American Dreams: Culture and Social Thought in the Depression Years.* New York, 1973.

Perkins, Maxwell E. *Editor to Author: The Letters of Maxwell E. Perkins,* edited by John Hall Wheelock. New York, 1950.

Phillipson, John S., ed. *Critical Essays on Thomas Wolfe.* Boston, 1985.

Pollock, Venetia. "New Novels." *Punch,* February 24, 1964, p. 294.

Prescott, Orville. "Books of the Times." *New York Times,* October 21, 1960, p. 31.

──────. "Money and the Dragon Woman." *New York Times,* March 25, 1964, p. 39.

Ransom, John Crowe. "Modern with the Southern Accent." *Virginia Quarterly Review*, XI (1935), 186-94.

Reeves, Paschal. *Thomas Wolfe: The Critical Reception*. New York, 1974.

"Relics and Angels." *New York Herald Tribune Review of Books*, September 8, 1929, pp. 19-20.

Rocks, James E. "Hamilton Basso and the World View from Pompey's Head." *South Atlantic Quarterly*, LXXI (1972), 326-41.

Rosenfeld, Isaac. "The Difficult Art of Fiction." *New Republic*, October 19, 1942, p. 520.

Rubin, Louis D., Jr. *The Faraway Country: Writers of the Modern South*. Seattle, 1963.

―――. *The Curious Death of the Novel: Essays in American Literature*. Baton Rouge, 1967.

―――. *A Gallery of Southerners*. Baton Rouge, 1982.

Rubin, Louis D., Jr., and C. Hugh Holman, eds. *Southern Literary Study: Problems and Possibilities*. Chapel Hill, 1975.

Rubin, Louis D., Jr., and James J. Fitzpatrick, eds. *The Lasting South: Fourteen Southerners Look at Their Home*. Chicago, 1957.

Rubin, Louis D., Jr., and Robert Jacobs, eds. *Southern Renascence: The Literature of the Modern South*. Baltimore, 1953.

―――, eds. *South: Modern Southern Literature in Its Cultural Setting*. New York, 1961.

Santayana, George. *The Philosophy of Santayana: Selections from the Works of George Santayana*, edited by Irwin Edman. New York, 1936.

Saxon, Lyle. "Uneasy Blood in Their Veins." *New York Herald Tribune Book Review*, November 1, 1936, p. 8.

Scarborough, Dorothy. "A Louisiana Senator." *New York Times Book Review*, February 25, 1935, pp. 8-9.

Scott, Evelyn. "Doctor's Choice." *Saturday Review of Literature*, August 5, 1939, p. 7.

Shi, David E. *Matthew Josephson: Bourgeois Bohemian*. New Haven, 1981.

Shrapnel, Norman. "Manner over Matter." *Manchester Guardian Weekly*, February 18, 1965, p. 11.

Simpson, Louis P. *The Dispossessed Garden: Pastoral and History in Southern Literature*. Baton Rouge, 1983.

Singal, D. J. *The War Within: From Victorian to Modernist Thought in the South, 1919-1945*. Chapel Hill, 1982.

Skaggs, Merrill Maguire. *The Folk of Southern Fiction*. Athens, Ga., 1972.

Smith, Henry N. "The Dilemma of Agrarianism." *Southwest Review*, XIX (1934), 205-32.

Snyder, Robert E. "The Concept of Demagoguery: Huey Long and His Literary Critics." *Louisiana Studies*, XV (1976), 61-83.

"Some Important Fall Authors Speak for Themselves." *New York Herald Tribune Book Review*, October 24, 1954, p. 4.

Spencer, Benjamin T. "Wherefore This Southern Fiction?" *Sewanee Review*, XLVII (1939), 512.

Spiller, Robert E., ed. *A Time of Harvest: American Literature, 1910–1960*. New York, 1962.

Spratling, William. *File on Spratling: An Autobiography*. Boston, 1967.

Stearns, Harold. *Civilization in the United States: An Inquiry by Thirty Americans*. 1922; rpr. Westport, Conn., 1971.

Stott, William. *Documentary Expression and Thirties America*. Oxford, 1973.

"Stripped-Down Novelist." *Newsweek*, September 19, 1949, p. 87.

Swanberg, W. A. *Citizen Hearst: A Biography of William Randolph Hearst*. New York, 1962.

Sweeney, Patricia. *Women in Southern Literature: An Index*. New York, 1986.

Tallack, Douglas. *Twentieth Century America: The Intellectual and Cultural Context*. London, 1991.

Tallant, Robert. *The Romantic New Orleanians*. New York, 1950.

Tate, Allen. *Jefferson Davis, His Rise and Fall: A Biographical Narrative*. New York, 1929.

Taylor, Joe Gray. *Louisiana: A Bicentennial History*. New York, 1976.

Thorp, Willard. *American Writing in the Twentieth Century*. Cambridge, Mass., 1960.

Tindall, George B. *The Emergence of the New South, 1913–1945*. Baton Rouge, 1967.

Tinker, Edward L. Review of *Beauregard*. *Review of Literature*, March 4, 1933, p. 466.

Townsend, Kim. *Sherwood Anderson: A Biography*. Boston, 1987.

Tunstall, Caroline. "Story of Secession Days in Old Pompey." *Herald Tribune Book Review*, June 7, 1959, p. 3.

Turner, Arlin. "The Southern Novel." *Southwest Review*, XXV (1940), 205.

Tuttleton, James W. *The Novel of Manners in America*. Chapel Hill, 1972.

Twelve Southerners. *I'll Take My Stand: The South and the Agrarian Tradition*. 1930; rpr. New York, 1962.

Vernon, Grenville. "Carolina's Best." *Commonweal*, XIX (May 1933), 50.

Wade, Mason. "Shorter Notices." *Nation*, November 28, 1936, p. 640.

Wagner, Linda W. *Dos Passos: Artist as American*. Austin, 1979.

Walker, Hugh. "Hero of Sumter." *Nashville Tennessean*, June 25, 1972, p. 3.

Walker, William, and Robert Welker, eds. *Reality and Myth: Essays in American Literature*. Nashville, 1964.

Warren, Robert Penn. "Not Local Color." *Virginia Quarterly Review*, VIII (1932), 153–60.

————. "T. S. Stribling: A Paragraph in the History of Critical Realism." *American Review,* II (1934), 463–86.

————. "Some Don'ts for Literary Regionalism." *American Review,* VIII (1936), 142–50.

Wellek, René. *A History of Modern Criticism, 1900–1950.* New Haven, 1986.

Welty, Eudora. *One Writer's Beginnings.* Cambridge, Mass., 1983.

Wheelock, John H., ed. *Editor to Author: The Letters of Maxwell E. Perkins.* New York, 1950.

Williams, T. H. *P. G. T. Beauregard: Napoleon in Gray.* Baton Rouge, 1955.

————. *Every Man a King: Huey Long.* Baton Rouge, 1964.

Wilson, Edmund. "Reveries and Surprises." *New Republic,* October 23, 1929, pp. 274–75.

————. *The Twenties.* New York, 1975.

————. *Letters on Literature and Politics, 1912–1972,* edited by Elena Wilson. London, 1977.

————. *The Thirties.* New York, 1980.

————. *The Sixties.* New York, 1993.

Wolfe, Thomas. *The Letters of Thomas Wolfe,* edited by Elizabeth Nowell. New York, 1956.

Woodburn, John. "Assistant Editor's Holiday." *Saturday Review of Literature,* September 24, 1949, p. 17.

Woodward, C. Vann. "The Historical Dimension." *Virginia Quarterly Review,* XXXII (1956), 258–67.

————. *The Burden of Southern History.* Baton Rouge, 1960.

————. *Thinking Back: The Perils of Writing History.* Baton Rouge, 1986.

Wright, Louis B. "Mythmakers and the Southern Dilemma." *Sewanee Review,* LIII (1945), 544–58.

Wyatt-Brown, Bertram. *Southern Honor: Ethics and Behavior in the Old South.* New York, 1982.

Yardley, Jonathan. "Rediscovering a Novel of Manners." *Washington Post Book Review,* June 30, 1985, p. 3.

Young, T. D. *The Past in the Present: A Thematic Study of Modern Southern Fiction.* Baton Rouge, 1981.

Index